Vice President, Social Sciences: Charles Linsmeier
Senior Publisher High School: Ann Heath
Executive Program Manager: Nathan Odell
Senior Development Editor: Donald Gecewicz

Assistant Editor: Corrina Santos
Editorial Assistant: Carla Duval
Senior Marketing Manager: Janie Pierce-Bratcher
Marketing Assistant: Tiffani Tang
Media Editor: Kim Morte
Executive Media Producer: Keri deManigold
Senior Media Project Manager: Michelle Camisa
Director of Design, Content Management: Diana Blume
Senior Cover Designer: William Boardman
Interior Designer: Lumina Datamatics, Inc.
Director, Content Management Enhancement: Tracey Kuehn
Senior Managing Editor: Michael Granger
Content Project Manager: Louis C. Bruno Jr.
Manager of Publishing Services: Andrea Cava
Senior Workflow Project Supervisor: Joe Ford
Production Supervisor: Robin Besofsky
Director of Rights and Permissions: Hilary Newman
Composition: Lumina Datamatics, Inc.
Printing and Binding: LSC Communications
Cover photo: Tristan Eaton, photo by Rey Rosa/The L.I.S.A. Project NYC

Library of Congress Control Number: 2018968515

ISBN-13: 978-1-319-23658-8
ISBN-10: 1-319-23658-8

Manufactured in the United States of America.

2   3   4   5   6   24   23   22   21   20   19

W. H. Freeman and Company
Bedford, Freeman & Worth
One New York Plaza
Suite 4600
New York, NY 10004-1562
highschool.bfwpub.com/AmGov1e

Foundational Documents
and Court Cases Reader

TO ACCOMPANY
American Government:
Stories of a Nation for the AP® Course

Karen Waples ■ **Pamela Lamb**
Katie Piper ■ **Benwari Singh**

bedford, freeman & worth
high school publishers
Boston | New York

Contents

About the Authors

Karen Waples
Holy Family High School, Broomfield, Colorado

Karen Waples has taught since 1999, now at Holy Family High School in Colorado. She teaches AP® U.S. Government and Politics and AP® Comparative Government and Politics. Karen is the co-author of *American Government: Stories of a Nation for the AP® Course*. She conducts AP® workshops and institutes throughout the country. Karen has served as a reader for the AP® U.S. History and AP® U.S. Government and Politics exams and has served as a reader, table leader, question leader, and exam leader for the AP® Comparative Government and Politics exam. Karen was a member of the Curriculum Redesign Committee for the AP® U.S. Government and Politics course. Karen was a trial attorney from 1985–1989. She received the Colorado Governor's Award for Excellence in Education in 1997 and was recognized as a Cherry Creek High School teacher of the year in 2002.

Pamela Lamb
Del Rio High School, Del Rio, Texas

Pamela Lamb has been teaching for thirty-four years, twenty-nine in AP® U.S. Government and Politics. She holds a B.A. in history and a M.A. in both history and political science. Pam has been a workshop consultant for the College Board since 1994 and has served as a reader, table leader, and question leader at the AP® U.S. Government and Politics reading.

Katie Piper
Bellevue High School, Bellevue, Washington

Katie Piper taught AP® U.S. Government and Politics for eleven years, and she is currently an instructional coach in Bellevue, Washington. She is a member of the College Board Instructional Design Committee for the AP® U.S. Government and Politics redesign and leads AP® institutes and workshops for teachers. She served as a teacher leader and designer in partnership with the University of Washington and Lucas Education Research to create a project-based curriculum for AP® U.S. Government and Politics. She has also coached AP® U.S. Government and Politics teachers on implementing project-based learning with the Buck Institute for Education.

Benwari Singh
Cherry Creek High School, Greenwood Village, Colorado

Benwari has taught social studies for twenty-six years in a variety of public-school settings, starting as a sixth-grade teacher in an urban school in Denver in 1992. For the last fifteen years, Benwari has taught AP® U.S. Government and Politics and AP® Comparative Government and Politics at Cherry Creek High School. In addition to his teaching duties, Benwari has served as a reader, table leader, and question leader at the AP® U.S. Government and Politics reading for fourteen years. He also served on the AP® U.S. Government and Politics test development committee for six years, including two as the co-chair of the committee.

To the Student: Your Key to the Structure of This Book

Welcome to the document reader that accompanies *American Government: Stories of a Nation for the AP® Course*. The AP® U.S. Government and Politics course requires that you understand nine foundational documents and fifteen Supreme Court cases. This reader will help you work through difficult language and understand the challenging concepts presented in each of these readings.

The nine foundational documents are reproduced in their entirety. You are expected to read each completely, understand their meaning, and be able to apply the documents in the multiple-choice and argumentation essay portions of the AP® exam.

The Foundational Documents

This reader organizes each foundational document into the following sections:

Focus on

This section explains why the document is important and tells you what to look for when you are reading it.

Overview of

This is a short outline, which briefly explains how the document is structured.

Reader Alert!

Pay close attention to the tips in this section, which will give you important information about challenging language, the arguments made, and the structure of the document.

Foundational Documents

Each document is printed in full. Within each document, look for the following features:

- **Sections and Headings:** Some of the documents are long. To make it easier to read, we have divided all of the documents into manageable chunks and added headings to help you understand the purpose of each section.
- **Vocabulary:** Difficult vocabulary is in italics. Look for the definitions in the margins.
- **Guiding Questions:** Questions throughout each section help you interact with the text.

Impact

This explanation summarizes the impact of the document in U.S. government and politics.

Check for Understanding

These questions give you the opportunity to make sure you fully understand the document.

Critical Thinking Question

This question takes you beyond the document and asks you to think critically and synthesize what you have learned.

The Supreme Court Cases

You are not expected to read full Supreme Court cases, so this reader contains excerpts of the fifteen required cases, designed to help you understand the most important aspects of these key decisions. Although you are not likely to be tested on the dissenting opinions, the dissents often point to wider issues or to public policy matters to consider. The required cases will appear in the multiple-choice portion of the exam, as well as on the SCOTUS free-response question.

Each Supreme Court case is organized into the following sections:

Focus on

This section explains why the case is important and tells you what to look for when you are reading it.

Reader Alert!

Pay close attention to the tips in this section, which will give you important information about challenging language, the arguments made, and the structure of the decision.

Facts of the Case

This section tells you what happened that led to the Supreme Court case. This is the background of "who did what" and how the case ended up in court.

Issue/Issues

This is the legal question or questions the Court was asked to resolve. Often, the issue is whether or not an action or law violates the Constitution.

Decision/Holding

This is usually the easiest part of the case. It's a sentence about who won.

Majority and Dissenting Opinions

These sections contain excerpts from the majority opinion of the Court, which will serve as precedent, as well as any important dissenting opinions. (The dissenting opinions are worth reading because they often point to weaknesses in the legal argument of the majority.) To make the decisions easier to read, we have divided them into manageable chunks and added headings to help you understand the purpose of each section. Also, look for:

- **Vocabulary:** Difficult vocabulary is in italics. Look for the definitions in the margins.
- **Guiding Questions:** Questions throughout each section help you interact with the text.

Impact

This explanation summarizes the impact of the case in U.S. government and politics.

Check for Understanding

These questions give you an opportunity to make sure you fully understand the opinions.

SCOTUS Practice Question

After each case, we've provided a practice question in the same format as the SCOTUS free-response essay, which will appear on the AP® exam. These questions require you to apply the required case to a nonrequired case, using your skills in critical thinking.

Foundational Documents

How to Master the Foundational Documents

Reading the foundational documents may seem intimidating. Most of them were written a long time ago, using outdated words. The Articles of Confederation and the Constitution, for example, are written in legalistic language, because they are governing documents that have the force of law.

The key to reading foundational documents is not to panic if you don't understand every word. The following strategies are designed to help you tackle the foundational documents. Not all of these strategies will work for everyone. Try them all, and use what works best for you.

Once you have fine-tuned your approach, reading historical documents will become easier, and you will be able to use these skills in college and beyond.

1. Get comfortable

Before you tackle difficult reading, eliminate distractions. Put your cell phone on silent, and put it in a drawer or in another room. Tell your family to leave you alone, or go to a library or another quiet place. Maybe you like to read outside. Put on comfy clothes, and grab your favorite beverage and a snack. Some students love to read, but even if you don't enjoy reading, you will feel better about it if you can create a setting you enjoy.

2. Before you read the document, get an overview

This document reader contains *Focus on, Overview,* and *Reader Alert!* sections to give you a preview of what you will be reading. In college, where you may be asked to read other historical and difficult documents, you may be able to find plain-English versions online. Be sure these versions come from a credible source. Remember that translations are a tool to help you understand difficult reading, but they *do not* replace reading the full document. This is very important, especially if you want to do well on the AP® Exam, where you will be given passages from nonrequired documents and be asked to interpret them. If you haven't developed the skills of parsing language and understanding arguments, you will struggle on the exam.

3. Highlight key words and passages to drown out the noise

Here is an example of what you might highlight in the passage from *Federalist* No. 10 defining faction: "By a faction, I understand a number of citizens, whether amounting to a majority or a minority of the whole, who are united and actuated by some common impulse of passion, or of interest, adversed to the rights of other citizens, or to the permanent and aggregate interests of the community."

3

When you review the highlighted text, you get the gist of what a faction is: a group that shares a common interest and that will cause harm to others. This isn't a perfect definition, but it gets the point across.

4. Use context clues

This document reader defines difficult and unusual terms, but you may still come across a term you don't understand. It would be time-consuming to find the definition of every word you don't fully understand, and doing so may be unrealistic. You may be able figure out what a word means by putting it in context. For example, the passage above, from *Federalist* No. 10 contains the phrase, "adversed to the rights of other citizens, or to the permanent and aggregate interests of the community." Madison's use of the word *adversed* seems weird, but the rest of the sentence indicates that it means *against*. Think of other ways you have seen similar terms used. Enemies are sometimes described as *adversaries*, so the term *adversed* has a negative connotation.

5. Don't just read—interact!

Reading is more than just moving your eyes over a page. The author's message has to sink into your consciousness. The document reader contains questions to help you understand each section. Pay attention to these questions, because they are designed to help you understand why each section is important and how the document is structured. When you are in college, you may have to add notes in the margin to help you interact with and remember each passage. When you take notes in the margin and highlight important passages, you don't have to re-read the document later for review. You can just refer to your notes and highlighting, and you have a built-in study guide.

6. Ask for help

Sometimes, despite all of your hard work, you just don't get it. Teachers aren't mind-readers, and your teacher may not know you are struggling in reading the documents. AP® students are often hesitant to admit when they don't understand something. AP® classes are filled with smart kids, but at some point, most students feel like they are the only person in the room who doesn't understand. Make an appointment with your teacher, make a list of the points in the document that you want to clarify, and get help. You may have a group of friends who are good at explaining things. Talking over the content clears up most misconceptions.

Experiment with these strategies to figure out what works best for you. And keep a positive attitude. Think of reading as your personal interaction with the author over time and space. This is one of the coolest aspects of reading.

The Declaration of Independence

Thomas Jefferson

▓ Focus on *the Declaration of Independence*

The Declaration of Independence was approved by the Second Continental Congress on July 4, 1776, proclaiming the separation of the thirteen British colonies in North America from the British government. It was based on a resolution proposed by Richard Henry Lee of Virginia that "these United Colonies are, and of right ought to be Free and Independent States." The Declaration of Independence announced to the world the colonies' intentions of breaking away from Britain and explained the colonies' actions to gain support for their cause.

▓ Overview of *the Declaration of Independence*

In the Declaration of Independence, Jefferson
* explains a theory of government based on the Enlightenment principle of natural law to justify independence.
* discusses a list of complaints against the king and "others."
* issues a declaration of war/statement of separation.

▓ Reader Alert!

Why and for whom was the Declaration of Independence written? The Declaration was written to let King George III, the British Parliament, and the rest of the world know the intentions of the colonists and to rationally explain why such a separation was both justified and required. The Founders believed that "dissolving the political bands" to Britain required, out of sheer dignity and respect to the rest of the world, an explanation.

Jefferson based his ideas for the Declaration of Independence on the principles of Enlightenment thought, especially those of John Locke:
* "All men are created equal."
* People are born with inalienable rights given by God, not the king. Among those rights are "life, liberty, and the pursuit of happiness." This statement by Jefferson is based on John Locke's "life, liberty and property."
* Governments are created by men, so Jefferson supported the notion of "consent of the governed."
* If a government did not act on behalf of the people, the people have not only a right, but a duty, to "alter or abolish" the government.

What is a declaration? A declaration is a formal statement or announcement.

[Introduction]

In Congress July 4, 1776
The unanimous Declaration of the thirteen
United States of America

Laws of Nature—natural law, rights that come from nature, not from government

impel—to force

1   When in the Course of human events, it becomes necessary for one people to dissolve the political bands which have connected them with another, and to assume among the powers of the earth, the separate and equal station to which the *Laws of Nature* and of Nature's God entitle them, a decent respect to the opinions of mankind requires that they should declare the causes which *impel* them to the separation.

[Preamble: A theory of government]

self-evident—obvious

In Enlightenment thought, people are born equal and no one is rightfully the ruler of others by birth—an argument in opposition to the divine right of kings

unalienable rights—rights that cannot be denied because they come from God, not government, or come simply from being human

deriving—getting

institute—create

prudence—carefulness

transient—fleeting or momentary

usurpations—taking power by force

despotism—dominance through threat of punishment and violence; dictatorship

tyranny—cruel or oppressive government

2   We hold these truths to be *self-evident*, that all men are created equal, that they are endowed by their Creator with certain *unalienable Rights*, that among these are Life, Liberty and the pursuit of Happiness.—That to secure these rights, Governments are instituted among Men, *deriving* their just powers from the consent of the governed,—That whenever any Form of Government becomes destructive of these ends, it is the Right of the People to alter or to abolish it, and to *institute* new Government, laying its foundation on such principles and organizing its powers in such form, as to them shall seem most likely to effect their Safety and Happiness. *Prudence*, indeed, will dictate that Governments long established should not be changed for light and *transient* causes; and accordingly all experience hath shewn, that mankind are more disposed to suffer, while evils are sufferable, than to right themselves by abolishing the forms to which they are accustomed. But when a long train of abuses and *usurpations*, pursuing invariably the same Object evinces a design to reduce them under absolute *Despotism*, it is their right, it is their duty, to throw off such Government, and to provide new Guards for their future security.—Such has been the patient sufferance of these Colonies; and such is now the necessity which constrains them to alter their former Systems of Government. The history of the present King of Great Britain is a history of repeated injuries and usurpations, all having in direct object the establishment of an absolute *Tyranny* over these States. To prove this, let Facts be submitted to a candid world.

[Indictment of George III: List of grievances]

He has refused his *Assent* to Laws, the most wholesome and necessary for the public good. ³

He has forbidden his Governors to pass Laws of immediate ⁴ and pressing importance, unless suspended in their operation till his *Assent* should be obtained; and when so suspended, he has utterly neglected to attend to them.

He has refused to pass other Laws for the accommodation of ⁵ large districts of people, unless those people would relinquish the right of Representation in the Legislature, a right *inestimable* to them and formidable to tyrants only.

He has called together legislative bodies at places unusual, ⁶ uncomfortable, and distant from the depository of their public Records, for the sole purpose of fatiguing them into compliance with his measures.

He has dissolved Representative Houses repeatedly, for opposing with manly firmness his invasions on the rights of the people. ⁷

He has refused for a long time, after such dissolutions, ⁸ to cause others to be elected; whereby the Legislative powers, *incapable of Annihilation*, have returned to the People at large for their exercise; the State remaining in the mean time exposed to all the dangers of invasion from without, and convulsions within.

He has endeavoured to prevent the population of these States; ⁹ for that purpose obstructing the Laws for Naturalization of Foreigners; refusing to pass others to encourage their migrations hither, and raising the conditions of new Appropriations of Lands.

He has obstructed the Administration of Justice, by refusing 10 his Assent to Laws for establishing Judiciary powers.

He has made Judges dependent on his Will alone, for the ten- 11 ure of their offices, and the amount and payment of their salaries.

He has erected a multitude of New Offices, and sent hither 12 swarms of Officers to harrass our people, and eat out their substance.

He has kept among us, in times of peace, Standing Armies 13 without the Consent of our legislatures.

He has affected to render the Military independent of and 14 superior to the Civil power.

He has combined with others to subject us to a jurisdiction 15 foreign to our constitution, and unacknowledged by our laws; giving his Assent to their Acts of pretended Legislation:

Why did Jefferson include this list of grievances?

assent—approval or acceptance

inestimable—too great to set a value on

incapable of annihilation—cannot be destroyed or suppressed

16   For Quartering large bodies of armed troops among us:

17   For protecting them, by a mock Trial, from punishment for any Murders which they should commit on the Inhabitants of these States:

18   For cutting off our Trade with all parts of the world:

19   For imposing Taxes on us without our Consent:

20   For depriving us in many cases, of the benefits of Trial by Jury:

21   For transporting us beyond Seas to be tried for pretended offences:

22   For abolishing the free System of English Laws in a neighbouring Province, establishing therein an Arbitrary government, and enlarging its Boundaries so as to render it at once an example and fit instrument for introducing the same absolute rule into these Colonies:

23   For taking away our Charters, abolishing our most valuable Laws, and altering fundamentally the Forms of our Governments:

24   For suspending our own Legislatures, and declaring themselves invested with power to legislate for us in all cases whatsoever.

25   He has abdicated Government here, by declaring us out of his Protection and waging War against us.

26   He has plundered our seas, ravaged our Coasts, burnt our towns, and destroyed the lives of our people.

27   He is at this time transporting large Armies of foreign Mercenaries to compleat the works of death, desolation and tyranny, already begun with circumstances of Cruelty & *perfidy* scarcely paralleled in the most barbarous ages, and totally unworthy the Head of a civilized nation.

perfidy—deceit

28   He has constrained our fellow Citizens taken Captive on the high Seas to bear Arms against their Country, to become the executioners of their friends and Brethren, or to fall themselves by their Hands.

29   He has excited domestic insurrections amongst us, and has endeavoured to bring on the inhabitants of our frontiers, the merciless Indian Savages, whose known rule of warfare, is an undistinguished destruction of all ages, sexes and conditions.

[Criticism of the British people]

30 In every stage of these Oppressions We have Petitioned for *Redress* in the most humble terms: Our repeated Petitions have been answered only by repeated injury. A Prince whose character

redress—remedy

is thus marked by every act which may define a Tyrant, is unfit to be the ruler of a free people.

Nor have We been wanting in attentions to our Brittish *breth-* 31
ren. We have warned them from time to time of attempts by their legislature to extend an *unwarrantable* jurisdiction over us. We have reminded them of the circumstances of our emigration and settlement here. We have appealed to their native justice and magnanimity, and we have conjured them by the ties of our common kindred to disavow these usurpations, which, would inevitably interrupt our connections and correspondence. They too have been deaf to the voice of justice and of *consanguinity.* We must, therefore, *acquiesce* in the necessity, which denounces our Separation, and hold them, as we hold the rest of mankind, Enemies in War, in Peace Friends.

brethren—fellow citizens

unwarrantable—unjustified

consanguinity—being of blood relation

acquiesce—let ourselves be persuaded

[Conclusion: Statement of Separation]

We, therefore, the Representatives of the United States of Amer- 32
ica, in General Congress, Assembled, appealing to the Supreme Judge of the world for the *rectitude* of our intentions, do, in the Name, and by Authority of the good People of these Colonies, solemnly publish and declare, That these United Colonies are, and of Right ought to be Free and Independent States; that they are *Absolved* from all Allegiance to the British Crown, and that all political connection between them and the State of Great Britain, is and ought to be totally dissolved; and that as Free and Independent States, they have full Power to levy War, conclude Peace, contract Alliances, establish Commerce, and to do all other Acts and Things which Independent States may of right do. And for the support of this Declaration, with a firm reliance on the protection of divine Providence, we mutually pledge to each other our Lives, our Fortunes and our sacred Honor.

rectitude—honor

absolved—set free

[Signers]

John Hancock, President
Attested, Charles Thomson, Secretary

Georgia	**North Carolina**
Button Gwinnett	William Hooper
Lyman Hall	Joseph Hewes
George Walton	John Penn

South Carolina
Edward Rutledge
Thomas Heyward, Jr.
Thomas Lynch, Jr.
Arthur Middleton

Maryland
Samuel Chase
William Paca
Thomas Stone
Charles Carroll of
    Carrollton

Virginia
George Wythe
Richard Henry Lee
Thomas Jefferson
Benjamin Harrison
Thomas Nelson, Jr.
Francis Lightfoot Lee
Carter Braxton

Pennsylvania
Robert Morris
Benjamin Rush
Benjamin Franklin
John Morton
George Clymer
James Smith
George Taylor
James Wilson
George Ross

Delaware
Caesar Rodney

George Read
Thomas McKean

New York
William Floyd
Philip Livingston
Francis Lewis
Lewis Morris

New Jersey
Richard Stockton
John Witherspoon
Francis Hopkinson
John Hart
Abraham Clark

New Hampshire
Josiah Bartlett
William Whipple
Matthew Thornton

Massachusetts
Samuel Adams
John Adams
Robert Treat Paine
Elbridge Gerry

Rhode Island
Stephen Hopkins
William Ellery

Connecticut
Roger Sherman
Samuel Huntington
William Williams
Oliver Wolcott

Impact of *the Declaration of Independence*

The Declaration of Independence created the United States of America. This document is a symbol of American democracy and one of the "charters of freedom." By issuing the Declaration of Independence in 1776, the thirteen American colonies officially ended their political ties to Great Britain. The words of the Declaration of Independence summarized the colonists' motivations for seeking independence and rallied support for the colonists in America and abroad. By declaring themselves an independent nation, the American colonists were able to gain an alliance with France and obtain French economic and military assistance in the war against Great Britain. The most important diplomatic effect was to allow for recognition of the newly proclaimed United States by foreign governments friendly to the colonists. The impact of the Declaration of Independence can be seen and felt within the United States and around the world. It is important to remember that the Declaration of Independence is a statement of political philosophy, and although it is often quoted in support of various causes, it is not a formal part of the law. Several portions of the U.S. Constitution and its amendments address the grievances Jefferson levied against the king.

Check for Understanding

1. Explain why the writers of the Declaration of Independence felt the need to declare their reasons for separating from the British government. (Paragraph 1)
2. Describe what Jefferson meant in his statement: "We hold these truths to be self-evident, that all men are created equal ...". (Paragraph 2)
3. Describe three complaints of the colonists against the king. (Paragraphs 3–29)
4. Explain why the signers of the Declaration of Independence pledged "to each other our Lives, our Fortunes and our sacred Honor." (Paragraph 32)

Critical Thinking Question

After winning independence from the British, the Founders created a new government under the Articles of Confederation and then the Constitution. Explain how the Constitution reflects the Declaration's assertion that government "[derives] its just powers from the consent of the governed."

The Articles of Confederation and Perpetual Union

John Dickinson (primary author)

The Articles of Confederation was the first plan for government for the United States. The document was drawn up in 1777 in response to the Lee Resolution (precursor to the Declaration of Independence), which called for American independence. While officially written by a committee with a representative from each colony, John Dickinson is credited as the main author of the original draft of the articles.

▌ Focus on *the Articles of Confederation*

The Articles of Confederation organized the United States as a confederation—in which most of the power remained with the states. The national government, consisting only of a Congress, was given very limited powers. This was a result of colonial experience under British rule leading up to the American Revolution. This limited power led to chaos, because the government could not tax, draft soldiers, or create a single currency for nationwide use. In the end, these problems created the conditions that led to Shays's Rebellion and the resulting ineffective response by the national government. This crisis led to a meeting to discuss amending the Articles that resulted in the drafting of a new constitution to replace the Articles of Confederation.

▌ Overview of *the Articles of Confederation*

The Articles of Confederation described:

- the powers reserved to the states.
- the war powers of the national government.
- how the states were to interact with one another.
- how representation and voting in Congress worked.

▌ Reader Alert!

Although John Dickinson and his committee are careful writers, the spelling, capitalization, and punctuation in their times were not the same as what we use now. A few pointers:

- Rhodeisland is the state of Rhode Island.
- Certain words like *defense, pretense,* and *expense* used to be spelled with the letter **c**, as in *expence.*

- Using *thro'* means that people no longer pronounced the **g** and **h** at the end of *through*. (Think of the pronunciation we use now.)
- The word *cloathed* is more familiar to us as *clothed*.
- The writers chose not to capitalize *united states*.
- Many of the signers abbreviated their names in ways that are no longer in common use. *Jno* means John. *Thos* means Thomas.

The Articles of Confederation and Perpetual Union

[Creating a confederacy]

To all to whom *these Presents* shall come, we the undersigned 1 Delegates of the States affixed to our Names, send greeting.

    Whereas the Delegates of the United States of America, in 2 Congress assembled, did, on the 15th day of November, in the Year of Our Lord One thousand Seven Hundred and Seventy seven, and in the Second Year of the Independence of America, agree to certain articles of Confederation and perpetual Union between the States of New-hampshire, Massachusetts-bay, Rhodeisland and Providence Plantations, Connecticut, New York, New Jersey, Pennsylvania, Delaware, Maryland, Virginia, North-Carolina, South-Carolina, and Georgia in the words following, viz. "Articles of Confederation and perpetual Union between the states of New-hampshire, Massachusetts-bay, Rhodeisland and Providence Plantations, Connecticut, New-York, New-Jersey, Pennsylvania, Delaware, Maryland, Virginia, North-Carolina, South-Carolina and Georgia".

Article I.

The *Stile* of this *confederacy* shall be "The United States of 3 America."

[On the assignment of powers]

Article II.

Each state retains its sovereignty, freedom, and independence, 4 and every Power, Jurisdiction and right, which is not by this confederation expressly delegated to the United States, in Congress assembled.

Article III.

The said states hereby *severally* enter into a firm league of friend- 5 ship with each other, for their common defence, the security of their Liberties, and their mutual and general welfare, binding

these presents—the present document; this written document

stile—an official or legal title, now spelled *style*

confederacy—a way of organizing power between national and subnational (state) governments in which the subnational governments retain the majority of power.

Explain how Article II guarantees that the states will retain most power in the Confederation.

Describe the purpose of the Articles of Confederation according to Article III.

severally—separately, individually

themselves to assist each other, against all force offered to, or attacks made upon them, or any of them, on account of religion, sovereignty, trade, or any other pretence whatever.

[Rules regarding interstate relations]
Article IV.

6   The better to secure and perpetuate mutual friendship and intercourse among the people of the different states in this union, the free inhabitants of each of these states, *paupers*, *vagabonds* and fugitives from justice excepted, shall be entitled to all privileges and immunities of free citizens in the several states; and the people of each state shall have free ingress and regress to and from any other state, and shall enjoy therein all the privileges of trade and commerce, subject to the same duties impositions and restrictions as the inhabitants thereof respectively, provided that such restriction shall not extend so far as to prevent the removal of property imported into any state, to any other state, of which the Owner is an inhabitant; provided also that no imposition, duties or restriction shall be laid by any state, on the property of the united states, or either of them. If any Person guilty of, or charged with treason, *felony*,—or other *high misdemeanor* in any state, shall flee from Justice, and be found in any of the united states, he shall, upon demand of the Governor or executive power, of the state from which he fled, be delivered up and removed to the state having jurisdiction of his offence. Full faith and credit shall be given in each of these states to the records, acts and judicial proceedings of the courts and magistrates of every other state.

[On the rules for congressional elections, terms, and voting]
Article V.

7   For the more convenient management of the general interests of the united states, delegates shall be annually appointed in such manner as the legislature of each state shall direct, to meet in Congress on the first Monday in November, in every year, with a power reserved to each state, to recal its delegates, or any of them, at any time within the year, and to send others in their stead, for the remainder of the Year.

8   No state shall be represented in Congress by less than two, nor by more than seven Members; and no person shall be capable of being a delegate for more than three years in any term of six

---

Describe three rules that regulated how states interacted with one another.

pauper—a poor person

vagabond—a homeless wanderer

felony; high misdemeanor—serious crimes

Explain how representatives to Congress were chosen.

Describe the number of representatives each state is allowed in Congress. Identify the number of votes each state received in Congress.

years; nor shall any person, being a delegate, be capable of holding any office under the united states, for which he, or another for his benefit receives any salary, fees or *emolument* of any kind.

Each state shall maintain its own delegates in a meeting of the states, and while they act as members of the committee of the states. In determining questions in the united states in Congress assembled, each state shall have one vote.

Freedom of speech and debate in Congress shall not be *impeached* or questioned in any Court, or place out of Congress, and the members of congress shall be protected in their persons from arrests and imprisonments, during the time of their going to and from, and attendance on congress, except for treason, felony, or breach of the peace.

[On the conduct of foreign policy]
Article VI.
No state, without the Consent of the united states in congress assembled, shall send any embassy to, or receive any embassy from, or enter into any conference agreement, alliance or treaty with any King prince or state; nor shall any person holding any office of profit or trust under the united states, or any of them, accept of any present, emolument, office or title of any kind whatever from any king, prince or foreign state; nor shall the united states in congress assembled, or any of them, grant any title of nobility.

No two or more states shall enter into any treaty, confederation or alliance whatever between them, without the consent of the united states in congress assembled, specifying accurately the purposes for which the same is to be entered into, and how long it shall continue.

No state shall lay any *imposts* or *duties*, which may interfere with any stipulations in treaties, entered into by the united states in congress assembled, with any king, prince or state, in *pursuance* of any treaties already proposed by congress, to the courts of France and Spain.

[On armies and armaments]

No vessels of war shall be kept up in time of peace by any state, except such number only, as shall be deemed necessary by the united states in congress assembled, for the defence of such state, or its trade; nor shall any body of forces be kept up by any state, in time of peace, except such number only, as in the judgment of

---

Describe the length of a congressional term.

emolument— payment, compensation

impeach—to charge with misconduct, to charge with a crime against the state

Explain why the Articles protected freedom of speech for members of Congress.

What restrictions did the Articles of Confederation place on the states regarding foreign relations?

impost—a tax or required payment (especially on imports)

duty—a tax on imported goods

pursuance— carrying out a plan or provision

Describe the military obligations placed on the states.

Describe the role of the national government in directing the states in their military obligations.

the united states, in congress assembled, shall be deemed requisite to garrison the forts necessary for the defence of such state; but every state shall always keep up a well regulated and disciplined militia, sufficiently armed and *accoutered*, and shall provide and constantly have ready for use, in public stores, a due number of field pieces and tents, and a proper quantity of arms, ammunition and camp equipage. No state shall engage in any war without the consent of the united states in congress assembled, unless such state be actually invaded by enemies, or shall have received certain advice of a resolution being formed by some nation of Indians to invade such state, and the danger is so imminent as not to admit of a delay till the united states in congress assembled can be consulted: nor shall any state grant commissions to any ships or vessels of war, nor *letters of marque or reprisal*, except it be after a declaration of war by the united states in congress assembled, and then only against the kingdom or state and the subjects thereof, against which war has been so declared, and under such regulations as shall be established by the united states in congress assembled, unless such state be infested by pirates, in which case vessels of war may be fitted out for that occasion, and kept so long as the danger shall continue, or until the united states in congress assembled, shall determine otherwise.

Article VII.

15 When land-forces are raised by any state for the common defence, all officers of or under the rank of colonel, shall be appointed by the legislature of each state respectively, by whom such forces shall be raised, or in such manner as such state shall direct, and all vacancies shall be filled up by the State which first made the appointment.

[On paying for the common defense]
Article VIII.

16 All charges of war, and all other expences that shall be incurred for the common defence or general welfare, and allowed by the united states in congress assembled, shall be defrayed out of a common treasury, which shall be supplied by the several states in proportion to the value of all land within each state, granted to or surveyed for any Person, as such land and the buildings and improvements thereon shall be estimated according to such mode as the united states in congress assembled, shall from time to time direct and appoint.

accoutered— equipped

letter of marque and reprisal—license to arm a privately owned ship to capture merchants and disrupt shipping of an enemy power

Explain how war was paid for under the Articles of Confederation. What was a weakness in this approach?

The taxes for paying that proportion shall be laid and levied by the authority and direction of the legislatures of the several states within the time agreed upon by the united states in congress assembled.

[On the powers of the national government]

Article IX.

The united states in congress assembled, shall have the sole and exclusive right and power of determining on peace and war, except in the cases mentioned in the sixth article—of sending and receiving ambassadors—entering into treaties and alliances, provided that no treaty of commerce shall be made whereby the legislative power of the respective states shall be restrained from imposing such imposts and duties on foreigners as their own people are subjected to, or from prohibiting the exportation or importation of any species of goods or commodities, whatsoever—of establishing rules for deciding in all cases, what captures on land or water shall be legal, and in what manner prizes taken by land or naval forces in the service of the united states shall be divided or appropriated—of granting letters of marque and reprisal in times of peace—appointing courts for the trial of piracies and felonies committed on the high seas and establishing courts for receiving and determining finally appeals in all cases of captures, provided that no member of congress shall be appointed a judge of any of the said courts. The united states in congress assembled shall also be the last resort on appeal in all disputes and differences now subsisting or that hereafter may arise between two or more states concerning boundary, jurisdiction or any other cause whatever; which authority shall always be exercised in the manner following. Whenever the legislative or executive authority or lawful agent of any state in controversy with another shall present a petition to congress stating the matter in question and praying for a hearing, notice thereof shall be given by order of congress to the legislative or executive authority of the other state in controversy, and a day assigned for the appearance of the parties by their lawful agents, who shall then be directed to appoint by joint consent, commissioners or judges to constitute a court for hearing and determining the matter in question: but if they cannot agree, congress shall name three persons out of each of the united states, and from the list of such persons each party shall alternately strike out one,

17 | Describe the war powers given to Congress by the Articles of Confederation.

How does the Congress resolve disputes between states?

Describe the two circumstances in which Congress could mediate disputes between the states.

by lot—using a random process, like a lottery

the petitioners beginning, until the number shall be reduced to thirteen; and from that number not less than seven, nor more than nine names as congress shall direct, shall in the presence of congress be drawn out *by lot*, and the persons whose names shall be so drawn or any five of them, shall be commissioners or judges, to hear and finally determine the controversy, so always as a major part of the judges who shall hear the cause shall agree in the determination: and if either party shall neglect to attend at the day appointed, without showing reasons, which congress shall judge sufficient, or being present shall refuse to strike, the congress shall proceed to nominate three persons out of each state, and the secretary of congress shall strike in behalf of such party absent or refusing; and the judgment and sentence of the court to be appointed, in the manner before prescribed, shall be final and conclusive; and if any of the parties shall refuse to submit to the authority of such court, or to appear or defend their claim or cause, the court shall nevertheless proceed to pronounce sentence, or judgment, which shall in like manner be final and decisive, the judgment or sentence and other proceedings being in either case transmitted to congress, and lodged among the acts of congress for the security of the parties concerned: provided that every commissioner, before he sits in judgment, shall take an oath to be administered by one of the judges of the supreme or superior court of the state, where the cause shall be tried, "well and truly to hear and determine the matter in question, according to the best of his judgment, without favour, affection or hope of reward:" provided also, that no state shall be deprived of territory for the benefit of the united states.

Explain why the mediation process laid out is so complicated.

18   All controversies concerning the private right of soil claimed under different grants of two or more states, whose jurisdictions as they may respect such lands, and the states which passed such grants are adjusted, the said grants or either of them being at the same time claimed to have originated antecedent to such settlement of jurisdiction, shall on the petition of either party to the congress of the united states, be finally determined as near as may be in the same manner as is before prescribed for deciding disputes respecting territorial jurisdiction between different states.

[On decision making about national issues related to finance and defense]

alloy—the mixture of metals (in a coin)

19 The united states in congress assembled shall also have the sole and exclusive right and power of regulating the *alloy* and value

of coin struck by their own authority, or by that of the respective states—fixing the standard of weights and measures throughout the united states—regulating the trade and managing all affairs with the Indians, not members of any of the states, provided that the legislative right of any state within its own limits be not infringed or violated—establishing or regulating post offices from one state to another, throughout all the united states, and exacting such postage on the papers passing thro' the same as may be *requisite* to defray the expences of the said office—appointing all officers of the land forces, in the service of the united states, excepting regimental officers—appointing all the officers of the naval forces, and commissioning all officers whatever in the service of the united states—making rules for the government and regulation of the said land and naval forces, and directing their operations.

requisite—required, needed

The united states in congress assembled shall have authority to appoint a committee, to sit in the recess of congress, to be denominated "A Committee of the States," and to consist of one delegate from each state; and to appoint such other committees and civil officers as may be necessary for managing the general affairs of the united states under their direction—to appoint one of their number to preside, provided that no person be allowed to serve in the office of president more than one year in any term of three years; to ascertain the necessary sums of money to be raised for the service of the united states, and to appropriate and apply the same for defraying the public expences to borrow money, or emit bills on the credit of the united states, transmitting every half year to the respective states an account of the sums of money so borrowed or emitted,—to build and equip a navy—to agree upon the number of land forces, and to make requisitions from each state for its quota, in proportion to the number of white inhabitants in such state; which requisition shall be binding, and thereupon the legislature of each state shall appoint the regimental officers, raise the men and cloth, arm and equip them in a soldier like manner, at the expence of the united states; and the officers and men so cloathed, armed and [e]quipped shall march to the place appointed, and within the time agreed on by the united states in congress assembled: But if the united states in congress assembled shall, on consideration of circumstances judge proper that any state should not raise men, or should raise a smaller number than its quota, and that any other state should raise a greater number of men than the quota thereof, such extra number shall

20 What is the purpose of the Committee of the States?

Describe the criteria used to determine how many troops each state had to provide during wartime. How could this number be changed?

be raised, officered, cloathed, armed and equipped in the same manner as the quota of such state, unless the legislature of such state shall judge that such extra number cannot be safely spared out of the same, in which case they shall raise officer, cloath, arm and equip as many of such extra number as they judge can be safely spared. And the officers and men so cloathed, armed and equipped, shall march to the place appointed, and within the time agreed on by the united states in congress assembled.

21   The united states in congress assembled shall never engage in a war, nor grant letters of marque and reprisal in time of peace, nor enter into any treaties or alliances, nor coin money, nor regulate the value thereof, nor ascertain the sums and expences necessary for the defence and welfare of the united states, or any of them, nor emit bills, nor borrow money on the credit of the united states, nor appropriate money, nor agree upon the number of vessels of war, to be built or purchased, or the number of land or sea forces to be raised, nor appoint a commander in chief of the army or navy, unless nine states assent to the same: nor shall a question on any other point, except for adjourning from day to day be determined, unless by the votes of a majority of the united states in congress assembled.

Identify the number of states need to approve spending decisions made in Congress.

[On meetings and publication of their transcripts]

22   The congress of the united states shall have power to adjourn to any time within the year, and to any place within the united states, so that no period of adjournment be for a longer duration than the space of six Months, and shall publish the Journal of their proceedings monthly, except such parts thereof relating to treaties, alliances or military operations, as in their judgment require secrecy; and the yeas and nays of the delegates of each state on any question shall be entered on the Journal, when it is desired by any delegate; and the delegates of a state, or any of them, at his or their request shall be furnished with a transcript of the said Journal, except such parts as are above excepted, to lay before the legislatures of the several states.

Article X.

What responsibilities fall to the Committee of the States?

23   The committee of the states, or any nine of them, shall be authorized to execute, in the recess of congress, such of the powers of congress as the united states in congress assembled, by the consent

of nine states, shall from time to time think expedient to vest them with; provided that no power be delegated to the said committee, for the exercise of which, by the articles of confederation, the voice of nine states in the congress of the united states assembled is requisite.

Article XI.

Canada acceding to this confederation, and joining in the measures of the united states, shall be admitted into, and entitled to all the advantages of this union: but no other colony shall be admitted into the same, unless such admission be agreed to by nine states.

24 Why did the procedure to admit Canada, if it chose to join the United States, differ from other possible additions?

[On paying the bills]

Article XII.

All bills of credit emitted, monies borrowed and debts contracted by, or under the authority of congress, before the assembling of the united states, in pursuance of the present confederation, shall be deemed and considered as a charge against the united states, for payment and satisfaction whereof the said united states, and the public faith are hereby solemnly pledged.

25 In Article XII, the national government assumed the debt accrued to that point. Why was doing so an important step in legitimizing the new government?

Article XIII.

Every state shall abide by the determinations of the united states in congress assembled, on all questions which by this confederation are submitted to them. And the Articles of this confederation shall be inviolably observed by every state, and the union shall be perpetual; nor shall any alteration at any time hereafter be made in any of them; unless such alteration be agreed to in a congress of the united states, and be afterwards confirmed by the legislatures of every state.

26

How could the Articles of Confederation be altered or revised?

And Whereas it hath pleased the Great Governor of the World to incline the hearts of the legislatures we respectively represent in congress, to approve of, and to authorize us to ratify the said articles of confederation and perpetual union. Know Ye that we the undersigned delegates, by virtue of the power and authority to us given for that purpose, do by *these presents*, in the name and in behalf of our respective constituents, fully and entirely ratify and confirm each and every of the said articles of confederation and perpetual union, and all and singular the matters and things therein contained: And we do further solemnly *plight* and engage the faith of our respective constituents, that they shall abide by

27

these presents—this document or legal instrument

plight—to pledge

the determinations of the united states in congress assembled, on all questions, which by the said confederation are submitted to them. And that the articles thereof shall be inviolably observed by the states we respectively represent, and that the union shall be perpetual.

28   In Witness whereof we have hereunto set our hands in Congress. Done at Philadelphia in the state of Pennsylvania the ninth day of July in the Year of our Lord one Thousand seven Hundred and Seventy-eight, and in the third year of the independence of America.

On the part of & behalf of the State of **New Hampshire:**

- Josiah Bartlett
- John Wentworth. Junr; August 8th, 1778

On the part and behalf of the State of **Rhode-Island and Providence Plantations:**

- William Ellery
- Henry Marchant
- John Collins

On the part and behalf of the State of **New York:**

- Jas Duane
- Fra: Lewis
- Wm Duer
- Gouvr Morris

On the part and behalf of the State of **Pennsylvania:**

- Robert Morris
- Daniel Roberdeau
- Jon. Bayard Smith
- William Clingan
- Joseph Reed; 22d July, 1778

On the part and behalf of the State of **Maryland:**

- John Hanson; March 1, 1781
- Daniel Carroll, do.

On the part and behalf of the State of **North Carolina:**

- John Penn; July 21st, 1778
- Corns Harnett
- Jno Williams

On the part and behalf of the State of **Georgia:**

- Jno Walton; 24th July, 1778
- Edwd Telfair
- Edwd Langworthy

On the part of & behalf of the State of **Massachusetts Bay:**

- John Hancock
- Samuel Adams
- Elbridge Gerry
- Francis Dana
- James Lovell
- Samuel Holten

On the part and behalf of the State of **Connecticut:**

- Roger Sherman
- Samuel Huntington
- Oliver Wolcott
- Titus Hosmer
- Andrew Adams

On the Part and in Behalf of the State of **New Jersey,** November 26th, 1778:

- Jno Witherspoon
- Nathl Scudder

On the part and behalf of the State of **Delaware:**

- Thos McKean; Febr 22d, 1779
- John Dickinson; May 5th, 1779
- Nicholas Van Dyke

On the part and behalf of the State of **Virginia:**

- Richard Henry Lee
- John Banister
- Thomas Adams
- Jno Harvie
- Francis Lightfoot Lee

On the part and behalf of the State of **South Carolina:**

- Henry Laurens
- William Henry Drayton
- Jno Mathews
- Richd Hutson
- Thos Heyward, junr.

Impact of *the Articles of Confederation*

The Articles of Confederation represents one strain of American political thought—one of extremely limited government. The Articles created a central government that was intentionally weak. The authors of the Articles were, like many of the Framers of the Constitution, distrustful of concentrated governmental authority. However, unlike the Framers, the authors of the Articles took this fear too far. The Articles were so weak that there was no choice but for the Articles to be scrapped and replaced with a Constitution that created a much stronger national government.

In the AP® U.S. Government and Politics course description, the Articles of Confederation are placed in Unit 1, Foundations of American Democracy, alongside the Declaration of Independence, the U.S. Constitution, *Federalist* No. 10, *Federalist* No. 51, and Brutus No. 1. Specifically, you should know the weaknesses and limitations of the Articles of Confederation and how these led to the creation of the U.S. Constitution.

Chapters 2 and 3 of the textbook introduced and focus on the Articles of Confederation and the U.S. Constitution.

Check for Understanding

1. Define confederation.
2. Explain how Article II creates the circumstances that led to confusion and chaos under the Articles of Confederation.
3. Describe two powers specifically given to the national government. Explain why these powers were given to the national government.
4. Other than Article II, describe other parts of the Articles of Confederation that made governing difficult.
5. What impact, if any, do you think the Articles of Confederation had on our relationships with other countries?

Critical Thinking Question

A fundamental issue in American political history has been the relationship between the states and the national government. Proponents of state power argue that states should have more powers because they are more accountable to the people and each state has a unique culture that cannot be addressed in national policy. On the other hand, proponents of national power argue that a citizen's rights and opportunities should not be a result of geographic chance and that without a uniform national policy in most areas, governing would be unwieldy. Should power in the United States reside mostly in the states? Why or why not? Describe one issue that is better left to the states and one issue that is better left to the national government, and explain your reasoning for each.

The Constitution of the United States

Focus on *the Constitution*

The Constitution of the United States replaced the Articles of Confederation as the framework of the national government. It was ratified after much controversy between the Federalists and the Antifederalists over the proper scope and power of the national government. It is the highest law of the land. It begins with the famous words of the preamble, which establish a democratic spirit, and it follows with Articles I through III that describe the powers of the three branches of government.

[Preamble]

We the People of the United States, in Order to form a more perfect Union, establish Justice, insure domestic Tranquility, provide for the common defence, promote the general Welfare, and secure the Blessings of Liberty to ourselves and our Posterity, do ordain and establish this Constitution for the United States of America.

Focus on *Article I*

Article I of the Constitution establishes a bicameral (two-house) legislature and outlines powers granted to Congress and powers denied to Congress. Notice that this article is long and detailed compared to Article II (the presidency) and III (the judiciary).

Overview of *Article I*

Article I of the Constitution

- specifies powers of the House, Senate, and states.
- specifies powers denied to Congress.
- describes elections of House and Senate.
- allows chambers to determine their own rules of proceedings.

Article. I.

Section. 1.

All legislative Powers herein granted shall be vested in a Congress of the United States, which shall consist of a Senate and House of Representatives.

Section. 2.

1 The House of Representatives shall be composed of Members chosen every second Year, by the People of the several States, and the Electors in each State shall have the Qualifications requisite for Electors of the most numerous Branch of the State Legislature.

2 No Person shall be a Representative who shall not have attained to the Age of twenty five Years, and been seven Years a Citizen of the United States, and who shall not, when elected, be an Inhabitant of that State in which he shall be chosen.

3 Representatives and direct Taxes shall be *apportioned* among the several States which may be included within this Union, according to their respective Numbers, which may be determined by adding to the whole Number of free Persons, including those bound to Service for a Term of Years, and excluding Indians not taxed, three fifths of all other Persons. The actual Enumeration shall be made within three Years after the first Meeting of the Congress of the United States, and within every subsequent Term of ten Years, in such Manner as they shall by Law direct. The Number of Representatives shall not exceed one for every thirty Thousand, but each State shall have at Least one Representative; and until such enumeration shall be made, the State of New Hampshire shall be entitled to chuse three, Massachusetts eight, Rhode-Island and Providence Plantations one, Connecticut five, New-York six, New Jersey four, Pennsylvania eight, Delaware one, Maryland six, Virginia ten, North Carolina five, South Carolina five, and Georgia three.

4 When vacancies happen in the Representation from any State, the Executive Authority thereof shall issue *Writs* of Election to fill such Vacancies.

5 The House of Representatives shall chuse their Speaker and other Officers; and shall have the sole Power of *Impeachment*.

Section. 3.

1 The Senate of the United States shall be composed of two Senators from each State, chosen by the Legislature thereof, for six Years; and each Senator shall have one Vote.

The U.S. Congress is *bicameral*, composed of two houses, the Senate and the House of Representatives.

Membership in the House was the only federal office that was directly elected when the Constitution was written.

A representative must be 25 years old when elected, a senator 30 years old, and a president 35 years old. Why do you think the Framers set these age requirements for these offices?

apportioned means "divided up." Every ten years, the U.S. Congress takes the total number of members of the House of Representatives and allots them among states based on population.

The federal government is required to take a census once every ten years.

writ—legal order

Impeachment is similar to an indictment or criminal charge. The Senate has the power to try the impeachment, decide guilt, and remove an official from office. Why did the Framers give the House the power of impeachment and the Senate the power to try the impeached?

Immediately after they shall be assembled in Consequence of the first Election, they shall be divided as equally as may be into three Classes. The Seats of the Senators of the first Class shall be vacated at the Expiration of the second Year, of the second Class at the Expiration of the fourth Year, and of the third Class at the Expiration of the sixth Year, so that one third may be chosen every second Year; and if Vacancies happen by Resignation, or otherwise, during the Recess of the Legislature of any State, the Executive thereof may make temporary Appointments until the next Meeting of the Legislature, which shall then fill such Vacancies.

No Person shall be a Senator who shall not have attained to the Age of thirty Years, and been nine Years a Citizen of the United States, and who shall not, when elected, be an Inhabitant of that State for which he shall be chosen.

The Vice President of the United States shall be President of the Senate, but shall have no Vote, unless they be equally divided.

The Senate shall chuse their other Officers, and also a President pro tempore, in the Absence of the Vice President, or when he shall exercise the Office of President of the United States.

The Senate shall have the sole Power to try all Impeachments. When sitting for that Purpose, they shall be on Oath or Affirmation. When the President of the United States is tried, the Chief Justice shall preside: And no Person shall be convicted without the Concurrence of two thirds of the Members present.

Judgment in Cases of Impeachment shall not extend further than to removal from Office, and disqualification to hold and enjoy any Office of honor, Trust or Profit under the United States: but the Party convicted shall nevertheless be liable and subject to Indictment, Trial, Judgment and Punishment, according to Law.

Section. 4.

The Times, Places and Manner of holding Elections for Senators and Representatives, shall be prescribed in each State by the Legislature thereof; but the Congress may at any time by Law make or alter such Regulations, except as to the Places of chusing Senators.

The Congress shall assemble at least once in every Year, and such Meeting shall be on the first Monday in December, unless they shall by Law appoint a different Day.

2 | Senators were chosen by state legislatures when the Constitution was originally written. The Seventeenth Amendment changed this, requiring direct election of senators.

Terms are staggered so that a third of the Senate is up for reelection every two years. By staggering Senate terms, a faction is prevented from sweeping all of the seats in one election year.

4 | The vice president has the responsibility of presiding over the Senate and breaking tie votes when necessary.

The president pro tempore nowadays is typically the most senior senator of the majority party and may preside over the Senate.

7 | An impeachment is a charge of wrongdoing, not a conviction. Why do you think the Framers required a two-thirds vote to convict following impeachment?

1 | States have power to conduct elections, but today this power is regulated by the federal government.

Section. 5.

Quorum refers to a minimum number required to conduct business. Note that a majority (more than half) is required most of the time to make a quorum.

1 Each House shall be the Judge of the Elections, Returns and Qualifications of its own Members, and a Majority of each shall constitute a *Quorum* to do Business; but a smaller Number may adjourn from day to day, and may be authorized to compel the Attendance of absent Members, in such Manner, and under such Penalties as each House may provide.

Most procedures of the House and Senate are not specified in the Constitution but by rules established in each chamber. This includes the filibuster rule in the Senate.

2 Each House may determine the Rules of its Proceedings, punish its Members for disorderly Behaviour, and, with the Concurrence of two thirds, expel a Member.

3 Each House shall keep a Journal of its Proceedings, and from time to time publish the same, excepting such Parts as may in their Judgment require Secrecy; and the Yeas and Nays of the Members of either House on any question shall, at the Desire of one fifth of those Present, be entered on the Journal.

One house is not allowed to adjourn without the other. This prevents one house from stopping the other's legislative proceedings.

4 Neither House, during the Session of Congress, shall, without the Consent of the other, adjourn for more than three days, nor to any other Place than that in which the two Houses shall be sitting.

Section. 6.

The House and the Senate determine their own salary. The Twenty-Seventh Amendment requires that if Congress increases its pay, the raise may not go into effect until after an election.

1 The Senators and Representatives shall receive a Compensation for their Services, to be ascertained by Law, and paid out of the Treasury of the United States. They shall in all Cases, except Treason, Felony and Breach of the Peace, be privileged from Arrest during their Attendance at the Session of their respective Houses, and in going to and returning from the same; and for any Speech or Debate in either House, they shall not be questioned in any other Place.

emolument—pay or salary

2 No Senator or Representative shall, during the Time for which he was elected, be appointed to any civil Office under the Authority of the United States, which shall have been created, or the *Emoluments* whereof shall have been encreased during such time; and no Person holding any Office under the United States, shall be a Member of either House during his Continuance in Office.

Revenue means money raised for the government, usually through taxes. Why was the House and not the Senate given the power to raise revenue?

Section. 7.

1 All Bills for raising *Revenue* shall originate in the House of Representatives; but the Senate may propose or concur with Amendments as on other Bills.

Every Bill which shall have passed the House of Representatives and the Senate, shall, before it become a Law, be presented to the President of the United States; If he approve he shall sign it, but if not he shall return it, with his Objections to that House in which it shall have originated, who shall enter the Objections at large on their Journal, and proceed to reconsider it. If after such Reconsideration two thirds of that House shall agree to pass the Bill, it shall be sent, together with the Objections, to the other House, by which it shall likewise be reconsidered, and if approved by two thirds of that House, it shall become a Law. But in all such Cases the Votes of both Houses shall be determined by yeas and Nays, and the Names of the Persons voting for and against the Bill shall be entered on the Journal of each House respectively. If any Bill shall not be returned by the President within ten Days (Sundays excepted) after it shall have been presented to him, the Same shall be a Law, in like Manner as if he had signed it, unless the Congress by their Adjournment prevent its Return, in which Case it shall not be a Law.

Every Order, Resolution, or Vote to which the Concurrence of the Senate and House of Representatives may be necessary (except on a question of *Adjournment*) shall be presented to the President of the United States; and before the Same shall take Effect, shall be approved by him, or being disapproved by him, shall be repassed by two thirds of the Senate and House of Representatives, according to the Rules and Limitations prescribed in the Case of a Bill.

Section. 8.

The Congress shall have Power To lay and collect Taxes, Duties, Imposts and Excises, to pay the Debts and provide for the common Defence and general Welfare of the United States; but all Duties, Imposts and Excises shall be uniform throughout the United States;

To borrow Money on the credit of the United States;

To *regulate Commerce* with foreign Nations, and among the several States, and with the Indian Tribes;

To establish an uniform Rule of *Naturalization*, and uniform Laws on the subject of Bankruptcies throughout the United States;

To coin Money, regulate the Value thereof, and of foreign Coin, and fix the Standard of Weights and Measures;

To provide for the Punishment of counterfeiting the Securities and current Coin of the United States;

This sentence gives the president the veto power. How hard is it politically for both houses of Congress to obtain the two-thirds vote to override a veto? How common is it for Congress to override a veto?

Congress has the power to override a president's veto by a two-thirds vote.

To become law, a bill must pass both houses of Congress and be signed by the president. If the president waits ten days without signing a bill and Congress adjourns, this becomes a *pocket veto.*

To adjourn is to dismiss. The president has to sign congressional legislation but does not have to approve of motions to adjourn or nonbinding resolutions.

The power to regulate commerce stated here is known as the "commerce clause" and has given the federal government broad powers.

naturalization—the process of granting citizenship

7   To establish Post Offices and post Roads;

8   To promote the Progress of Science and useful Arts, by securing for limited Times to Authors and Inventors the exclusive Right to their respective Writings and Discoveries;

9   To constitute Tribunals inferior to the supreme Court;

10   To define and punish Piracies and Felonies committed on the high Seas, and Offences against the Law of Nations;

Congress has the power to declare war, but the president acts as commander in chief of the armed forces. Why do you think the Framers distributed power this way?

11   To declare War, grant *Letters of Marque and Reprisal,* and make Rules concerning Captures on Land and Water;

12   To raise and support Armies, but no Appropriation of Money to that Use shall be for a longer Term than two Years;

13   To provide and maintain a Navy;

14   To make Rules for the Government and Regulation of the land and naval Forces;

letter of marque and reprisal—license to arm a privately owned ship to capture merchants and disrupt shipping of an enemy power

15   To provide for calling forth the Militia to execute the Laws of the Union, suppress Insurrections and repel Invasions;

16   To provide for organizing, arming, and disciplining, the Militia, and for governing such Part of them as may be employed in the Service of the United States, reserving to the States respectively, the Appointment of the Officers, and the Authority of training the Militia according to the discipline prescribed by Congress;

cession—breaking away

17   To exercise exclusive Legislation in all Cases whatsoever, over such District (not exceeding ten Miles square) as may, by *Cession* of particular States, and the Acceptance of Congress, become the Seat of the Government of the United States, and to exercise like Authority over all Places purchased by the Consent of the Legislature of the State in which the Same shall be, for the Erection of Forts, Magazines, Arsenals, dock-Yards, and other needful Buildings;—And

This is sometimes called the *elastic clause* because the words *necessary and proper* are interpreted to give the federal government many powers not specifically stated in the Constitution.

18   To make all Laws which shall be *necessary and proper* for carrying into Execution the foregoing Powers, and all other Powers vested by this Constitution in the Government of the United States, or in any Department or Officer thereof.

Section. 9.

Importation of slaves after 1808 was banned even before slavery was formally abolished.

1   The Migration or Importation of such Persons as any of the States now existing shall think proper to admit, shall not be prohibited by the Congress prior to the Year one thousand eight hundred and eight, but a Tax or duty may be imposed on such Importation, not exceeding ten dollars for each Person.

The Privilege of the *Writ of Habeas Corpus* shall not be suspended, unless when in Cases of Rebellion or Invasion the public Safety may require it. 2

No *Bill of Attainder* or *ex post facto Law* shall be passed. 3

No *Capitation*, or other direct, Tax shall be laid, unless in Proportion to the Census or enumeration herein before directed to be taken. 4

No Tax or Duty shall be laid on Articles exported from any State. 5

No Preference shall be given by any Regulation of Commerce or Revenue to the Ports of one State over those of another: nor shall Vessels bound to, or from, one State, be obliged to enter, clear, or pay Duties in another. 6

No Money shall be drawn from the Treasury, but in Consequence of Appropriations made by Law; and a regular Statement and Account of the Receipts and Expenditures of all public Money shall be published from time to time. 7

No Title of Nobility shall be granted by the United States: And no Person holding any Office of Profit or Trust under them, shall, without the Consent of the Congress, accept of any present, Emolument, Office, or Title, of any kind whatever, from any King, Prince, or foreign State. 8

Section. 10.

No State shall enter into any Treaty, Alliance, or Confederation; grant Letters of Marque and Reprisal; coin Money; emit Bills of Credit; make any Thing but gold and silver Coin a Tender in Payment of Debts; pass any Bill of Attainder, ex post facto Law, or Law impairing the Obligation of Contracts, or grant any Title of Nobility. 1

No State shall, without the Consent of the Congress, lay any Imposts or Duties on Imports or Exports, except what may be absolutely necessary for executing it's inspection Laws: and the net Produce of all Duties and Imposts, laid by any State on Imports or Exports, shall be for the Use of the Treasury of the United States; and all such Laws shall be subject to the Revision and Controul of the Congress. 2

No State shall, without the Consent of Congress, lay any Duty of Tonnage, keep Troops, or Ships of War in time of Peace, enter into any Agreement or Compact with another State, or with a foreign Power, or engage in War, unless actually invaded, or in such imminent Danger as will not admit of delay. 3

A *writ of habeas corpus* protects rights of the accused, especially against unlawful detention. This clause is designed to prevent abuse of power.

A *bill of attainder* is a vote of guilt taken by a legislature. This practice is forbidden because only the courts have the power to determine guilt.

An *ex post facto law* imposes a punishment for an activity that took place before the law went into effect.

By use of the word *capitation*, this clause required Congress to levy taxes based on a state's population rather than income.

■ Focus on *Article II*

Article II describes the qualifications required to be president, the process of electing the president, and the powers of the president. Scholars argue that presidential power has grown over time, but that the growth in power is *not* due to the powers of the president stated in the Constitution. Compared to Article I, which describes the legislature, Article II is much shorter and identifies a few responsibilities of the office. Today, citizens expect much more of the president that what is stated in Article II.

■ Overview of *Article II*

Article II of the Constitution

- defines the president's term as four years.
- outlines how the electors will to select the president and vice president.
- identifies age and residency requirements to be president.
- identifies powers of the president, including serving as commander in chief, negotiating treaties, and heading the executive branch.

Originally, the Constitution did not limit the number of four-year terms a president could serve. The Twenty-Second Amendment ratified in 1951 limits the president to two four-year terms.

Paragraphs 2, 3, and 4 are the rules for the Electoral College that determines who becomes president.

The Twelfth Amendment changed the way electors voted for president and vice president. Instead of voting for two persons, the Twelfth Amendment requires one ballot for president and one ballot for vice president.

Article. II.

Section. 1.

1 The executive Power shall be vested in a President of the United States of America. He shall hold his Office during the Term of four Years, and, together with the Vice President, chosen for the same Term, be elected, as follows

2 Each State shall appoint, in such Manner as the Legislature thereof may direct, a Number of Electors, equal to the whole Number of Senators and Representatives to which the State may be entitled in the Congress: but no Senator or Representative, or Person holding an Office of Trust or Profit under the United States, shall be appointed an Elector.

3 The Electors shall meet in their respective States, and vote by Ballot for two Persons, of whom one at least shall not be an Inhabitant of the same State with themselves. And they shall make a List of all the Persons voted for, and of the Number of Votes for each; which List they shall sign and certify, and transmit sealed to the Seat of the Government of the United States, directed to the President of the Senate. The President of the Senate shall, in the Presence of the Senate and House of Representatives, open all the Certificates, and the Votes shall then be counted. The

Person having the greatest Number of Votes shall be the President, if such Number be a Majority of the whole Number of Electors appointed; and if there be more than one who have such Majority, and have an equal Number of Votes, then the House of Representatives shall immediately chuse by Ballot one of them for President; and if no Person have a Majority, then from the five highest on the List the said House shall in like Manner chuse the President. But in chusing the President, the Votes shall be taken by States, the Representation from each State having one Vote; A quorum for this Purpose shall consist of a Member or Members from two thirds of the States, and a Majority of all the States shall be necessary to a Choice. In every Case, after the Choice of the President, the Person having the greatest Number of Votes of the Electors shall be the Vice President. But if there should remain two or more who have equal Votes, the Senate shall chuse from them by Ballot the Vice President.

> If no candidate receives more than half of the electoral votes, the House decides the election using a rule of one vote for each state.

> In the event that no one candidate receives more than half of the vote, the Senate chooses the vice president.

4   The Congress may determine the Time of chusing the Electors, and the Day on which they shall give their Votes; which Day shall be the same throughout the United States.

> The rules of the Electoral College require that a candidate receive a majority. Because of the development of our two-party system, referral to the House of Representatives has happened only a few times in U.S. history.

5   No Person except a natural born Citizen, or a Citizen of the United States, at the time of the Adoption of this Constitution, shall be eligible to the Office of President; neither shall any Person be eligible to that Office who shall not have attained to the Age of thirty five Years, and been fourteen Years a Resident within the United States.

6   In Case of the Removal of the President from Office, or of his Death, Resignation, or Inability to discharge the Powers and Duties of the said Office, the Same shall devolve on the Vice President, and the Congress may by Law provide for the Case of Removal, Death, Resignation or Inability, both of the President and Vice President, declaring what Officer shall then act as President, and such Officer shall act accordingly, until the Disability be removed, or a President shall be elected.

> Congressional legislation determines the order of succession in the event that both the president and vice president are unable to serve.

7   The President shall, at stated Times, receive for his Services, a Compensation, which shall neither be encreased nor diminished during the Period for which he shall have been elected, and he shall not receive within that Period any other *Emolument* from the United States, or any of them.

> Known as the *emoluments clause,* this means that while in office, the president cannot receive compensations or gifts for services from foreign governments or others.

8   Before he enter on the Execution of his Office, he shall take the following Oath or Affirmation:—"I do solemnly swear (or affirm) that I will faithfully execute the Office of President of the

United States, and will to the best of my Ability, preserve, protect and defend the Constitution of the United States."

Section. 2.

The president is commander in chief of the military. Article I gives the Congress the power to declare war.

1 The President shall be Commander in Chief of the Army and Navy of the United States, and of the Militia of the several States, when called into the actual Service of the United States; he may require the Opinion, in writing, of the principal Officer in each of the executive Departments, upon any Subject relating to the Duties of their respective Offices, and he shall have Power to grant Reprieves and *Pardons* for Offences against the United States, except in Cases of Impeachment.

The president is the sole official in the United States with the power to grant *pardons* (forgiveness) for individuals convicted of crimes.

This paragraph identifies formal powers of the president, including the power to negotiate treaties and appoint Cabinet officials. Both of these require consent of the Senate. Why do you think the framers of the Constitution required consent of the Senate for these two powers?

2 He shall have Power, by and with the Advice and Consent of the Senate, to make Treaties, provided two thirds of the Senators present concur; and he shall nominate, and by and with the Advice and Consent of the Senate, shall appoint Ambassadors, other public Ministers and Consuls, Judges of the supreme Court, and all other Officers of the United States, whose Appointments are not herein otherwise provided for, and which shall be established by Law: but the Congress may by Law vest the Appointment of such inferior Officers, as they think proper, in the President alone, in the Courts of Law, or in the Heads of Departments.

3 The President shall have Power to fill up all Vacancies that may happen during the Recess of the Senate, by granting Commissions which shall expire at the End of their next Session.

Section. 3.

Section 3 requires the president to deliver a State of the Union Address.

1 He shall from time to time give to the Congress Information of the State of the Union,

2 and recommend to their Consideration such Measures as he shall judge necessary and expedient;

3 he may, on extraordinary Occasions, convene both Houses, or either of them, and in Case of Disagreement between them, with Respect to the Time of Adjournment, he may adjourn them to such Time as he shall think proper;

4 he shall receive Ambassadors and other public Ministers;

5 he shall take Care that the Laws be faithfully executed,

6 and shall Commission all the Officers of the United States.

Section. 4.

What is meant by a *high crime*? Why do you think the writers of the Constitution omitted a definition or list of specific impeachable offenses?

The President, Vice President and all civil Officers of the United States, shall be removed from Office on Impeachment for, and Conviction of, Treason, Bribery, or other *high Crimes* and Misdemeanors.

▓ **Focus on** *Article III*

Article III describes the judicial branch of government. Like Article II, Article III is brief and leaves room for interpretation. Notice that there is no mention of the power of judicial review in Article III, nor does it set the number of lower-court judges or Supreme Court justices.

▓ **Overview of** *Article III*

Article III of the Constitution

- establishes a Supreme Court.
- allows Congress to create lower federal courts.
- gives federal judges life-long terms (although they can be impeached).
- outlines jurisdiction of the federal courts with regard to the Constitution and federal law.
- identifies a limited number of cases of original jurisdiction for the Supreme Court.

Article. III.

Section. 1.

The judicial Power of the United States, shall be vested in one supreme Court, and in such inferior Courts as the Congress may from time to time ordain and establish. The Judges, both of the supreme and inferior Courts, shall hold their Offices during good Behaviour, and shall, at stated Times, receive for their Services, a Compensation, which shall not be diminished during their Continuance in Office.

The Supreme Court is created, but judicial review is not defined. Congress is given the power to create inferior (lower) courts.

Note that the standard for impeachment of a federal judge is "good behavior," and failure to adhere to this standard could warrant impeachment. This language is different from impeachment of a president, which can occur for "high crimes and misdemeanors." Why do you think the framers had different standards for federal judges when compared to presidents?

Section. 2.

The judicial Power shall extend to all Cases, in Law and Equity, arising under this Constitution, the Laws of the United States, and Treaties made, or which shall be made, under their Authority;— to all Cases affecting Ambassadors, other public Ministers and Consuls;—to all Cases of admiralty and maritime Jurisdiction;— to Controversies to which the United States shall be a Party;—to Controversies between two or more States;—between a State and Citizens of another State,—between Citizens of different States,— between Citizens of the same State claiming Lands under Grants of different States, and between a State, or the Citizens thereof, and foreign States, Citizens or Subjects.

original jurisdiction—the first court where a case is tried

appellate jurisdiction—capability to review a lower court's decision

2   In all Cases affecting Ambassadors, other public Ministers and Consuls, and those in which a State shall be Party, the supreme Court shall have *original Jurisdiction*. In all the other Cases before mentioned, the supreme Court shall have *appellate Jurisdiction*, both as to Law and Fact, with such Exceptions, and under such Regulations as the Congress shall make.

3   The Trial of all Crimes, except in Cases of Impeachment, shall be by Jury; and such Trial shall be held in the State where the said Crimes shall have been committed; but when not committed within any State, the Trial shall be at such Place or Places as the Congress may by Law have directed.

Section. 3.

treason—the crime of betraying one's country

1   *Treason* against the United States, shall consist only in levying War against them, or in adhering to their Enemies, giving them Aid and Comfort. No Person shall be convicted of Treason unless on the Testimony of two Witnesses to the same overt Act, or on Confession in open Court.

attainder— hereditary guilt passed to the next generation or other relatives

2   The Congress shall have Power to declare the Punishment of Treason, but no *Attainder* of Treason shall work Corruption of Blood, or Forfeiture except during the Life of the Person attainted.

Focus on *Article IV*

Article IV describes the obligations states have to one another and provides a guarantee of a republican (democratic) government.

Overview of *Article IV*

Article IV provides that states have the following obligations to one another:

- Recognition of laws, acts, records, and judicial proceedings (full faith and credit)
- Nondiscrimination against citizens from other states (privileges and immunities)
- Extradition of criminals to the state where the crime happened

Article IV guarantees each state its own democratically elected government, sets up rules for the admission of new states, and promises military protection of the states.

Article. IV.

Section. 1.

Full Faith and Credit shall be given in each State to the public Acts, Records, and judicial Proceedings of every other State. And the Congress may by general Laws prescribe the Manner in which such Acts, Records and Proceedings shall be proved, and the Effect thereof.

The full faith and credit clause requires that states recognize other states' laws and judgments. For example, a driver's license in one state is valid in another state

Section. 2.

The Citizens of each State shall be entitled to all Privileges and Immunities of Citizens in the several States. [1]

A Person charged in any State with Treason, Felony, or other Crime, who shall flee from Justice, and be found in another State, shall on Demand of the executive Authority of the State from which he fled, be delivered up, to be removed to the State having Jurisdiction of the Crime. [2]

The privileges and immunities clause prevents states from treating citizens from other states differently.

No Person held to Service or Labour in one State, under the Laws thereof, escaping into another, shall, in Consequence of any Law or Regulation therein, be discharged from such Service or Labour, but shall be delivered up on Claim of the Party to whom such Service or Labour may be due. [3]

This clause required states to return runaway slaves and was abolished with the ratification of the Thirteenth Amendment.

Section. 3.

New States may be admitted by the Congress into this Union; but no new State shall be formed or erected within the Jurisdiction of any other State; nor any State be formed by the Junction of two or more States, or Parts of States, without the Consent of the Legislatures of the States concerned as well as of the Congress. [1]

The Congress shall have Power to dispose of and make all needful Rules and Regulations respecting the Territory or other Property belonging to the United States; and nothing in this Constitution shall be so construed as to Prejudice any Claims of the United States, or of any particular State. [2]

Section. 4.

The United States shall guarantee to every State in this Union a *Republican Form of Government,* [1]

and shall protect each of them against Invasion; and on Application of the Legislature, or of the Executive (when the Legislature cannot be convened), against domestic Violence. [2]

Republican form of government in this section means a democratically elected state government.

Focus on *Article V*

Article V outlines the difficult process for amending the Constitution.

Overview of *Article V*

Article V outlines the process of amending the Constitution. There are two ways to propose an amendment and two ways to ratify an amendment. For an amendment to go into force, it must be both proposed and ratified. Any combination of proposal and ratification will successfully amend the Constitution. In other words, there are four formal ways to amend the Constitution.

Amendments to the Constitution may be proposed by:
* a two-thirds vote in both houses of Congress, or
* two thirds of the states calling a Convention.

Amendments to the Constitution may be ratified by
* a three-fourths vote of state legislatures, or
* a three-fourths vote of state conventions.

The method using two-thirds vote in both houses of Congress is the most common way of proposing amendments. All twenty-seven of the current amendments were proposed this way. No constitutional convention has been held to amend the Constitution.

A *ratifying convention* is a citizen vote. Proposed constitutional amendments can be ratified by either three-fourths of state legislatures or three-fourths of state ratifying conventions, in which a special convention of representatives is held to vote on the proposal.

Article. V.

The Congress, whenever two thirds of both Houses shall deem it necessary, shall propose Amendments to this Constitution, or, on the Application of the Legislatures of two thirds of the several States, shall call a Convention for proposing Amendments, which, in either Case, shall be valid to all Intents and Purposes, as Part of this Constitution, when ratified by the Legislatures of three fourths of the several States, or by *Conventions* in three fourths thereof, as the one or the other Mode of Ratification may be proposed by the Congress; Provided that no Amendment which may be made prior to the Year One thousand eight hundred and eight shall in any Manner affect the first and fourth Clauses in the Ninth Section of the first Article; and that no State, without its Consent, shall be deprived of its equal Suffrage in the Senate.

Focus on *Article VI*

The supremacy clause is at the center of this article. It was unpopular with the Anti-federalists, who believed that the state government should have more power than the central government.

▨ **Overview of** *Article VI*

Article VI states:

* Federal laws and the Constitution are the supreme law of the land.
* Debt from the Confederation is absorbed by the federal government.
* Lawmakers of the Confederation were required to take an oath of affirmation to support the Constitution.

Article. VI.

All Debts contracted and Engagements entered into, before the   1
Adoption of this Constitution, shall be as valid against the United
States under this Constitution, as under the Confederation.

    This Constitution, and the Laws of the United States which   2
shall be made in Pursuance thereof; and all Treaties made, or
which shall be made, under the Authority of the United States,
shall be the supreme Law of the Land; and the Judges in every
State shall be bound thereby, any Thing in the Constitution or
Laws of any State to the Contrary notwithstanding.

    The Senators and Representatives before mentioned, and the   3
Members of the several State Legislatures, and all executive and
judicial Officers, both of the United States and of the several States,
shall be bound by Oath or Affirmation, to support this Constitution; but no religious Test shall ever be required as a Qualification
to any Office or public Trust under the United States.

> 2   The supremacy clause was a concern of the Antifederalists, who favored stronger state governments.

▨ **Overview of** *Article VII*

Approval by nine of the thirteen states was required to ratify the Constitution.

Article. VII.

The Ratification of the Conventions of nine States, shall be sufficient for the Establishment of this Constitution between the States
so ratifying the Same.

    done in Convention by the Unanimous Consent of the States
present the Seventeenth Day of September in the Year of our Lord
one thousand seven hundred and Eighty seven and of the Inde-
pendance of the United States of America the Twelfth In witness
whereof We have hereunto subscribed our Names,

G°. Washington
Presidt and deputy from Virginia

Delaware
Geo: Read
Gunning Bedford jun
John Dickinson
Richard Bassett
Jaco: Broom

Maryland
James McHenry
Dan of St Thos. Jenifer
Danl. Carroll

Virginia
John Blair
James Madison Jr.

North Carolina
Wm. Blount
Richd. Dobbs Spaight
Hu Williamson

South Carolina
J. Rutledge
Charles Cotesworth Pinckney
Charles Pinckney
Pierce Butler

Georgia
William Few
Abr Baldwin

New Hampshire
John Langdon
Nicholas Gilman

Massachusetts
Nathaniel Gorham
Rufus King

Connecticut
Wm. Saml. Johnson
Roger Sherman

New York
Alexander Hamilton

New Jersey
Wil: Livingston
David Brearley
Wm. Paterson
Jona: Dayton

Pennsylvania
B Franklin
Thomas Mifflin
Robt. Morris
Geo. Clymer
Thos. FitzSimons
Jared Ingersoll
James Wilson
Gouv Morris

The Word, "the," being interlined between the seventh and eighth Lines of the first Page, The Word "Thirty" being partly written on an Erazure in the fifteenth Line of the first Page, The Words "is tried" being interlined between the thirty second and thirty third Lines of the first Page and the Word "the" being interlined between the forty third and forty fourth Lines of the second Page.

Attest William Jackson Secretary

The U.S. Bill of Rights and Other Amendments

Focus on *the Bill of Rights*

The Bill of Rights is made up of the first ten amendments to the United States Constitution, which were proposed as a package after the Constitution was ratified. Notice that many of the amendments protect individuals from abuse of power by the government. The addition of a bill of rights was controversial at the time the document was written. On the one hand, the Federalists argued that the bill of rights would weaken the national government. On the other hand, some feared that identifying certain rights would mean that others weren't protected. The Bill of Rights was withheld from the original document, and Federalists promised Antifederalists that, if the Constitution was ratified, the Bill of Rights would be sent immediately to the states for ratification.

Reader Alert!

The following text is a transcription of the first ten amendments to the Constitution in their original form. These amendments were ratified December 15, 1791.

The Preamble to The Bill of Rights

Congress of the United States begun and held at the City of New-York, on Wednesday the fourth of March, one thousand seven hundred and eighty nine.

THE Conventions of a number of the States, having at the time of their adopting the Constitution, expressed a desire, in order to prevent misconstruction or abuse of its powers, that further declaratory and restrictive clauses should be added: And as extending the ground of public confidence in the Government, will best ensure the *beneficent* ends of its institution.

beneficent—seeking to do good

RESOLVED by the Senate and House of Representatives of the United States of America, in Congress assembled, two thirds of both Houses concurring, that the following Articles be proposed to the Legislatures of the several States, as amendments to the Constitution of the United States, all, or any of which Articles, when ratified by three fourths of the said Legislatures, to be valid to all intents and purposes, as part of the said Constitution; viz.

ARTICLES in addition to, and Amendment of the Constitution of the United States of America, proposed by Congress, and ratified by the Legislatures of the several States, pursuant to the fifth Article of the original Constitution.

The First Amendment provides for freedom of speech and religion. It is considered a hallmark of American liberty

Amendment I

Congress shall make no law respecting an establishment of religion, or prohibiting the free exercise thereof; or abridging the freedom of speech, or of the press; or the right of the people peaceably to assemble, and to petition the Government for a redress of grievances.

The Second Amendment has been interpreted to protect the right of individuals to own firearms.

Amendment II

A well regulated Militia, being necessary to the security of a free State, the right of the people to keep and bear Arms, shall not be infringed.

Amendment III

No Soldier shall, in time of peace be quartered in any house, without the consent of the Owner, nor in time of war, but in a manner to be prescribed by law.

What do you think constitutes an unreasonable search? Notice that much of the language in the Bill of Rights is subject to interpretation.

Amendment IV

The right of the people to be secure in their persons, houses, papers, and effects, against unreasonable searches and seizures, shall not be violated, and no Warrants shall issue, but upon probable cause, supported by Oath or affirmation, and particularly describing the place to be searched, and the persons or things to be seized.

capital crime— offense subject to the death penalty

Indictment by a grand jury requires a determination by a jury that there is enough evidence to begin a prosecution. This is required in federal trials but has not been incorporated into state law.

Amendment V

No person shall be held to answer for a *capital*, or otherwise infamous crime, unless on a presentment or indictment of a Grand Jury, except in cases arising in the land or naval forces, or in the Militia, when in actual service in time of War or public danger; nor shall any person be subject for the same offence to be twice put in jeopardy of life or limb; nor shall be compelled in any criminal case to be a witness against himself, nor be deprived of life, liberty, or property, without due process of law; nor shall private property be taken for public use, without just compensation.

The Sixth Amendment assures a right to speedy trial and assistance of counsel. In *Gideon v. Wainwright*, the Supreme Court ruled that states are required to provide lawyers to defendants who could not afford them.

compulsory process— the right to a subpoena compelling a witness to testify

Amendment VI

In all criminal prosecutions, the accused shall enjoy the right to a speedy and public trial, by an impartial jury of the State and district wherein the crime shall have been committed, which district shall have been previously ascertained by law, and to be informed of the nature and cause of the accusation; to be confronted with the witnesses against him; to have *compulsory process* for obtaining witnesses in his favor, and to have the Assistance of Counsel for his defence.

Amendment VII

In Suits at common law, where the value in controversy shall exceed twenty dollars, the right of trial by jury shall be preserved, and no fact tried by a jury, shall be otherwise re-examined in any Court of the United States, than according to the rules of the common law.

Amendment VIII

Excessive bail shall not be required, nor excessive fines imposed, nor *cruel and unusual* punishments inflicted.

Amendment IX

The enumeration in the Constitution, of certain rights, shall not be construed to deny or disparage others retained by the people.

Amendment X

The powers not delegated to the United States by the Constitution, nor prohibited by it to the States, are reserved to the States respectively, or to the people.

Amendments 11 through 27

Amendment XI

Passed by Congress March 4, 1794. Ratified February 7, 1795.

The Judicial power of the United States shall not be construed to extend to any suit in law or equity, commenced or prosecuted against one of the United States by Citizens of another State, or by Citizens or Subjects of any Foreign State.

Amendment XII

Passed by Congress December 9, 1803. Ratified June 15, 1804.

The Electors shall meet in their respective states and vote by ballot for President and Vice-President, one of whom, at least, shall not be an inhabitant of the same state with themselves; they shall name in their ballots the person voted for as President, and in distinct ballots the person voted for as Vice-President, and they shall make distinct lists of all persons voted for as President, and of all persons voted for as Vice-President, and of the number of votes for each, which lists they shall sign and certify, and transmit sealed to the seat of the government of the United States, directed to the President of the Senate;—the President of the Senate shall, in the presence of the Senate and House of Representatives, open all the certificates and the votes shall then be counted;—The person having the greatest number of votes for President, shall be the President, if such number

---

The Seventh Amendment allows litigants in civil cases to request a trial by jury.

What is *cruel and unusual* punishment? How have these standards evolved over time?

There may be other rights not identified in the Bill of Rights that are retained by the people. The Ninth Amendment was written because of concerns that articulating rights might imply that rights omitted were not rights.

The Tenth Amendment is the basis for federalism–which means that states have some powers protected from encroachment by the federal government.

The Eleventh Amendment protects states from being sued in federal courts. The principle of sovereign immunity means that state government may not be sued for wrongdoing.

A portion of Article II, section 1 of the Constitution was superseded by the Twelfth Amendment.

The Twelfth Amendment establishes the rule for the elector's vote in the electoral college, replacing the language of Article II, section 1, clause 3. Originally the electors voted for two persons without designating president or vice president. This change requires a specific candidate be identified for a specific office.

The sentence in brackets was superseded by section 3 of the Twentieth Amendment.

be a majority of the whole number of Electors appointed; and if no person have such majority, then from the persons having the highest numbers not exceeding three on the list of those voted for as President, the House of Representatives shall choose immediately, by ballot, the President. But in choosing the President, the votes shall be taken by states, the representation from each state having one vote; a quorum for this purpose shall consist of a member or members from two-thirds of the states, and a majority of all the states shall be necessary to a choice. [And if the House of Representatives shall not choose a President whenever the right of choice shall devolve upon them, before the fourth day of March next following, then the Vice-President shall act as President, as in case of the death or other constitutional disability of the President.—] The person having the greatest number of votes as Vice-President, shall be the Vice-President, if such number be a majority of the whole number of Electors appointed, and if no person have a majority, then from the two highest numbers on the list, the Senate shall choose the Vice-President; a quorum for the purpose shall consist of two-thirds of the whole number of Senators, and a majority of the whole number shall be necessary to a choice. But no person constitutionally ineligible to the office of President shall be eligible to that of Vice-President of the United States.

Amendment XIII
Passed by Congress January 31, 1865. Ratified December 6, 1865.

A portion of Article IV, section 2, of the Constitution was superseded by the Thirteenth Amendment.

Section 1.
Neither slavery nor involuntary servitude, except as a punishment for crime whereof the party shall have been duly convicted, shall exist within the United States, or any place subject to their jurisdiction.

Section 2.
Congress shall have power to enforce this article by appropriate legislation.

Amendment XIV
Passed by Congress June 13, 1866. Ratified July 9, 1868.

The Fourteenth Amendment grants U.S. citizenship rights to everyone born in the United States.

The due process clause is sometimes referred to as the "second bill of rights." The language "no state" in combination with "due process of law" has been used selectively by the Supreme Court to apply much of the Bill of Rights to state actions.

Section 1.
All persons born or naturalized in the United States, and subject to the jurisdiction thereof, are citizens of the United States and of the State wherein they reside. No State shall make or enforce any law which shall abridge the privileges or immunities of citizens of the United States; nor shall any State deprive any person of life,

liberty, or property, without due process of law; nor deny to any person within its jurisdiction the equal protection of the laws.

Section 2.

Representatives shall be apportioned among the several States according to their respective numbers, counting the whole number of persons in each State, excluding Indians not taxed. But when the right to vote at any election for the choice of electors for President and Vice-President of the United States, Representatives in Congress, the Executive and Judicial officers of a State, or the members of the Legislature thereof, is denied to any of the male inhabitants of such State, being twenty-one years of age, and citizens of the United States, or in any way abridged, except for participation in rebellion, or other crime, the basis of representation therein shall be reduced in the proportion which the number of such male citizens shall bear to the whole number of male citizens twenty-one years of age in such State.

> Article I, section 2, of the Constitution was modified by section 2 of the Fourteenth Amendment.

> The age was changed by section 1 of the Twenty-Sixth Amendment.

Section 3.

No person shall be a Senator or Representative in Congress, or elector of President and Vice-President, or hold any office, civil or military, under the United States, or under any State, who, having previously taken an oath, as a member of Congress, or as an officer of the United States, or as a member of any State legislature, or as an executive or judicial officer of any State, to support the Constitution of the United States, shall have engaged in insurrection or rebellion against the same, or given aid or comfort to the enemies thereof. But Congress may by a vote of two-thirds of each House, remove such disability.

Section 4.

The validity of the public debt of the United States, authorized by law, including debts incurred for payment of pensions and bounties for services in suppressing *insurrection* or rebellion, shall not be questioned. But neither the United States nor any State shall assume or pay any debt or obligation incurred in aid of insurrection or rebellion against the United States, or any claim for the loss or emancipation of any slave; but all such debts, obligations and claims shall be held illegal and void.

> *insurrection*—violent uprising against a government

Section 5.

The Congress shall have the power to enforce, by appropriate legislation, the provisions of this article.

Amendment XV

Passed by Congress February 26, 1869. Ratified February 3, 1870.

This amendment guaranteed voting rights to former slaves and to African Americans. Southern states chose to circumvent this, passing laws that barred many African Americans from voting.

Section 1.

The right of citizens of the United States to vote shall not be denied or abridged by the United States or by any State on account of race, color, or previous condition of servitude—

Section 2.

The Congress shall have the power to enforce this article by appropriate legislation.

Amendment XVI

Passed by Congress July 2, 1909. Ratified February 3, 1913.

This amendment granted Congress the power to tax income. Article I, section 9, of the Constitution was modified by the amendment.

The Congress shall have power to lay and collect taxes on incomes, from whatever source derived, without apportionment among the several States, and without regard to any census or enumeration.

Amendment XVII

Passed by Congress May 13, 1912. Ratified April 8, 1913.

Article I, section 3, of the Constitution was modified by the Seventeenth Amendment. After its ratification, senators were directly elected.

The Senate of the United States shall be composed of two Senators from each State, elected by the people thereof, for six years; and each Senator shall have one vote. The electors in each State shall have the qualifications requisite for electors of the most numerous branch of the State legislatures.

executive authority— governor's office

When vacancies happen in the representation of any State in the Senate, the *executive authority* of such State shall issue writs of election to fill such vacancies: Provided, That the legislature of any State may empower the executive thereof to make temporary appointments until the people fill the vacancies by election as the legislature may direct.

This amendment shall not be so construed as to affect the election or term of any Senator chosen before it becomes valid as part of the Constitution.

Amendment XVIII

Passed by Congress December 18, 1917. Ratified January 16, 1919. Repealed by Amendment 21.

Section 1.

After one year from the ratification of this article the manufacture, sale, or transportation of intoxicating liquors within, the importation thereof into, or the exportation thereof from the United States and all territory subject to the jurisdiction thereof for beverage purposes is hereby prohibited.

Section 2.

The Congress and the several States shall have concurrent power to enforce this article by appropriate legislation.

Section 3.

This article shall be inoperative unless it shall have been ratified as an amendment to the Constitution by the legislatures of the several States, as provided in the Constitution, within seven years from the date of the submission hereof to the States by the Congress.

Amendment XIX

Passed by Congress June 4, 1919. Ratified August 18, 1920.

The right of citizens of the United States to vote shall not be denied or abridged by the United States or by any State on account of sex.

Congress shall have power to enforce this article by appropriate legislation.

The Nineteenth Amendment grants women the right to vote and is the only place in the Constitution where women are mentioned.

Amendment XX

Passed by Congress March 2, 1932. Ratified January 23, 1933.

Section 1.

The terms of the President and the Vice President shall end at noon on the 20th day of January, and the terms of Senators and Representatives at noon on the 3d day of January, of the years in which such terms would have ended if this article had not been ratified; and the terms of their successors shall then begin.

Article I, section 4, of the Constitution was modified by section 2 of this amendment. In addition, a portion of the Twelfth Amendment was superseded by section 3.

Section 2.

The Congress shall assemble at least once in every year, and such meeting shall begin at noon on the 3d day of January, unless they shall by law appoint a different day.

Section 3.

If, at the time fixed for the beginning of the term of the President, the President elect shall have died, the Vice President elect shall become President. If a President shall not have been chosen before the time fixed for the beginning of his term, or if the President elect shall have failed to qualify, then the Vice President elect shall act as President until a President shall have qualified; and the

Congress may by law provide for the case wherein neither a President elect nor a Vice President elect shall have qualified, declaring who shall then act as President, or the manner in which one who is to act shall be selected, and such person shall act accordingly until a President or Vice President shall have qualified.

Section 4.

The Congress may by law provide for the case of the death of any of the persons from whom the House of Representatives may choose a President whenever the right of choice shall have devolved upon them, and for the case of the death of any of the persons from whom the Senate may choose a Vice President whenever the right of choice shall have devolved upon them.

Section 5.

Sections 1 and 2 shall take effect on the 15th day of October following the ratification of this article.

Section 6.

This article shall be inoperative unless it shall have been ratified as an amendment to the Constitution by the legislatures of three-fourths of the several States within seven years from the date of its submission.

Amendment XXI

Passed by Congress February 20, 1933. Ratified December 5, 1933.

Section 1.

The eighteenth article of amendment to the Constitution of the United States is hereby repealed.

Section 2.

The transportation or importation into any State, Territory, or possession of the United States for delivery or use therein of intoxicating liquors, in violation of the laws thereof, is hereby prohibited.

Section 3.

This article shall be inoperative unless it shall have been ratified as an amendment to the Constitution by conventions in the several States, as provided in the Constitution, within seven years from the date of the submission hereof to the States by the Congress.

Of the twenty-seven amendments, only one, repeal of Prohibition, was sent to state ratifying conventions for a vote.

Amendment XXII

Passed by Congress March 21, 1947. Ratified February 27, 1951.

Section 1.

No person shall be elected to the office of the President more than twice, and no person who has held the office of President, or acted as President, for more than two years of a term to which some other person was elected President shall be elected to the office of the President more than once. But this Article shall not apply to any person holding the office of President when this Article was proposed by the Congress, and shall not prevent any person who may be holding the office of President, or acting as President, during the term within which this Article becomes operative from holding the office of President or acting as President during the remainder of such term.

Section 2.

This article shall be inoperative unless it shall have been ratified as an amendment to the Constitution by the legislatures of three-fourths of the several States within seven years from the date of its submission to the States by the Congress.

This amendment was ratified shortly after the presidency of Franklin D. Roosevelt, the only president to serve more than two terms. George Washington set the tradition of serving for two terms only. Limiting the president to two terms was discussed at the Constitutional Convention, but term limits for the presidency were not instituted until the Twenty-Second Amendment was ratified.

Amendment XXIII

Passed by Congress June 16, 1960. Ratified March 29, 1961.

Section 1.

The District constituting the seat of Government of the United States shall appoint in such manner as the Congress may direct:

A number of electors of President and Vice President equal to the whole number of Senators and Representatives in Congress to which the District would be entitled if it were a State, but in no event more than the least populous State; they shall be in addition to those appointed by the States, but they shall be considered, for the purposes of the election of President and Vice President, to be electors appointed by a State; and they shall meet in the District and perform such duties as provided by the twelfth article of amendment.

Section 2.

The Congress shall have power to enforce this article by appropriate legislation.

Washington, D.C., is not a state. The District of Columbia does not have voting representation in Congress, but the Twenty-Third Amendment gave D.C. three electors, allowing residents to vote for president.

Amendment XXIV

Passed by Congress August 27, 1962. Ratified January 23, 1964.

Section 1.

The right of citizens of the United States to vote in any primary or other election for President or Vice President, for electors for

Poll taxes were one method of disenfranchising African American voters in the South. This amendment abolished the poll tax.

President or Vice President, or for Senator or Representative in Congress, shall not be denied or abridged by the United States or any State by reason of failure to pay any poll tax or other tax.

Section 2.

The Congress shall have power to enforce this article by appropriate legislation.

Amendment XXV

Passed by Congress July 6, 1965. Ratified February 10, 1967.

Section 1.

In case of the removal of the President from office or of his death or resignation, the Vice President shall become President.

Section 2.

Whenever there is a vacancy in the office of the Vice President, the President shall nominate a Vice President who shall take office upon confirmation by a majority vote of both Houses of Congress.

Article II, section 1, of the Constitution was modified by the Twenty-Fifth Amendment.

Section 3.

Whenever the President transmits to the President pro tempore of the Senate and the Speaker of the House of Representatives his written declaration that he is unable to discharge the powers and duties of his office, and until he transmits to them a written declaration to the contrary, such powers and duties shall be discharged by the Vice President as Acting President.

Section 4.

Whenever the Vice President and a majority of either the principal officers of the executive departments or of such other body as Congress may by law provide, transmit to the President pro tempore of the Senate and the Speaker of the House of Representatives their written declaration that the President is unable to discharge the powers and duties of his office, the Vice President shall immediately assume the powers and duties of the office as Acting President.

Thereafter, when the President transmits to the President pro tempore of the Senate and the Speaker of the House of Representatives his written declaration that no inability exists, he shall resume the powers and duties of his office unless the Vice President and a majority of either the principal officers of the executive department or of such other body as Congress may by law provide, transmit within four days to the President pro tempore of the Senate and the Speaker of the House of Representatives their written declaration that the President is unable to discharge the powers and duties of his office. Thereupon Congress shall decide the issue, assembling within forty-eight hours for that purpose if not in session. If the Congress, within twenty-one days after receipt of the latter written declaration, or, if Congress is not in session, within twenty-one days after Congress is required to assemble, determines by two-thirds vote of both Houses that the President is unable to discharge the powers and duties of his office, the Vice President shall continue to discharge the same as Acting President; otherwise, the President shall resume the powers and duties of his office.

Amendment XXVI
Passed by Congress March 23, 1971. Ratified July 1, 1971.

Section 1.
The right of citizens of the United States, who are eighteen years of age or older, to vote shall not be denied or abridged by the United States or by any State on account of age.

Section 2.
The Congress shall have power to enforce this article by appropriate legislation.

Amendment XXVII
Originally proposed Sept. 25, 1789. Ratified May 7, 1992.

No law, varying the compensation for the services of the Senators and Representatives, shall take effect, until an election of Representatives shall have intervened.

After the War in Vietnam, there were increasing calls for allowing 18 year olds the right to vote. Amendment 14, section 2, of the Constitution was modified by section 1 of the Twenty-Sixth Amendment. It provides 18 year olds with the right to vote.

The Twenty-Seventh Amendment was proposed when the Constitution was originally written but was not ratified until 1992. It provides that if Congress votes to raise its pay, the pay raise does not go into effect until after the next election.

Check for Understanding

1. The U.S. Constitution is widely respected in the United States and abroad. Why do you think it carries such a high level of respect?
2. When the Constitution was written, the Antifederalists were concerned that the language in the Constitution would give the federal government too much power. What clauses of the Constitution have allowed the federal government's power to expand?
3. A *supermajority* is defined as a vote requirement that exceeds a majority. What actions in the U.S. Constitution require a supermajority vote? Why did

the Framers of the Constitution require supermajority votes for these actions (and not just a majority)? What is the practical impact of requiring a supermajority vote?

4. Why do you think the federal judges were given life terms in the Constitution? What is the impact on policymaking of giving federal judges a life term?

5. How does the Constitution enable the expansion of power of the presidency? Are there sufficient checks on presidential power?

Critical Thinking Question

The Constitution created a democratic form of government that has survived for more than 200 years. The amendment process is one reason that the Constitution has been able to change with the times. What amendment to the Constitution would you like to see ratified? Explain how your proposal would strengthen our democracy.

Brutus No. 1

Author Unknown

▤ Focus on *Brutus No. 1*

Although the Antifederalists agreed that the Articles of Confederation did not establish an effective government, they believed the Constitution went too far in creating a powerful central government. Brutus No. 1 is the first in a series of essays opposed to ratification of the Constitution. It was first published on October 18, 1787, in the *New York Journal*. The author's identity is still not known. The author most likely was a leading Antifederalist.

Brutus No. 1 expresses the fear that that representation of the people's interests could not be maintained as the country grew in size, population, and power. The essay argues that, once elected and comfortable in their jobs, representatives would not relinquish power. Furthermore, representing large and diverse districts would alienate representatives from their constituents' wishes.

One of the greatest worries expressed in Brutus No. 1 is that the economic power of the national government to tax and to regulate interstate commerce would give the national government unlimited power and be used to abolish state powers. This fear was only made worse by the necessary and proper clause and the supremacy clauses of the proposed Constitution, all of which could be used by the national government to take away the power of the states. Brutus No. 1 also discusses the dangers of a standing army.

▤ Overview of *Brutus No. 1*

In the essay, Brutus

- argues that governments rarely give power back to citizens once it has been relinquished.
- describes a difference between a confederation and a federation.
- explains that the necessary and proper and supremacy clauses give the national government too much power.
- supports the argument that Congress has too many economic powers.
- explains how the federal courts might destroy liberty and take away the powers of state courts.
- describes how democracy cannot be protected in a large republic.
- explains that large republics are too diverse to meet the needs of the public good.
- describes how standing armies lead to tyranny.
- describes how large republics lead to corruption.

▦ Reader Alert!

The author of Brutus No. 1 repeats the same arguments in different places. For example, the author argues twice that the necessary and proper and supremacy clauses will result in too much expansion of federal government power. Similarly, the author mentions the dangers of a standing army in two different places. Perhaps the author circled back to his earlier arguments to emphasize his points. In any event, as you read Brutus No. 1, if you feel like you have seen an argument before, you probably have.

[Thoughts on the proposed constitution]

To the Citizens of the State of New-York.

1   When the public is called to investigate and decide upon a question in which not only the present members of the community are deeply interested, but upon which the happiness and misery of generations yet unborn is in great measure suspended, the benevolent mind cannot help feeling itself peculiarly interested in the result.

dispassionate—
rational and
unemotional

Why was Brutus No. 1
written?

2   In this situation, I trust the feeble efforts of an individual, to lead the minds of the people to a wise and prudent determination, cannot fail of being acceptable to the candid and *dispassionate* part of the community. Encouraged by this consideration, I have been induced to offer my thoughts upon the present important crisis of our public affairs.

[On problems with the Articles of Confederation]

Note the concession
that the Articles of
Confederation are not
effective.

Why does Brutus
No. 1 concede that
the country faces
problems under
the Articles of
Confederation?

*expedient—*a means
of attaining something

3   Perhaps this country never saw so critical a period in their political concerns. We have felt the feebleness of the ties by which these United-States are held together, and the want of sufficient energy in our present confederation, to manage, in some instances, our general concerns. Various *expedients* have been proposed to remedy these evils, but none have succeeded. At length a Convention of the states has been assembled, they have formed a constitution which will now, probably, be submitted to the people to ratify or reject, who are the fountain of all power, to whom alone it of right belongs to make or unmake constitutions, or forms of government, at their pleasure.

[On why the decision whether or not to ratify the Constitution is important]

The most important question that was ever proposed to your decision, or to the decision of any people under heaven, is before you, and you are to decide upon it by men of your own election, chosen specially for this purpose. If the constitution, offered to [your acceptance], be a wise one, calculated to preserve the invaluable blessings of liberty, to secure the inestimable rights of mankind, and promote human happiness, then, if you accept it, you will lay a lasting foundation of happiness for millions yet unborn; generations to come will rise up and call you blessed. You may rejoice in the prospects of this vast extended continent becoming filled with freemen, who will assert the dignity of human nature. You may solace yourselves with the idea, that society, in this favoured land, will fast advance to the highest point of perfection; the human mind will expand in knowledge and virtue, and the golden age be, in some measure, realised. But if, on the other hand, this form of government contains principles that will lead to the subversion of liberty—if it tends to establish a despotism, or, what is worse, a tyrannic aristocracy; then, if you adopt it, this only remaining *asylum* or liberty will be [shut] up, and posterity will *execrate* your memory.

[On why citizens should not give up too much power to the government]

Momentous then is the question you have to determine, and you are called upon by every motive which should influence a noble and virtuous mind, to examine it well, and to make up a wise judgment. It is insisted, indeed, that this constitution must be received, be it ever so imperfect. If it has its defects, it is said, they can be best amended when they are experienced. But remember, when the people once part with power, they can seldom or never resume it again but by force. Many instances can be produced in which the people have voluntarily increased the powers of their rulers; but few, if any, in which rulers have willingly abridged their authority. This is a sufficient reason to induce you to be careful, in the first instance, how you deposit the powers of government.

4

With these few introductory remarks I shall proceed to a consideration of this constitution:

5

Why does the author of Brutus No. 1 believe that the decision to ratify the Constitution is "the most important question that was ever proposed...?"

asylum—protection

execrate—curse

According to Brutus, why should citizens think twice before they voluntarily increase the government's power?

[On the end of the confederation]

6   The first question that presents itself on the subject is, whether a confederated government be the best for the United States or not? Or in other words, whether the thirteen United States should be reduced to one great republic, governed by one legislature, and under the direction of one executive and judicial; or whether they should continue thirteen confederated republics, under the direction and controul of a supreme federal head for certain defined national purposes only?

7   This enquiry is important, because, although the government reported by the convention does not go to a perfect and entire consolidation, yet it approaches so near to it, that it must, if executed, certainly and infallibly terminate in it.

Why does Brutus No. 1 emphasize that the Constitution creates a federal government, abolishing the confederation?

[Argument that the necessary and proper and supremacy clauses give the national government too much power]

8   This government is to possess absolute and uncontroulable power, legislative, executive and judicial, with respect to every object to which it extends, for by the last clause of section 8th, article Ist, it is declared "that the Congress shall have power to make all laws which shall be necessary and proper for carrying into execution the foregoing powers, and all other powers vested by this constitution, in the government of the United States; or in any department or office thereof." And by the 6th article, it is declared "that this constitution, and the laws of the United States, which shall be made in pursuance thereof, and the treaties made, or which shall be made, under the authority of the United States, shall be the supreme law of the land; and the judges in every state shall be bound thereby, any thing in the constitution, or law of any state to the contrary notwithstanding." It appears from these articles that there is no need of any intervention of the state governments, between the Congress and the people, to execute any one power vested in the general government, and that the constitution and laws of every state are nullified and declared void, so far as they are or shall be inconsistent with this constitution, or the laws made in pursuance of it, or with treaties made under the authority of the United States.—The government then, so far as it extends, is a complete one, and not a confederation. It is as much

How will the necessary and proper clause result in uncontrolled power in the Congress?

How does the supremacy clause nullify the power of the states?

one complete government as that of New-York or Massachusetts, has as absolute and perfect powers to make and execute all laws, to appoint officers, institute courts, declare offences, and annex penalties, with respect to every object to which it extends, as any other in the world. So far therefore as its powers reach, all ideas of confederation are given up and lost. It is true this government is limited to certain objects, or to speak more properly, some small degree of power is still left to the states, but a little attention to the powers vested in the general government, will convince every candid man, that if it is capable of being executed, all that is reserved for the individual states must very soon be annihilated, except so far as they are barely necessary to the organization of the general government.

[On why the Constitution gives Congress too much power over the economy]

[paragraph 8 continued] The powers of the general legislature extend to every case that is of the least importance—there is nothing valuable to human nature, nothing dear to freemen, but what is within its power. It has authority to make laws which will affect the lives, the liberty, and property of every man in the United States; nor can the constitution or laws of any state, in any way prevent or impede the full and complete execution of every power given. The legislative power is competent to lay taxes, duties, imposts, and *excises;*—there is no limitation to this power, unless it be said that the clause which directs the use to which those taxes, and duties shall be applied, may be said to be a limitation; but this is no restriction of the power at all, for by this clause they are to be applied to pay the debts and provide for the common defence and general welfare of the United States; but the legislature have authority to contract debts at their discretion; they are the sole judges of what is necessary to provide for the common defence, and they only are to determine what is for the general welfare: this power therefore is neither more nor less, than a power to lay and collect taxes, imposts, and excises, at their pleasure; not only the power to lay taxes unlimited, as to the amount they may require, but it is perfect and absolute to raise them in any mode they please. No state legislature, or any power in the state governments, have any more to do in carrying

excise—a tax on certain goods, commodities, or licenses to do business

this into effect, than the authority of one state has to do with that of another. In the business therefore of laying and collecting taxes, the idea of confederation is totally lost, and that of one entire republic is embraced. It is proper here to remark, that the authority to lay and collect taxes is the most important of any power that can be granted; it connects with it almost all other powers, or at least will in process of time draw all other after it; it is the great mean of protection, security, and defence, in a good government, and the great engine of oppression and tyranny in a bad one. This cannot fail of being the case, if we consider the contracted limits which are set by this constitution, to the late governments, on this article of raising money. No state can emit paper money—lay any duties, or imposts, on imports, or exports, but by consent of the Congress; and then the net produce shall be for the benefit of the United States. The only mean therefore left, for any state to support its government and discharge its debts, is by direct taxation; and the United States have also power to lay and collect taxes, in any way they please. Every one who has thought on the subject, must be convinced that but small sums of money can be collected in any country, by direct taxe[s], when the foederal government begins to exercise the right of taxation in all its parts, the legislatures of the several states will find it impossible to raise monies to support their governments. Without money they cannot be supported, and they must dwindle away, and, as before observed, their powers absorbed in that of the general government.

Do you agree that the power to lay and collect taxes is the most important power that can be granted to the federal government?

How does the federal government's power of taxation limit the state's ability to raise money to support their governments?

[Argument that the federal courts will destroy the powers of state courts]

9 It might be here shewn, that the power in the federal legislative, to raise and support armies at pleasure, as well in peace as in war, and their controul over the militia, tend, not only to a consolidation of the government, but the destruction of liberty.—I shall not, however, dwell upon these, as a few observations upon the judicial power of this government, in addition to the preceding, will fully *evince* the truth of the position.

evince—indicate

10   The judicial power of the United States is to be vested in a supreme court, and in such inferior courts as Congress may from time to time ordain and establish. The powers of these courts are very extensive; their jurisdiction comprehends all civil causes, except such as arise between citizens of the same state; and it

extends to all cases in law and equity arising under the constitution. One *inferior court* must be established, I presume, in each state at least, with the necessary executive officers appendant thereto. It is easy to see, that in the common course of things, these courts will eclipse the dignity, and take away from the respectability, of the state courts. These courts will be, in themselves, totally independent of the states, deriving their authority from the United States, and receiving from them fixed salaries; and in the course of human events it is to be expected, that they will swallow up all the powers of the courts in the respective states.

inferior court—a lower court, whose decisions can be reviewed by the highest court

What evidence does Brutus No. 1 use to support the argument that federal courts will "swallow up" all of the powers of the state courts?

[On why the necessary and proper clause and other enumerated powers will give Congress the opportunity to destroy state powers]

How far the clause in the 8th section of the Ist article may oper- 11
ate to do away all idea of confederated states, and to effect an entire consolidation of the whole into one general government, it is impossible to say. The powers given by this article are very general and comprehensive, and it may receive a construction to justify the passing almost any law. A power to make all laws, which shall be necessary and proper, for carrying into execution, all powers vested by the constitution in the government of the United States, or any department or officer thereof, is a power very comprehensive and definite, and may, for ought I know, be exercised in a such manner as entirely to abolish the state legislatures. Suppose the legislature of a state should pass a law to raise money to support their government and pay the state debt, may the Congress repeal this law, because it may prevent the collection of a tax which they may think proper and necessary to lay, to provide for the general welfare of the United States? For all laws made, in pursuance of this constitution, are the supreme lay of the land, and the judges in every state shall be bound thereby, any thing in the constitution or laws of the different states to the contrary notwithstanding.—By such a law, the government of a particular state might be overturned at one stroke, and thereby be deprived of every means of its support.

It is not meant, by stating this case, to insinuate that the 12
constitution would warrant a law of this kind; or unnecessarily to alarm the fears of the people, by suggesting, that the federal

legislature would be more likely to pass the limits assigned them by the constitution, than that of an individual state, further than they are less responsible to the people. But what is meant is, that the legislature of the United States are vested with the great and uncontroulable powers, of laying and collecting taxes, duties, imposts, and excises; of regulating trade, raising and supporting armies, organizing, arming, and disciplining the militia, instituting courts, and other general powers. And are by this clause invested with the power of making all laws, proper and necessary, for carrying all these into execution; and they may so exercise this power as entirely to annihilate all the state governments, and reduce this country to one single government. And if they may do it, it is pretty certain they will; for it will be found that the power retained by individual states, small as it is, will be a clog upon the wheels of the government of the United States; the latter therefore will be naturally inclined to remove it out of the way. Besides, it is a truth confirmed by the unerring experience of ages, that every man, and every body of men, invested with power, are ever disposed to increase it, and to acquire a superiority over every thing that stands in their way. This disposition, which is implanted in human nature, will operate in the federal legislature to lessen and ultimately to subvert the state authority, and having such advantages, will most certainly succeed, if the federal government succeeds at all. It must be very evident then, that what this constitution wants of being a complete consolidation of the several parts of the union into one complete government, possessed of perfect legislative, judicial, and executive powers, to all intents and purposes, it will necessarily acquire in its exercise and operation.

[On why a federal system cannot protect freedom in a large republic]

13 Let us now proceed to enquire, as I at first proposed, whether it be best the thirteen United States should be reduced to one great republic, or not? It is here taken for granted, that all agree in this, that whatever government we adopt, it ought to be a free one; that it should be so framed as to secure the liberty of the citizens of America, and such an one as to admit of a full, fair, and equal representation of the people. The question then will be, whether a government thus constituted, and founded on such principles, is practicable, and can be exercised over the whole United States, reduced into one state?

Which enumerated powers of Congress are likely to lead to uncontrollable power?

Under what circumstances is Congress likely to take power away from the states?

What viewpoint does the author of Brutus No. 1 have about human nature?

On what point do both the Federalists and the Antifederalists agree?

If respect is to be paid to the opinion of the greatest and 14 wisest men who have ever thought or wrote on the science of government, we shall be constrained to conclude, that a free republic cannot succeed over a country of such immense extent, containing such a number of inhabitants, and these encreasing in such rapid progression as that of the whole United States. Among the many illustrious authorities which might be produced to this point, I shall content myself with quoting only two. The one is the baron de Montesquieu, spirit of laws, chap. xvi. vol. I [book VIII]. "It is natural to a republic to have only a small territory, otherwise it cannot long subsist. In a large republic there are men of large fortunes, and consequently of less moderation; there are trusts too great to be placed in any single subject; he has interest of his own; he soon begins to think that he may be happy, great and glorious, by oppressing his fellow citizens; and that he may raise himself to grandeur on the ruins of his country. In a large republic, the public good is sacrificed to a thousand views; it is subordinate to exceptions, and depends on accidents. In a small one, the interest of the public is easier perceived, better understood, and more within the reach of every citizen; abuses are of less extent, and of course are less protected." Of the same opinion is the marquis Beccarari.

> Do you agree that a large republic with many diverse views makes it difficult to make decisions for the public good?

> *Note*: Cesare Beccaria was an influential criminologist and legal philosopher who was opposed to torture and capital punishment.

History furnishes no example of a free republic, any thing 15 like the extent of the United States. The Grecian republics were of small extent; so also was that of the Romans. Both of these, it is true, in process of time, extended their conquests over large territories of country; and the consequence was, that their governments were changed from that of free governments to those of the most tyrannical that ever existed in the world.

> What historical examples does Brutus No. 1 use to support the argument that democracy cannot survive in large republics?

Not only the opinion of the greatest men, and the experience 16 of mankind, are against the idea of an extensive republic, but a variety of reasons may be drawn from the reason and nature of things, against it. In every government, the will of the sovereign is the law. In despotic governments, the supreme authority being lodged in one, his will is law, and can be as easily expressed to a large extensive territory as to a small one. In a pure democracy the people are the sovereign, and their will is declared by themselves; for this purpose they must all come together to deliberate, and decide. This kind of government cannot be exercised, therefore, over a country of any considerable extent; it must be confined to a single city, or at least limited to such bounds as that

Why does pure democracy function best in small territories?

the people can conveniently assemble, be able to debate, understand the subject submitted to them, and declare their opinion concerning it.

[On why representatives cannot represent the will of the people in a large republic]

17 In a free republic, although all laws are derived from the consent of the people, yet the people do not declare their consent by themselves in person, but by representatives, chosen by them, who are supposed to know the minds of their constituents, and to be possessed of integrity to declare this mind.

18   In every free government, the people must give their assent to the laws by which they are governed. This is the true criterion between a free government and an arbitrary one. The former are ruled by the will of the whole, expressed in any manner they may agree upon; the latter by the will of one, or a few. If the people are to give their assent to the laws, by persons chosen and appointed by them, the manner of the choice and the number chosen, must be such, as to possess, be disposed, and consequently qualified to declare the sentiments of the people; for if they do not know, or are not disposed to speak the sentiments of the people, the people do not govern, but the sovereignty is in a few. Now, in a large extended country, it is impossible to have a representation, possessing the sentiments, and of integrity, to declare the minds of the people, without having it so numerous and unwieldly, as to be subject in great measure to the inconveniency of a democratic government.

Why is it difficult for members of the legislature to represent their constituents' wishes in a large territory?

19   The territory of the United States is of vast extent; it now contains near three millions of souls, and is capable of containing much more than ten times that number. Is it practicable for a country, so large and so numerous as they will soon become, to elect a representation, that will speak their sentiments, without their becoming so numerous as to be incapable of transacting public business? It certainly is not.

[On why a large republic is too diverse to promote the public good]

20 In a republic, the manners, sentiments, and interests of the people should be similar. If this be not the case, there will be a constant clashing of opinions; and the representatives of one part will be

continually striving against those of the other. This will retard the operations of government, and prevent such conclusions as will promote the public good. If we apply this remark to the condition of the United States, we shall be convinced that it forbids that we should be one government. The United States includes a variety of climates. The productions of the different parts of the union are very variant, and their interests, of consequence, diverse. Their manners and habits differ as much as their climates and productions; and their sentiments are by no means coincident. The laws and customs of the several states are, in many respects, very diverse, and in some opposite; each would be in favor of its own interests and customs, and, of consequence, a legislature, formed of representatives from the respective parts, would not only be too numerous to act with any care or decision, but would be composed of such *heterogenous* and *discordant* principles, as would constantly be contending with each other.

heterogenous—diverse

discordant—disagreeing

In what ways was the large republic of the United States diverse, and how does this diversity hinder the operation of government?

[On the difficulty of executing laws in a large republic]

The laws cannot be executed in a republic, of an extent equal to that of the United States, with promptitude. 21

The magistrates in every government must be supported in the execution of the laws, either by an armed force, maintained at the public expence for that purpose; or by the people turning out to aid the magistrate upon his command, in case of resistance. 22

What three reasons does Brutus No. 1 give to explain why it will be difficult to carry out laws in a large republic?

[On why standing armies support tyranny]

In *despotic* governments, as well as in all the monarchies of Europe, standing armies are kept up to execute the commands of the prince or the magistrate, and are employed for this purpose when occasion requires: But they have always proved the destruction of liberty, and [are] abhorrent to the spirit of a free republic. In England, where they depend upon the parliament for their annual support, they have always been complained of as oppressive and unconstitutional, and are seldom employed in executing of the laws; never except on extraordinary occasions, and then under the direction of a civil magistrate. 23

despotic—tyrannical

A free republic will never keep a standing army to execute its laws. It must depend upon the support of its citizens. But when a 24 government is to receive its support from the aid of the citizens, it must be so constructed as to have the confidence, respect, and affection of the people. Men who, upon the call of the magistrate, offer themselves to execute the laws, are influenced to do it either by affection to the government, or from fear; where a standing army is at hand to punish offenders, every man is actuated by the latter principle, and therefore, when the magistrate calls, will obey: but, where this is not the case, the government must rest for its support upon the confidence and respect which the people have for their government and laws.

Why does a standing army cause citizens to support the government out of fear, instead of confidence and respect?

[On why people lose confidence in their rulers in a large republic]

[paragraph 24 continued] The body of the people being attached, the government will always be sufficient to support and execute its laws, and to operate upon the fears of any faction which may be opposed to it, not only to prevent an opposition to the execution of the laws themselves, but also to compel the most of them to aid the magistrate; but the people will not be likely to have such confidence in their rulers, in a republic so extensive as the United States, as necessary for these purposes. The confidence which the people have in their rulers, in a free republic, arises from their knowing them, from their being responsible to them for their conduct, and from the power they have of displacing them when they misbehave: but in a republic of the extent of this continent, the people in general would be acquainted with very few of their rulers: the people at large would know little of their proceedings, and it would be extremely difficult to change them. The people in Georgia and New-Hampshire would not know one another's mind, and therefore could not act in concert to enable them to effect a general change of representatives. The different parts of so extensive a country could not possibly be made acquainted with the conduct of their representatives, nor be informed of the reasons upon which measures were founded. The consequence will be, they will have no confidence in their legislature, suspect them of ambitious views, be jealous of every measure they adopt, and will not support the laws they pass. Hence the government will be nerveless and inefficient, and no way will be left to render it otherwise, but by establishing an armed force to execute the laws at the point of the bayonet—a government of all others the most to be dreaded.

Brutus No. 1 argues that citizens will not be acquainted with their rulers in a large republic. How might this lead to fear and suspicion of government, and even the possibility of military rule?

[On why legislatures cannot represent citizens' wishes in a large republic]

In a republic of such vast extent as the United-States, the legisla- 25 ture cannot attend to the various concerns and wants of its different parts. It cannot be sufficiently numerous to be acquainted with the local condition and wants of the different districts, and if it could, it is impossible it should have sufficient time to attend to and provide for all the variety of cases of this nature, that would be continually arising.

Much of the argument in Brutus No. 1 focuses on the impact of a large republic on citizens. Note that this argument focuses on the impact on representatives and why it will be difficult for them to meet the needs of constituents.

[On why large republics lead to corruption]

In so extensive a republic, the great officers of government would 26 soon become above the controul of the people, and abuse their power to the purpose of *aggrandizing* themselves, and oppressing them. The trust committed to the executive offices, in a country of the extent of the United-States, must be various and of magnitude. The command of all the troops and navy of the republic, the appointment of officers, the power of pardoning offences, the collecting of all the public revenues, and the power of expending them, with a number of other powers, must be lodged and exercised in every state, in the hands of a few. When these are attended with great honor and *emolument* , as they always will be in large states, so as greatly to interest men to pursue them, and to be proper objects for ambitious and designing men, such men will be ever restless in their pursuit after them. They will use the power, when they have acquired it, to the purposes of gratifying their own interest and ambition, and it is scarcely possible, in a very large republic, to call them to account for their misconduct, or to prevent their abuse of power.

aggrandize—to enhance power or wealth

emolument—profit

Why it is easier for an official to engage in corruption in a large republic?

[Conclusion—Why the Constitution should not be ratified]

These are some of the reasons by which it appears, that a free 27 republic cannot long subsist over a country of the great extent of these states. If then this new constitution is calculated to consolidate the thirteen states into one, as it evidently is, it ought not to be adopted.

Though I am of opinion, that it is a sufficient objection to 28 this government, to reject it, that it creates the whole union into

obviate—to remove

obtrude—to intrude into

How does Brutus No. 1 conclude the argument that the Constitution should not be ratified?

one government, under the form of a republic, yet if this objection was *obviated*, there are exceptions to it, which are so material and fundamental, that they ought to determine every man, who is a friend to the liberty and happiness of mankind, not to adopt it. I beg the candid and dispassionate attention of my countrymen while I state these objections—they are such as have *obtruded* themselves upon my mind upon a careful attention to the matter, and such as I sincerely believe are well founded. There are many objections, of small moment, of which I shall take no notice—perfection is not to be expected in any thing that is the production of man—and if I did not in my conscience believe that this scheme was defective in the fundamental principles—in the foundation upon which a free and equal government must rest—I would hold my peace.

Impact of *Brutus No. 1*

Brutus No. 1 was the first in a series of essays that created a powerful movement in the states against ratifying the Constitution. The arguments in Brutus No. 1 made people think about whether or not they wanted a federal government with so many powers, and debates raged in state legislatures about whether a strong central government would take away the rights of the states and infringe on the liberties of citizens. Although not directly addressed in Brutus No. 1, the Antifederalists later argued that a Bill of Rights should be added to protect the liberties of citizens. Although the Antifederalists lost their battle against ratification of the Constitution, in 1792, the first ten amendments to the Constitution were adopted as the Bill of Rights.

Check for Understanding

1. Describe the argument that the necessary and proper and supremacy clauses would be used by the federal government to destroy the powers of the state governments.
2. Identify the specific powers listed in Brutus No. 1 to support the argument that the Constitution gives Congress too much power over the economy.
3. Explain the argument made in Brutus No. 1 that the federal courts would destroy the power of the state courts.
4. Describe two arguments made by Brutus No. 1 to support the claim that large republics cannot protect democracy.
5. Explain how Brutus No. 1 supports the argument that a standing army will lead to tyranny.

▣ Critical Thinking Question

Brutus No. 1 argues against a large and diverse republic, stating, "[i]n a republic, the manners, sentiments, and interests of the people should be similar." Yet, the United States has always been a heterogeneous nation. To what degree has the United States, as a large and diverse nation, managed to overcome the argument made in Brutus No. 1 that democracy works best in countries where people share similar characteristics and viewpoints?

Federalist No. 10

The Same Subject Continued: The Union as a Safeguard against Domestic Faction and Insurrection

James Madison

The Federalist Papers were a series of essays written by Alexander Hamilton, John Jay, and James Madison. These essays were written as a response to essays that were opposed to the new Constitution published in New York newspapers during the ratification debate in the fall of 1787. In all, Hamilton, Jay, and Madison published 85 essays under the pseudonym Publius that explored the benefits of the new Constitution and advocated that New Yorkers should support ratification.

Focus on *Federalist* No. 10

Federalist No. 10, written by James Madison and published November 23, 1787, is generally considered to be the most important of the *Federalist* essays. In *Federalist* No. 10, Madison explains how the Constitution would "control and break the violence of faction." This essay has been used to explain how the Constitution balances various groups that might harm the community, preventing any one of them from becoming too powerful and taking away the liberty of others.

Overview of *Federalist* No. 10

In the essay, Madison

- defines a faction.
- describes why factions are inevitable in a democracy.
- describes the causes of faction.
- explains why it is impossible to prevent the causes of faction.
- explains how the Constitution creates a republic that can control the effects of the "mischiefs of faction."
- explains why factions are easier to control in a large republic.

▦ Reader Alert!

Although Madison writes in outdated language, his argument is linear and logical. Madison first discusses the causes of faction before addressing how the Constitution controls the effects of faction. If you pay close attention to the simple way the argument is organized, it will be easier for you to understand the arguments Madison lays out in the document.

[On the necessity of a new constitution]

To the People of the State of New York:

AMONG the numerous advantages promised by a well- 1 constructed Union, none deserves to be more accurately developed than its tendency to break and control the violence of faction. The friend of popular governments never finds himself so much alarmed for their character and fate, as when he contemplates their propensity to this dangerous vice. He will not fail, therefore, to set a due value on any plan which, without violating the principles to which he is attached, provides a proper cure for it. The instability, injustice, and confusion introduced into the public councils, have, in truth, been the mortal diseases under which popular governments have everywhere perished; as they continue to be the favorite and fruitful topics from which the adversaries to liberty derive their most *specious* declamations. The valuable improvements made by the American constitutions on the popular models, both ancient and modern, cannot certainly be too much admired; but it would be an unwarrantable partiality, to contend that they have as effectually *obviated* the danger on this side, as was wished and expected. Complaints are everywhere heard from our most considerate and virtuous citizens, equally the friends of public and private faith, and of public and personal liberty, that our governments are too unstable, that the public good is disregarded in the conflicts of rival parties, and that measures are too often decided, not according to the rules of justice and the rights of the minor party, but by the superior force of an interested and overbearing majority. However anxiously we may wish that these complaints had no foundation, the evidence, of known facts will not permit us to deny that they are in some degree true. It will be found, indeed, on a candid review of our situation, that some of the distresses under which we labor have been erroneously charged on the operation of our governments;

> Why does Madison argue for a new form of government?

> *specious*—a false statement that seems to be true

> *obviate*—to anticipate and prevent

but it will be found, at the same time, that other causes will not alone account for many of our heaviest misfortunes; and, particularly, for that prevailing and increasing distrust of public engagements, and alarm for private rights, which are echoed from one end of the continent to the other. These must be chiefly, if not wholly, effects of the unsteadiness and injustice with which a factious spirit has tainted our public administrations.

[On the definition of faction]

Note this concession to the Antifederalists.

How does Madison define faction so that all factions are groups, but not all groups are factions?

adversed—opposed to

2 By a faction, I understand a number of citizens, whether amounting to a majority or a minority of the whole, who are united and actuated by some common impulse of passion, or of interest, *adversed* to the rights of other citizens, or to the permanent and aggregate interests of the community.

[On the difficulty in removing the causes of faction]

How does this short paragraph preview the structure of Madison's argument?

What are the methods for eliminating the causes of faction?

3 There are two methods of curing the mischiefs of faction: the one, by removing its causes; the other, by controlling its effects.

4   There are again two methods of removing the causes of faction: the one, by destroying the liberty which is essential to its existence; the other, by giving to every citizen the same opinions, the same passions, and the same interests.

Why is it impossible to eliminate either cause?

aliment— nourishment

5   It could never be more truly said than of the first remedy, that it was worse than the disease. Liberty is to faction what air is to fire, an *aliment* without which it instantly expires. But it could not be less folly to abolish liberty, which is essential to political life, because it nourishes faction, than it would be to wish the annihilation of air, which is essential to animal life, because it imparts to fire its destructive agency.

How does Madison describe human nature?

insuperable— impossible to overcome

How does the unequal distribution of wealth and property cause factions to form?

6   The second expedient is as impracticable as the first would be unwise. As long as the reason of man continues fallible, and he is at liberty to exercise it, different opinions will be formed. As long as the connection subsists between his reason and his self-love, his opinions and his passions will have a reciprocal influence on each other; and the former will be objects to which the latter will attach themselves. The diversity in the faculties of men, from which the rights of property originate, is not less an *insuperable* obstacle to a uniformity of interests. The protection of these faculties is the first object of government. From the protection of different and

unequal *faculties* of acquiring property, the possession of different degrees and kinds of property immediately results; and from the influence of these on the sentiments and views of the respective proprietors, ensues a division of the society into different interests and parties.

faculties—powers

The latent causes of faction are thus sown in the nature of man; and we see them everywhere brought into different degrees of activity, according to the different circumstances of civil society. A zeal for different opinions concerning religion, concerning government, and many other points, as well of speculation as of practice; an attachment to different leaders ambitiously contending for pre-eminence and power; or to persons of other descriptions whose fortunes have been interesting to the human passions, have, in turn, divided mankind into parties, inflamed them with mutual animosity, and rendered them much more disposed to *vex* and oppress each other than to co-operate for their common good. So strong is this propensity of mankind to fall into mutual animosities, that where no substantial occasion presents itself, the most frivolous and fanciful distinctions have been sufficient to kindle their unfriendly passions and excite their most violent conflicts. But the most common and durable source of factions has been the various and unequal distribution of property. Those who hold and those who are without property have ever formed distinct interests in society. Those who are creditors, and those who are debtors, fall under a like discrimination. A landed interest, a manufacturing interest, a mercantile interest, a moneyed interest, with many lesser interests, grow up of necessity in civilized nations, and divide them into different classes, actuated by different sentiments and views. The regulation of these various and interfering interests forms the principal task of modern legislation, and involves the spirit of party and faction in the necessary and ordinary operations of the government.

7

How does this paragraph relate to separation of powers and checks and balances?

vex—to bother or annoy

No man is allowed to be a judge in his own cause, because his interest would certainly bias his judgment, and, not improbably, corrupt his integrity. With equal, nay with greater reason, a body of men are unfit to be both judges and parties at the same time; yet what are many of the most important acts of legislation, but so many judicial determinations, not indeed concerning the rights of single persons, but concerning the rights of large bodies of citizens? And what are the different classes of legislators but advocates and parties to the causes which they determine? Is a

8

law proposed concerning private debts? It is a question to which the creditors are parties on one side and the debtors on the other. Justice ought to hold the balance between them. Yet the parties are, and must be, themselves the judges; and the most numerous party, or, in other words, the most powerful faction must be expected to prevail. Shall domestic manufactures be encouraged, and in what degree, by restrictions on foreign manufactures? are questions which would be differently decided by the landed and the manufacturing classes, and probably by neither with a sole regard to justice and the public good. The apportionment of taxes on the various descriptions of property is an act which seems to require the most exact impartiality; yet there is, perhaps, no legislative act in which greater opportunity and temptation are given to a predominant party to trample on the rules of justice. Every shilling with which they overburden the *inferior number*, is a shilling saved to their own pockets.

> Why are legislators tempted to make laws that will benefit themselves? Why will the most powerful faction, or the majority, probably win?

> *inferior number*—the minority whose rights will be trampled

[On the temptations of leaders]

9   It is in vain to say that enlightened statesmen will be able to adjust these clashing interests, and render them all subservient to the public good. Enlightened statesmen will not always be at the helm. Nor, in many cases, can such an adjustment be made at all without taking into view indirect and remote considerations, which will rarely prevail over the immediate interest which one party may find in disregarding the rights of another or the good of the whole.

> How does Madison address the potential for bad leaders and the temptation for people to act in their immediate interest?

[From causes of faction to controlling their effects]

10   The inference to which we are brought is, that the CAUSES of faction cannot be removed, and that relief is only to be sought in the means of controlling its EFFECTS.

> How does this short paragraph serve as a transition in Madison's argument?

[On republican government as a control on factions]

11   If a faction consists of less than a majority, relief is supplied by the republican principle, which enables the majority to defeat its sinister views by regular vote. It may clog the administration, it may convulse the society; but it will be unable to execute and mask its violence under the forms of the Constitution. When a majority

is included in a faction, the form of popular government, on the other hand, enables it to sacrifice to its ruling passion or interest both the public good and the rights of other citizens. To secure the public good and private rights against the danger of such a faction, and at the same time to preserve the spirit and the form of popular government, is then the great object to which our inquiries are directed. Let me add that it is the great *desideratum* by which this form of government can be rescued from the *opprobrium* under which it has so long labored, and be recommended to the esteem and adoption of mankind.

Why is a faction of the majority more dangerous than a smaller faction?

desideratum—requirement

opprobrium—harsh criticism

By what means is this object attainable? Evidently by one of two only. Either the existence of the same passion or interest in a majority at the same time must be prevented, or the majority, having such coexistent passion or interest, must be rendered, by their number and local situation, unable to *concert* and carry into effect schemes of oppression. If the impulse and the opportunity be suffered to coincide, we well know that neither moral nor religious motives can be relied on as an adequate control. They are not found to be such on the injustice and violence of individuals, and lose their efficacy in proportion to the number combined together, that is, in proportion as their efficacy becomes needful.

12

concert—band together

What are the two ways of controlling a faction of the majority?

From this view of the subject it may be concluded that a pure democracy, by which I mean a society consisting of a small number of citizens, who assemble and administer the government in person, can admit of no cure for the mischiefs of faction. A common passion or interest will, in almost every case, be felt by a majority of the whole; a communication and concert result from the form of government itself; and there is nothing to check the inducements to sacrifice the weaker party or an obnoxious individual. Hence it is that such democracies have ever been spectacles of turbulence and contention; have ever been found incompatible with personal security or the rights of property; and have in general been as short in their lives as they have been violent in their deaths. *Theoretic politicians*, who have patronized this species of government, have erroneously supposed that by reducing mankind to a perfect equality in their political rights, they would, at the same time, be perfectly equalized and assimilated in their possessions, their opinions, and their passions.

13

How does direct democracy harm the rights of the minority?

theoretic politicians—leaders who are more interested in theory than practical solutions

A republic, by which I mean a government in which the scheme of representation takes place, opens a different prospect, and promises the cure for which we are seeking. Let us examine

14

How does Madison define a republic?

the points in which it varies from pure democracy, and we shall comprehend both the nature of the cure and the efficacy which it must derive from the Union.

[On the difference between a republic and direct democracy]

What are the two differences between a direct democracy and a republic?

15 The two great points of difference between a democracy and a republic are: first, the delegation of the government, in the latter, to a small number of citizens elected by the rest; secondly, the greater number of citizens, and greater sphere of country, over which the latter may be extended.

[On the advantages of republican government]

16 The effect of the first difference is, on the one hand, to refine and enlarge the public views, by passing them through the medium of a chosen body of citizens, whose wisdom may best discern the true interest of their country, and whose patriotism and love of justice will be least likely to sacrifice it to temporary or partial considerations. Under such a regulation, it may well happen that the public voice, pronounced by the representatives of the people, will be more *consonant* to the public good than if pronounced by the people themselves, convened for the purpose. On the other hand, the effect may be inverted. Men of factious tempers, of local prejudices, or of sinister designs, may, by intrigue, by corruption, or by other means, first *obtain the suffrages*, and then betray the interests, of the people. The question resulting is, whether small or extensive republics are more favorable to the election of proper guardians of the public weal; and it is clearly decided in favor of the latter by two obvious considerations:

How does representative government guard against the passions of citizens?

consonant—in agreement with

obtain the suffrages—get people's votes

17   In the first place, it is to be remarked that, however small the republic may be, the representatives must be raised to a certain number, in order to guard against the *cabals* of a few; and that, however large it may be, they must be limited to a certain number, in order to guard against the confusion of a multitude. Hence, the number of representatives in the two cases not being in proportion to that of the two constituents, and being proportionally greater in the small republic, it follows that, if the proportion of fit characters be not less in the large than in the small republic, the former will present a greater option, and consequently a greater probability of a fit choice.

cabal—a secret political group

How does Madison use comparison and contrast?

In the next place, as each representative will be chosen by a greater number of citizens in the large than in the small republic, it will be more difficult for unworthy candidates to practice with success the vicious arts by which elections are too often carried; and the suffrages of the people being more free, will be more likely to centre in men who possess the most attractive merit and the most diffusive and established characters.

18

Why are large republics more likely to have representatives who are fit to serve?

[Argument for a large republic]

It must be confessed that in this, as in most other cases, there is a *mean*, on both sides of which inconveniences will be found to lie. By enlarging too much the number of *electors*, you render the representatives too little acquainted with all their local circumstances and lesser interests; as by reducing it too you render him unduly attached to these, and too little fit to comprehend and pursue great and national objects. The federal Constitution forms a happy combination in this respect; the great and aggregate interests being referred to the national, the local and particular to the State legislatures.

19

mean—an average; in this case, a legislature that is the right size

electors—citizens who elect representatives

How does federalism lead to legislatures that are the right size to get things done?

The other point of difference is, the greater number of citizens and extent of territory which may be brought within the compass of republican than of democratic government; and it is this circumstance principally which renders factious combinations less to be dreaded in the former than in the latter. The smaller the society, the fewer probably will be the distinct parties and interests composing it; the fewer the distinct parties and interests, the more frequently will a majority be found of the same party; and the smaller the number of individuals composing a majority, and the smaller the compass within which they are placed, the more easily will they concert and execute their plans of oppression. Extend the sphere, and you take in a greater variety of parties and interests; you make it less probable that a majority of the whole will have a common motive to invade the rights of other citizens; or if such a common motive exists, it will be more difficult for all who feel it to discover their own strength, and to act in unison with each other. Besides other impediments, it may be remarked that, where there is a consciousness of unjust or dishonorable purposes, communication is always checked by distrust in proportion to the number whose concurrence is necessary.

20

How does a large republic, with numerous factions, prevent a faction from taking control of government?

Hence, it clearly appears, that the same advantage which a republic has over a democracy, in controlling the effects of faction,

21

How is Madison's argument in favor of a large country similar to his argument in favor of a large republic?

endowments—attributes

palpable—tangible

How does Madison refute an argument made in Brutus No. 1?

What is Madison's conclusion about the proper structure of government?

incident—resulting from

is enjoyed by a large over a small republic,—is enjoyed by the Union over the States composing it. Does the advantage consist in the substitution of representatives whose enlightened views and virtuous sentiments render them superior to local prejudices and schemes of injustice? It will not be denied that the representation of the Union will be most likely to possess these requisite *endowments*. Does it consist in the greater security afforded by a greater variety of parties, against the event of any one party being able to outnumber and oppress the rest? In an equal degree does the increased variety of parties comprised within the Union, increase this security. Does it, in fine, consist in the greater obstacles opposed to the concert and accomplishment of the secret wishes of an unjust and interested majority? Here, again, the extent of the Union gives it the most *palpable* advantage.

22   The influence of factious leaders may kindle a flame within their particular States, but will be unable to spread a general conflagration through the other States. A religious sect may degenerate into a political faction in a part of the Confederacy; but the variety of sects dispersed over the entire face of it must secure the national councils against any danger from that source. A rage for paper money, for an abolition of debts, for an equal division of property, or for any other improper or wicked project, will be less apt to pervade the whole body of the Union than a particular member of it; in the same proportion as such a malady is more likely to taint a particular county or district, than an entire State.

[Conclusion]

23 In the extent and proper structure of the Union, therefore, we behold a republican remedy for the diseases most *incident* to republican government. And according to the degree of pleasure and pride we feel in being republicans, ought to be our zeal in cherishing the spirit and supporting the character of Federalists.

▪ **Impact of** *Federalist* No. 10

Federalist No. 10 is generally seen as the defining statement of the Framers' dislike of interest groups, because many political scientists view Madison's definition of faction as synonymous with interest groups. Remember that the Federalists and Antifederalists were not political parties, which had not formed yet in the United States. Today, political parties and interest groups are generally viewed as factions in modern American politics.

In the AP® U.S. Government and Politics course description, *Federalist* No. 10 is placed in Unit 1, Foundations of American Democracy. *Federalist* No. 10 argued that the Constitution, specifically the creation of a large republic and federalism, help protect the liberty of American citizens. *Federalist* No. 10 was used as an argument in favor of the ratification of the Constitution in the debate between the Federalists and the Antifederalists.

Specifically, the curriculum requires you to use *Federalist* No. 10, alongside the Constitution and Brutus No. 1, to describe the competing views on how to structure the American political system. On one side were those who believed in participatory democracy (Brutus No. 1) and on the other side were those who believed in pluralist democracy (*Federalist* No. 10).

The Constitution, *Federalist* No. 10, and Brutus No. 1 are covered in Chapter 2. Federalism is covered in Chapter 3. *Federalist* No. 10 helps explain interest group and party competition in modern American politics. Political parties are covered in Chapter 14, and interest groups are covered in Chapter 15.

Check for Understanding

1. Define faction in your own words (paragraph 2).
2. Describe the two methods of curing the mischiefs of faction (paragraph 4).
3. Describe the two remedies for controlling the effects of faction (paragraphs 17 and 20).
4. Explain why factions are more easily controlled in republics than in direct democracies (paragraphs 17–19).
5. Explain why factions are more easily controlled in large republics (paragraphs 20–22).

Critical Thinking Question

Madison argued that the Constitution would prevent dangerous factions from gaining too much power and taking away the liberty of citizens. However, the United States has changed significantly due to the availability of mass media, the nature of political parties, and the role of money in politics. To what extent are Madison's predictions about republican government still valid today?

Federalist No. 51

The Structure of the Government Must Furnish the Proper Checks and Balances between the Different Departments

James Madison

The Federalist Papers were a series of essays written by Alexander Hamilton, John Jay, and James Madison. These essays were written as a response to essays that were opposed to the new Constitution published in New York newspapers during the ratification debate in the fall of 1787. In all, Hamilton, Jay, and Madison published 85 essays under the pseudonym Publius that explored the benefits of the new Constitution and advocated that New Yorkers should support ratification.

Focus on *Federalist* No. 51

Federalist No. 51 was written in 1788 as a response to an Antifederalist paper entitled Centinel 1 that had been published in fall of 1787. This essay criticized the three-branch system of government that the Constitution created, claiming that this model would make it too difficult for the people to effectively hold government officials accountable as compared to a one-branch model (what existed under the Articles of Confederation).

Federalist No. 51 explains the purpose and function of both separation of powers and checks and balances within the three branches. Madison describes the need for a government strong enough to organize and control a society full of imperfect people but that also keeps their imperfect leaders in check. This writing is the classic explanation and defense of the "Madisonian Model" of government still in operation today.

Overview of *Federalist* No. 51

In the essay, Madison

- describes the purpose of a separation of powers.
- explains why human nature is such that a government must be designed to prevent abuse of power.
- describes a need for balancing the power of the legislature and the executive.
- explains the purpose of checks and balances.
- describes how these principles apply in our federal system of government with distinct state and national powers.

▨ Reader Alert!

Federalist No. 51 is as dense and as full of dated vocabulary as the other Federalist Papers. However, it also contains often-quoted pieces of political philosophy such as the sentence, "If men were angels, no government would be necessary." Don't get hung up on any one line of the document, and instead try to absorb its basic message about the intent and purpose of separation of powers and checks and balances. As you read, evaluate—based on the evidence you see of our political system today, whether or not the Constitution designed a system that works as the Founders intended.

[On separation of powers in practice]

To the People of the State of New York:

To what expedient then shall we finally resort, for maintaining in practice the necessary *partition* of power among the several departments, as laid down in the constitution? The only answer that can be given is, that as all these exterior provisions are found to be inadequate, the defect must be supplied, by so contriving the interior structure of the government, as that its several constituent parts may, by their mutual relations, be the means of keeping each other in their proper places. Without presuming to undertake a full developement of this important idea, I will hazard a few general observations, which may perhaps place it in a clearer light, and enable us to form a more correct judgment of the principles and structure of the government planned by the convention.

> 1   *partition*—structure dividing a space, a division into parts

> What constitutional principle is described in this passage?

In order to lay a due foundation for that separate and distinct exercise of the different powers of government, which, to a certain extent, is admitted on all hands to be essential to the preservation of liberty, it is evident that each department should have a will of its own; and consequently should be so constituted, that the members of each should have as little agency as possible in the appointment of the members of the others. Were this principle rigorously adhered to, it would require that all the appointments for the supreme executive, legislative, and judiciary magistracies, should be drawn from the same fountain of authority, the people, through channels having no communication whatever with one another. Perhaps such a plan of constructing the several departments, would be less difficult in practice, than it may in contemplation appear. Some difficulties, however, and some additional expense, would attend the execution of it. Some *deviations*, therefore, from the principle must be admitted. In the constitution of

> 2   What *second*, related but distinct, constitutional principle is described here?

> *deviation*—departing from an established course

the judiciary department in particular, it might be inexpedient to insist rigorously on the principle; first, because peculiar qualifications being essential in the members, the primary consideration ought to be to select that mode of choice which best secures these qualifications; secondly, because the permanent tenure by which the appointments are held in that department, must soon destroy all sense of dependence on the authority conferring them.

3   It is equally evident, that the members of each department should be as little dependent as possible on those of the others, for the *emoluments* annexed to their offices. Were the executive magistrate, or the judges, not independent of the legislature in this particular, their independence in every other, would be merely *nominal*.

[On ambition and human nature]

4   But the great security against a gradual concentration of the several powers in the same department, consists in giving to those who administer each department, the necessary constitutional means, and personal motives, to resist *encroachments* of the others. The provision for defence must in this, as in all other cases, be made *commensurate* to the danger of attack. Ambition must be made to counteract ambition. The interest of the man, must be connected with the constitutional rights of the place. It may be a reflection on human nature, that such devices should be necessary to control the abuses of government. But what is government itself, but the greatest of all reflections on human nature? If men were angels, no government would be necessary. If angels were to govern men, neither external nor internal controls on government would be necessary. In framing a government which is to be administered by men over men, the great difficulty lies in this: you must first enable the government to control the governed; and in the next place oblige it to control itself. A dependence on the people is, no doubt, the primary control on the government; but experience has taught mankind the necessity of *auxiliary* precautions.

5   This policy of supplying, by opposite and rival interests, the defect of better motives, might be traced through the whole system of human affairs, private as well as public. We see it particularly displayed in all the subordinate distributions of power; where the constant aim is, to divide and arrange the several offices in such a manner as that each may be a check on the other; that the private interest of every individual may be a *centinel* over the public

Margin notes:

How does Madison make the argument that the judiciary's permanent tenure means that they cannot have any dependence on the "authority conferring them"—those that nominated and/or confirmed them?

emoluments—payments

nominal—in name only; insignificant

encroachments—attempt to take over; intrusion

commensurate—equal

How is government a reflection on human nature?

What is Madison saying about human nature and goodness in this famous passage?

What is the main way that government is built on dependence on the people?

auxiliary—supplementary; additional

centinel—person who keeps guard (sentinel)

rights. These inventions of prudence cannot be less requisite in the distribution of the supreme powers of the state.

[On the power of the legislature compared to the executive]

But it is not possible to give to each department an equal power 6 of self-defence. In republican government, the legislative authority necessarily predominates. The remedy for this inconveniency is, to divide the legislature into different branches; and to render them, by different modes of election, and different principles of action, as little connected with each other, as the nature of their common functions, and their common dependence on the society, will admit. It may even be necessary to guard against dangerous encroachments by still further precautions. As the weight of the legislative authority requires that it should be thus divided, the weakness of the executive may require, on the other hand, that it should be fortified. An absolute negative on the legislature, appears, at first view, to be the natural defence with which the executive magistrate should be armed. But perhaps it would be neither altogether safe, nor alone sufficient. On ordinary occasions, it might not be exerted with the requisite firmness; and on extraordinary occasions, it might be perfidiously abused. May not this defect of an absolute negative be supplied by some qualified connexion between this weaker department, and the weaker branch of the stronger department, by which the latter may be led to support the constitutional rights of the former, without being too much detached from the rights of its own department?

If the principles on which these observations are founded be 7 just, as I persuade myself they are, and they be applied as a *criterion* to the several state constitutions, and to the federal constitution, it will be found, that if the latter does not perfectly correspond with them, the former are infinitely less able to bear such a test.

[Conclusion]

There are moreover two considerations particularly applicable to 8 the federal system of America, which place that system in a very interesting point of view.

First. In a single republic, all the power surrendered by the 9 people, is submitted to the administration of a single government; and the usurpations are guarded against, by a division of

---

Why would Madison assume that a legislature naturally dominates in a republican system of government? Does the legislature seem to dominate the three branches today? Why or why not?

What are some ways the Constitution divides power between the House of Representatives and the Senate? Under the original Constitution, how did the election of Senators differ from the election of members of the House of Representatives?

Why would Madison assume that the executive, on the other hand, would be weak and in need of strengthening within the system?

What specific checks and balances does Madison appear to be describing here?

criterion—a principle or standard by which something can be judged

the government into distinct and separate departments. In the *compound* republic of America, the power surrendered by the people, is first divided between two distinct governments, and then the portion allotted to each subdivided among distinct and separate departments. Hence a double security arises to the rights of the people. The different governments will control each other; at the same time that each will be controled by itself.

compound—made up of parts

10   *Second.* It is of great importance in a republic, not only to guard the society against the oppression of its rulers; but to guard one part of the society against the injustice of the other part. Different interests necessarily exist in different classes of citizens. If a majority be united by a common interest, the rights of the minority will be insecure. There are but two methods of providing against this evil: the one, by creating a will in the community independent of the majority, that is, of the society itself; the other, by comprehending in the society so many separate descriptions of citizens, as will render an unjust combination of a majority of the whole very improbable, if not impracticable. The first method prevails in all governments possessing an hereditary or self-appointed authority. This, at best, is but a *precarious* security; because a power independent of the society may as well *espouse* the unjust views of the major, as the rightful interests of the minor party, and may possibly be turned against both parties. The second method will be exemplified in the federal republic of the United States. Whilst all authority in it will be derived from, and dependent on the society, the society itself will be broken into so many parts, interests, and classes of citizens, that the rights of individuals, or of the minority, will be in little danger from interested combinations of the majority. In a free government, the security for civil rights must be the same as that for religious rights. It consists in the one case in the multiplicity of interests, and in the other, in the multiplicity of *sects*. The degree of security in both cases will depend on the number of interests and sects; and this may be presumed to depend on the extent of country and number of people comprehended under the same government. This view of the subject must particularly recommend a proper federal system to all the sincere and considerate friends of republican government: since it shows, that in exact proportion as the territory of the union may be formed into more *circumscribed* confederacies, or states, oppressive combinations of a majority will be facilitated; the best security under the republican form, for the rights of every class of citizens, will be diminished; and consequently, the stability and

precarious— insecure, rickety

espouse—advocate, put forth

sect—a religious group, often out of the mainstream

circumscribed— narrowly drawn, small, limited

independence of some member of the government, the only other security, must be proportionally increased. Justice is the end of government. It is the end of civil society. It ever has been, and ever will be, pursued, until it be obtained, or until liberty be lost in the pursuit. In a society, under the forms of which the stronger faction can readily unite and oppress the weaker, anarchy may as truly be said to reign, as in a state of nature, where the weaker individual is not secured against the violence of the stronger: and as, in the latter state, even the stronger individuals are prompted, by the uncertainty of their condition, to submit to a government which may protect the weak, as well as themselves: so, in the former state, will the more powerful factions or parties be gradually induced, by a like motive, to wish for a government which will protect all parties, the weaker as well as the more powerful. It can be little doubted, that if the state of Rhode Island was separated from the confederacy, and left to itself, the insecurity of rights under the popular form of government within such narrow limits, would be displayed by such reiterated oppressions of factious majorities, that some power altogether independent of the people, would soon be called for by the voice of the very factions whose misrule had proved the necessity of it. In the extended republic of the United States, and among the great variety of interests, parties, and sects, which it embraces, a coalition of a majority of the whole society could seldom take place upon any other principles, than those of justice and the general good: whilst there being thus less danger to a minor from the will of the major party, there must be less pretext also, to provide for the security of the former, by introducing into the government a will not dependent on the latter: or, in other words, a will independent of the society itself. It is no less certain than it is important, notwithstanding the contrary opinions which have been entertained, that the larger the society, provided it lie within a practicable sphere, the more duly capable it will be of self-government. And happily for the *republican cause*, the practicable sphere may be carried to a very great extent, by a judicious modification and mixture of the *federal principle*.

Summarize Madison's message in this long paragraph about how checks and balances help prevent tyranny of the majority.

How would a larger federal system aid the process of self-government?

Impact of *Federalist* No. 51 on U.S. political philosophy and the design of the branches of government

Federalist No. 51 is considered a classic piece of political philosophy because it is a defense of a constitutional system that was designed to safeguard against human nature's bad tendencies and imperfections. It will first be introduced in Unit 1, and you will have to understand this document in the context of the debate about federal power and the design of the new Constitution that went on between Federalists and Antifederalists.

It's important to spiral back to this document in Unit 2, the chapters that describe the three branches of government, because their interaction is precisely what *Federalist* No. 51 is all about. You can examine what branches of government seem more or less empowered today within the three-branch system, and in doing so, you can reflect on whether Madison was correct in his assumptions about where power should be enhanced or restrained in designing the system. Think about the effectiveness of the Madisonian Model in our age of gridlock in policymaking. Is gridlock the fault of a design flaw in the three-branch system, or is the nature of party polarization today to blame? Would Madison even see gridlock in congressional politics as a problem? He did, after all, want a cautious and deliberate decision-making body.

Finally, this document discusses the way in which the Constitution was designed to protect against abuse of minorities by the majority. This is a focus in Unit 3, Civil Rights and Civil Liberties, and you can return to this document as one example of how the government has sought to prevent tyranny of the majority over time.

Check for Understanding

1. Describe Madison's argument for the necessity of separating power between the branches of government.
2. Explain how checks and balances are different from separation of powers.
3. Describe Madison's argument based in human nature for why government needs to be strong, but not too strong.
4. Explain why Madison believes the legislature might need to be weakened, and describe his proposed remedy for weakening the legislature.
5. Describe two examples of check and balances that are referred to in the reading.

Critical Thinking Question

Madison explained that because neither men, nor those that lead them, are "angels," government must be strong enough to preserve order, but not so strong that power can be abused. Thus he helped to create a system with three separate branches of government with the power to check one another. But in this age of growing presidential strength, party polarization and congressional gridlock, is the Madisonian model functioning as intended?

Federalist No. 70

The Executive Department Further Considered

Alexander Hamilton

The Federalist Papers were a series of essays written by Alexander Hamilton, John Jay, and James Madison. These essays were written as a response to essays that were opposed to the new Constitution published in New York newspapers during the ratification debate in the fall of 1787. In all, Hamilton, Jay, and Madison published 85 essays under the pseudonym Publius that explored the benefits of the new Constitution and advocated that New Yorkers should support ratification.

During the Constitutional Convention, Alexander Hamilton proposed a plan for a new government based on that of the British monarchy and parliament, an alternative plan to the Virginia and New Jersey Plans. Often referred to as the "British Plan," Hamilton proposed a powerful single executive who served for life, or during good behavior. Hamilton believed that a lengthy term—life or good behavior—would give stability to the executive office. Hamilton argued that limited terms would make it hard for the executive to achieve policy goals and would encourage politicians to focus on reelection, rather than governing.

Although Hamilton's plan was rejected, a unitary executive was supported by the delegates to the convention. Hamilton was influenced by several Enlightenment theorists. Hamilton's call for energy in the executive, as described in *Federalist* No. 70, reflects Montesquieu's preference for a "vigor" in the executive. As part of the Federalists' effort to encourage the ratification of the Constitution, Hamilton published *Federalist* No. 70 to convince the states of the necessity of unity in the executive branch.

▊ Focus on *Federalist* No. 70

Federalist No. 70, written by Alexander Hamilton and published March 18, 1788, is the fourth of eleven essays written by Hamilton on the topic of the executive. In *Federalist* No. 70, Hamilton emphasizes the importance of having a single executive instead of the plural executive, or executive council, preferred by the Antifederalists. Hamilton suggests that a strong (energetic) executive leader is necessary because "Energy in the executive is the leading character in the definition of good government." A single executive could best protect against foreign attacks, administer the law, protect private property, and secure liberty. Furthermore, a single executive is needed to provide accountability. Hamilton contends that a plural executive would cause disputes within the executive branch, leading to delays in administering laws and a lack of accountability to the public.

◼ Overview of *Federalist* No. 70

In the essay, Hamilton

- defines good government.
- describes why a unitary executive is necessary to achieve good government.
- describes four ingredients of an energetic executive.
- explains why an energetic executive is necessary to good government.
- explains why a plural executive is bad for a strong union.

◼ Reader Alert!

This essay concerning the powers of the executive department is the most famous Federalist Paper concerning the presidency. Although lengthy and containing uncommon vocabulary, Hamilton's arguments are based on history and logic. Hamilton argues for a single "energetic" executive as necessary to create good government, discusses the "ingredients" necessary to create a strong executive, and provides historical evidence to support his claim. Hamilton also offers reasons for not having a plural executive, and this essay is a direct response to the Antifederalist preference for an executive council.

advocates—supporters

vigorous—energetic; strong

republican—democratic

Note how Hamilton challenges the Antifederalist argument for a plural executive.

supposition—belief

destitute—not having

How does Hamilton define good government?

faction—a party or group that would harm the community or take away rights

anarchy—disorder or lawlessness

tyranny—oppressive government

[On the need for a strong executive]

1   There is an idea, which is not without its *advocates*, that a *vigorous* executive is inconsistent with the genius of *republican* government. The enlightened well-wishers to this species of government must at least hope that the *supposition* is *destitute* of foundation; since they can never admit its truth, without at the same time admitting the condemnation of their own principles. Energy in the executive is a leading character in the definition of good government. It is essential to the protection of the community against foreign attacks; it is not less essential to the steady administration of the laws; to the protection of property against those irregular and high-handed combinations which sometimes interrupt the ordinary course of justice; to the security of liberty against the enterprises and assaults of ambition, of *faction*, and of *anarchy*. Every man the least conversant in Roman history knows how often that republic was obliged to take refuge in the absolute power of a single man, under the formidable title of dictator, as well against the intrigues of ambitious individuals who aspired to the *tyranny*, and the

seditions of whole classes of the community whose conduct threatened the existence of all government, as against the invasions of external enemies who menaced the conquest and destruction of Rome.

> *sedition*—incitement to rebellion

There can be no need, however, to multiply arguments or examples on this head. A *feeble* executive implies a feeble execution of the government. A feeble execution is but another phrase for a bad execution; and a government ill executed, whatever it may be in theory, must be, in practice, a bad government. [2]

> *feeble*—weak
>
> Note that Hamilton equates a strong executive with good government and argues that a weak executive will lead to a bad form of government.

[Ingredients for strong executive]

Taking it for granted, therefore, that all men of sense will agree in the necessity of an energetic executive; it will only remain to inquire, what are the ingredients which constitute this energy? How far can they be combined with those other ingredients which constitute safety in the republican sense? And how far does this combination characterize the plan which has been reported by the convention? [3]

The ingredients which constitute energy in the executive are unity; duration; an adequate provision for its support; and competent powers. [4]

> What ingredients make a strong executive?

The ingredients which constitute safety in the republican sense are a due dependence on the people, secondly a due responsibility. [5]

> What two ingredients create a safe republic?

Those politicians and statesmen who have been the most celebrated for the soundness of their principles and for the justness of their views have declared in favor of a single executive and a numerous legislature. They have with great *propriety,* considered energy as the most necessary qualification of the former, and have regarded this as most applicable to power in a single hand; while they have, with equal propriety, considered the latter as best adapted to deliberation and wisdom, and best calculated to *conciliate* the confidence of the people and to secure their privileges and interests. [6]

> *propriety*—conforming to conventionally accepted standards of behavior
>
> *conciliate*—calm

That unity is conducive to energy will not be disputed. Decision, activity, secrecy, and dispatch will generally characterize the proceedings of one man in a much more eminent degree than the proceedings of any greater number; and in proportion as the number is increased, these qualities will be diminished. [7]

This unity may be destroyed in two ways: either by vesting the power in two or more *magistrates* of equal dignity and [8]

> *magistrate*—judge

ostensibly—to all appearances

votary—a person who has made a pledge or vow

liable—accountable

authority, or by vesting it *ostensibly* in one man, subject in whole or in part to the control and co-operation of others, in the capacity of counselors to him. Of the first, the two consuls of Rome may serve as an example; of the last, we shall find examples in the constitutions of several of the States. New York and New Jersey, if I recollect right, are the only States which have entrusted the executive authority wholly to single men. Both these methods of destroying the unity of the executive have their partisans; but the *votaries* of an executive council are the most numerous. They are both *liable,* if not to equal, to similar objections, and may in most lights be examined in conjunction.

[On historical examples of plural executives]

History has taught us that an executive with multiple people does not work.

mischief—harm or disruption

dissention—disagreement

specimen—example; case

prudent—acting with or showing care and thought for the future

patrician—an aristocrat or noble of ancient Rome

plebian—plebeian, a commoner of ancient Rome

9   The experience of other nations will afford little instruction on this head. As far, however, as it teaches anything, it teaches us not to be enamored of plurality in the executive. We have seen that the Achaeans on an experiment of two Praetors, were induced to abolish one. The Roman history records many instances of *mischiefs* to the republic from the *dissentions* between the consuls, and between the military tribunes, who were at times substituted to the consuls. But it gives us no *specimens* of any peculiar advantages derived to the state from the circumstance of the plurality of those magistrates. That the dissentions between them were not more frequent or more fatal is matter of astonishment, until we advert to the singular position in which he republic was almost continually placed and to the *prudent* policy pointed out by the circumstances of the state, and pursued by the consuls, of making a division of the government between them. The *patricians* engaged in a perpetual struggle with the *plebians* for the preservation of their ancient authorities and dignities; the consuls, who were generally chosen out of the former body, were commonly united by the personal interest they had in the defense of the privileges of their order. In addition to this motive of union, after the arms of the republic had considerably expanded the bounds of its empire, it became an established custom with the consuls to divide the administration between themselves by lot—one of them remaining at Rome to govern the city and its environs; the other taking the command in the more distant provinces. This expedient must no doubt have had great influence in preventing those collisions and rivalships which might otherwise have embroiled the peace of the republic.

[On the dangers of a plural executive]

But quitting the dim light of historical research, and attaching
ourselves purely to the dictates of reason and good sense, we shall
discover much greater cause to reject than to approve the idea of
plurality in the executive, under any modification whatever.

Wherever two or more persons are engaged in any common
enterprise or pursuit, there is always danger of difference of opinion. If it be a public trust or office in which they are clothed with
equal dignity and authority, there is peculiar danger of personal
emulation and even animosity. From either, and especially from
all these causes, the most bitter dissentions are apt to spring.
Whenever these happen, they lessen the respectability, weaken the
authority, and distract the plans and operations of those whom
they divide. If they should unfortunately assail the supreme executive magistracy of a country, consisting of a plurality of persons,
they might *impede* or frustrate the most important measures of
the government in the most critical emergencies of the state. And
what is still worse, they might split the community into the most
violent and irreconcilable factions, adhering differently to the different individuals who composed the magistracy.

Men often oppose a thing merely because they have had no
agency in planning it, or because it may have been planned by
those whom they dislike. But if they have been consulted, and
have happened to disapprove, opposition then becomes, in their
estimation an indispensable duty of self-love. They seem to think
themselves bound in honor, and by all the motives of personal
infallibility, to defeat the success of what has been resolved upon,
contrary to their sentiments. Men of upright, *benevolent* tempers
have too many opportunities of remarking, with horror, to what
desperate lengths this disposition is sometimes carried, and how
often the great interests of society are sacrificed to the vanity,
to the conceit, and to the *obstinacy* of individuals, who have
credit enough to make their passions and their *caprices* interesting to mankind. Perhaps the question now before the public
may, in its consequences, afford *melancholy* proofs of the effects
of this despicable *frailty,* or rather detestable vice, in the human
character.

Upon the principles of a free government, inconveniences from
the source just mentioned must necessarily be submitted to in the
formation of the legislature; but it is unnecessary, and therefore
unwise, to introduce them into the constitution of the executive.

10 Hamilton provides reasons other than history why we should not have a plural executive.

11

emulation—effort to match or surpass a person or achieve-ment, typically by imitation

impede—delay or prevent some or something by obstructing them

Why is it dangerous to give two people equal power?

12

Under what circumstances are people likely to oppose something?

infallibility—the inability to be wrong

benevolent—kind, even-tempered

obstinacy—stubbornness

caprice—a sudden change of mood or behavior

melancholy—a feeling of sadness, typically with no obvious cause

frailty—weakness

13

pernicious—having a harmful effect

promptitude—acting quickly and without delay

salutary—beneficial

circumspection—being cautious and unwilling to take risks

palliate—alleviate; lessen

It is here too that they may be most *pernicious*. In the legislature, *promptitude* of decision is oftener an evil than a benefit. The differences of opinion, and the jarrings of parties in that department of the government, though they may sometimes obstruct *salutary* plans, yet often promote deliberation and *circumspection,* and serve to check excesses in the majority. When a resolution too is once taken, the opposition must be at an end. That resolution is a law, and resistance to it punishable. But no favorable circumstances *palliate* or atone for the disadvantages of dissention in the executive department. Here they are pure and unmixed. There is no point at which they cease to operate. They serve to embarrass and weaken the execution of the plan or measure to which they relate, from the first step to the final conclusion of it. They constantly counteract those qualities in the executive which are the most necessary ingredients in its composition—vigor and expedition, and this without any counterbalancing good. In the conduct of war, in which the energy of the executive is the bulwark of the national security, everything would be to be apprehended from its plurality.

concurrence—two or more events or circumstances happening at the same time

ostensible—presumed

cabal—a secret political group or faction

dilatoriness—inability to act swiftly

14   It must be confessed that these observations apply with principal weight to the first case supposed—that is, to a plurality of magistrates of equal dignity and authority, a scheme, the advocates for which are not likely to form a numerous sect; but they apply, though not with equal yet with considerable weight to the project of a council, whose *concurrence* is made constitutionally necessary to the operations of the *ostensible* executive. An artful *cabal* in that council would be able to distract and to enervate the whole system of administration. If no such cabal should exist, the mere diversity of views and opinions would alone be sufficient to tincture the exercise of the executive authority with a spirit of habitual feebleness and *dilatoriness.*

[On responsibility and accountability]

What is Hamilton's strongest argument against multiple executives or an executive council?

15   But one of the weightiest objections to a plurality in the executive, and which lies as much against the last as the first plan is that it tends to conceal faults and destroy responsibility. Responsibility is of two kinds—to censure and to punishment. The first is the most important of the two, especially in an elective office. Men in public trust will much oftener act in such a manner as to render them unworthy of being any longer trusted, than in such a manner as to make him obnoxious to legal punishment. But the multiplication

of the executive adds to the difficulty of detection in either case. It often becomes impossible, amidst mutual accusations, to determine on whom the blame or the punishment of a *pernicious* measure, or series of pernicious measures, ought really to fall. It is shifted from one to another with so much *dexterity,* and under such plausible appearances, that the public opinion is left in suspense about the real author. The circumstances which may have led to any national miscarriage or misfortune are sometimes so complicated that where there are a number of actors who may have had different degrees and kinds of agency, though we may clearly see upon the whole that there has been mismanagement, yet it may be impracticable to pronounce to whose account the evil which may have been incurred is truly chargeable.

pernicious—harmful

dexterity—skill in performing tasks

"I was overruled by my council. The council were so divided 16 in their opinions that it was impossible to obtain any better resolution on the point." These and similar pretexts are constantly at hand, whether true or false. And who is there that will either take the trouble or incur the *odium* of a strict scrutiny into the secret springs of the transaction? Should there be found a citizen zealous enough to undertake the unpromising task, if there happened to be a collusion between the parties concerned, how easy is it to cloth the circumstances with so much ambiguity as to render it uncertain what was the precise conduct of any of those parties?

odium—general or widespread hatred or disgust directed toward someone as a result of their actions.

In the single instance in which the governor of this state is 17 coupled with a council—that is, in the appointment to offices, we have seen the mischiefs of it in the view now under consideration. Scandalous appointments to important offices have been made. Some cases indeed have been so flagrant that ALL PARTIES have agreed in the impropriety of the thing. When inquiry has been made, the blame has been laid by the governor on the members of the council; who on their part have charged it upon his nomination; while the people remain altogether at a loss to determine by whose influence their interests have been committed to hands so unqualified and so manifestly improper. In tenderness to individuals, I forbear to descend to particulars.

It is evident from these considerations that the plurality of the 18 executive tends to deprive the people of the two greatest securities they can have for the faithful exercise of any delegated power, *first,* the restraints of public opinion, which lose their efficacy as well on account of the division of the censure attendant on bad measures among a number as on account of the uncertainty on whom it ought to fall; and, *second*, the opportunity of discovering with facility and clearness the misconduct of the persons they trust, in order either to their removal from office or to their actual punishment in cases which admit of it.

19   In England, the king is a perpetual magistrate; and it is a *maxim* which has obtained for the sake of the public peace that he is unaccountable for his administration, and his person sacred. Nothing, therefore, can be wiser in that kingdom than to annex to the king a constitutional council, who may be responsible to the nation for the advice they give. Without this, there would be no responsibility whatever in the executive department—an idea inadmissible in a free government. But even there the king is not bound by the resolutions of his council, though they are answerable for the advice they give. He is the absolute master of his own conduct in the exercise of his office and may observe or disregard the council given to him at his sole discretion.

maxim— an accepted belief

20   But in a republic where every magistrate ought to be personally responsible for his behavior in office, the reason which in the British Constitution dictates the propriety of a council not only ceases to apply, but turns against the institution. In the monarchy of Great Britain, it furnishes a substitute for the prohibited responsibility of the Chief Magistrate, which serves in some degree as a hostage to the national justice for his good behavior. In the American republic, it would serve to destroy, or would greatly diminish, the intended and necessary responsibility of the Chief Magistrate himself.

21   The idea of a council to the executive, which has so generally obtained in the State constitutions, has been derived from that maxim of republican jealousy which considers power as safer in the hands of a number of men than of a single man. If the maxim should be admitted to be applicable to the case, I should contend that the advantage on that side would not counterbalance the numerous disadvantages on the opposite side. But I do not think the rule at all applicable to the executive power. I clearly concur in opinion, in this particular, with a writer whom the celebrated *Junius* pronounces to be "deep, solid and ingenious," that "the executive power is more easily confined when it is one"; that it is far more safe there should be a single object for the jealousy and watchfulness of the people; and, in a word, that all multiplication of the executive is rather dangerous than friendly to liberty.

Junius—Junius was the pseudonym of a writer who contributed a series of letters to the *Public Advertiser*, from 21 January 1769 to 21 January 1772.

22   A little consideration will satisfy us that the species of security sought for in the multiplication of the executive is unattainable.

Numbers must be so great as to render combination difficult, or they are rather a source of danger than of security. The united credit and influence of several individuals must be more formidable to liberty than the credit and influence of either of them separately. When power, therefore, is placed in the hands of so small a number of men as to admit of their interests and views being easily combined in a common enterprise, by an artful leader, it becomes more liable to abuse and more dangerous when abused, than if it be lodged in the hands of one man, who, from the very circumstance of his being alone, will be more narrowly watched and more readily suspected, and who cannot unite so great a mass of influence as when he is associated with others. The *decemvirs* of Rome, whose name denotes their number, were more to be dreaded in their *usurpation* than any ONE of them would have been. No person would think of proposing an executive much more numerous than that body; from six to a dozen have been suggested for the number of the council. The extreme of these numbers is not too great for an easy combination; and from such a combination America would have more to fear than from the ambition of any single individual. A council to a magistrate, who is himself responsible for what he does, are generally nothing better than a clog upon his good intentions, are often the instruments and accomplices of his bad, and are almost always a cloak to his faults.

decemvirs—Latin for "ten men"; an official commission of ten

usurpation—illegal seizure by force

I forbear to dwell upon the subject of expense; though it be 23 evident that if the council should be numerous enough to answer the principal end aimed at by the institution, the salaries of the members, who must be drawn from their homes to reside at the seat of government, would form an item in the catalogue of public expenditures too serious to be incurred for an object of *equivocal* utility.

equivocal—open to more than one interpretation

I will only add that, prior to the appearance of the Constitu- 24 tion, I rarely met with an intelligent man from any of the States who did not admit, as the result of experience, that the UNITY of the executive of this State was one of the best of the distinguishing features of our Constitution.

◼ **Impact of** *Federalist* No. 70

In the AP® U.S. Government and Politics course description, *Federalist* No. 70 is placed in Unit 2, Interactions Among the Branches of Government. In *Federalist* No. 70, Hamilton argued for a single executive as opposed to a plural executive or executive council as the Antifederalists preferred.

Hamilton wrote *Federalist* numbers 67 through 77 on topics relating to the executive branch. Some of those essays cover the method of electing the president, duration in office, and powers of the president.

The arguments in *Federalist* No. 70 are still relevant today. After the attacks of September 11, 2001, the powers of the chief executive and the need for surveillance to prevent future terrorism have taken on a more fundamental, and often controversial, role in the pursuit of national security. The U.S. Department of Justice has recently argued that foreign policy is most effectively conducted with a single hand, meaning that Congress should defer to the president's authority, especially in times of crisis.

The Supreme Court has also referred to *Federalist* No. 70 as an authority on the importance of presidential accountability. In its 1997 opinion in *Clinton v. Jones*, the Court considered whether a sitting president could delay addressing civil litigation until the end of his term. The Court cited *Federalist* No. 70, stating that the president must be held accountable for his actions and, therefore, cannot be granted immunity from civil litigation.

Check for Understanding

1. Discuss the benefits that a strong executive provides to a republican government. (Paragraph 1)
2. Discuss how a weak executive creates a bad government. (Paragraph 2)
3. Describe what, according to Hamilton, is the most necessary quality for a president. (Paragraph 3)
4. Identify the four ingredients of an energetic executive. (Paragraph 4)
5. Explain how a shared presidency allows the executive to avoid responsibility. (Paragraphs 11–12)
6. Explain why a plural executive or executive council would lead to bad government. (Paragraphs 14–16; 21–24)

Critical Thinking Question

Based on several observations, historian Arthur M. Schlesinger, Jr., wrote of the "imperial presidency," claiming that the U.S. presidency had exceeded its constitutional limits and was uncontrollable. Today, the term "imperial presidency" is often used to describe the modern presidency of the United States, a presidency characterized by an executive who exceeds his role and utilizes greater power than the Constitution allows. In *Federalist* No. 70, Hamilton wrote that "energy in the executive" was one of the most important parts of the executive department. This "energy" has been cited as a justification for the expansion of presidential power, especially in the twentieth century. How might critics of the "imperial presidency" react to Hamilton's arguments in *Federalist* No. 70?

Federalist No. 78

A View of The Constitution of the Judicial Department in Relation to the Tenure of Good Behaviour

Alexander Hamilton

The Federalist Papers were a series of essays written by Alexander Hamilton, John Jay, and James Madison. These essays were written as a response to essays that were opposed to the new Constitution published in New York newspapers during the ratification debate in the fall of 1787. In all, Hamilton, Jay, and Madison published 85 essays under the pseudonym Publius that explored the benefits of the new Constitution and advocated that New Yorkers should support ratification.

Federalist No. 78 was written by Hamilton to rebut the arguments of the Antifederalist writings under the pseudonym Brutus. In this essay, Hamilton addresses some of the issues raised by Brutus, specifically Brutus' arguments concerning what he viewed as the unlimited power of the judicial branch, the lifetime tenure limited only by lack of "good behavior," and the far-reaching scope of federal judicial power.

Focus on Federalist No. 78

Federalist No. 78, written by Alexander Hamilton and published May 28, 1788, is the first of six essays written by Hamilton on the topic of the judiciary. In Federalist No. 78, Hamilton explains the importance of having an independent judiciary. Hamilton justifies the structure of the judiciary under the new Constitution, addressing the concerns of the Antifederalists over the scope and power of the federal judiciary, especially that of unelected, independent judges who would be appointed for life.

Overview of Federalist No. 78

In the essay, Hamilton

- explains and justifies the structure and role of the federal judiciary.
- argues for lifetime tenure for federal judges based on "good behavior."
- establishes the importance of having an independent judiciary.
- argues for the authority of the judiciary to overturn the acts of the executive and legislative branches (judicial review).
- explains the supremacy of the Constitution over statutory (legislative) law.

▦ Reader Alert!

Hamilton's arguments are based on responding to the Antifederalist concerns that the judiciary is too independent and lacks accountability. *Federalist* No. 78 asserts that the judiciary is established to protect the Constitution and describes the powers of judicial review. *Federalist* No. 78 is often quoted by Supreme Court justices.

[On the necessity of a judiciary]

To the People of the State of New York:

1   We proceed now to an examination of the judiciary department of the proposed government.

2   In unfolding the defects of the existing Confederation, the *utility* and necessity of a federal *judicature* have been clearly pointed out. It is the less necessary to *recapitulate* the considerations there urged as the propriety of the institution in the abstract is not disputed; the only questions which have been raised being relative to the manner of constituting it, and to its extent. To these points, therefore, our observations shall be confined.

utility—usefulness

judicature—judiciary

recapitulate—summarize or restate the main points

After studying the defects of the Articles of Confederation, the structure and powers of the judiciary have to be addressed.

[On the structure of a judiciary]

3   The manner of constituting it seems to embrace these several objects: 1st. The mode of appointing the judges. 2nd. The tenure by which they are to hold their places. 3d. The partition of the judiciary authority between different courts and their relations to each other.

What must be included in the structure of the judiciary?

4   *First.* As to the mode of appointing the judges: this is the same with that of appointing the officers of the Union in general and has been so fully discussed in the two last numbers that nothing can be said here which would not be useless repetition.

5   *Second.* As to the tenure by which the judges are to hold their places: this chiefly concerns their duration in office; the provisions for their support, and the precautions for their responsibility.

6   According to the plan of the convention, all the judges who may be appointed by the United States are to hold their offices *during good behavior*; which is conformable to the most approved of the State constitutions, and among the rest, to that of this State. Its propriety having been drawn into question by the *adversaries* of that plan is no light symptom of the rage for objection which disorders their imaginations and judgments. The standard of good behavior for the continuance in office of the judicial *magistracy* is

adversary—opponent

magistracy—the administrator of the law

certainly one of the most valuable of the modern improvements in the practice of government. In a monarchy it is an excellent barrier to the *despotism* of the prince; in a republic it is a no less excellent barrier to the encroachments and oppressions of the representative body. And it is the best expedient which can be devised in any government to secure a steady, upright and impartial administration of the laws.

[Whether it is the "Least Dangerous Branch"]

Whoever attentively considers the different departments of power must perceive that, in a government in which they are separated from each other, the judiciary, from the nature of its functions, will always be the least dangerous to the political rights of the Constitution; because it will be least in a capacity to annoy or injure them. The executive not only dispenses the honors but holds the sword of the community. The legislature not only commands the purse but prescribes the rules by which the duties and rights of every citizen are to be regulated. The judiciary, on the contrary, has no influence over either the sword or the purse; no direction either of the strength or of the wealth of the society, and can take no active resolution whatever. It may truly be said to have neither FORCE nor WILL but merely judgment; and must ultimately depend upon the aid of the executive arm even for the *efficacy* of its judgments.

How does Hamilton support his argument that the judicial branch would be the least powerful of the three branches of government?

efficacy—success

This simple view of the matter suggests several important consequences. It proves *incontestably* that the judiciary is beyond comparison the weakest of the three departments of power; that it can never attack with success either of the other two; and that all possible care is *requisite* to enable it to defend itself against their attacks. It equally proves that though individual oppression may now and then proceed from the courts of justice, the general liberty of the people can never be endangered from that quarter: I mean, so long as the judiciary remains truly distinct from both the legislative and executive. For I agree that "there is no liberty if the power of judging be not separated from the legislative and executive powers." And it proves, in the last place, that as liberty can have nothing to fear from the judiciary alone, but would have everything to fear from its union with either of the other departments; that as all the effects of such a union must ensue

incontestably—undeniably

requisite—necessary

nominal—existing in name only; minimal or minor

feebleness—weakness

citadel—stronghold

peculiarly—unusually

bills of attainder—a legislative act that singles out an individual or group for punishment without a trial

ex post facto laws—a law that retroactively makes criminal an act that was not criminal at the time it occurred.

tenor—meaning or content of something

judicial review—the process by which executive and legislative actions are subject to review by the judiciary

perplexity—confusion

from a dependence of the former on the latter, notwithstanding a *nominal* and apparent separation; that as, from the natural *feebleness* of the judiciary, it is in continual jeopardy of being overpowered, awed or influenced by its coordinate branches; and that as nothing can contribute so much to its firmness and independence as permanency in office, this quality may therefore be justly regarded as an indispensable ingredient in its constitution, and in a great measure as the *citadel* of the public justice and the public security.

9   The complete independence of the courts of justice is *peculiarly* essential in a limited Constitution. By a limited Constitution, I understand one which contains certain specified exceptions to the legislative authority; such, for instance, as that it shall pass no *bills of attainder,* no *ex post facto laws,* and the like. Limitations of this kind can be preserved in practice no other way than through the medium of the courts of justice, whose duty it must be to declare all acts contrary to the manifest *tenor* of the Constitution void. Without this, all the reservations of particular rights or privileges would amount to nothing.

[On the meaning and purpose of judicial review]

10   Some *perplexity* respecting the right of the courts to pronounce legislative acts void, because contrary to the Constitution, has arisen from an imagination that the doctrine would imply a superiority of the judiciary to the legislative power. It is urged that the authority which can declare the acts of another void must necessarily be superior to the one whose acts may be declared void. As this doctrine is of great importance in all the American constitutions, a brief discussion of the grounds on which it rests cannot be unacceptable.

11   There is no position which depends on clearer principles than that every act of a delegated authority, contrary to the tenor of the commission under which it is exercised, is void. No legislative act therefore contrary to the constitution can be valid. To deny this would be to affirm that the deputy is greater than his principal; that the servant is above his master; that the representatives of the people are superior to the people themselves; that men acting by virtue of powers may do not only what their powers do not authorize, but what they forbid.

If it be said that the legislative body are themselves the consti- 12 tutional judges of their own powers and that the construction they put upon them is *conclusive* upon the other departments it may be answered that this cannot be the natural presumption where it is not to be collected from any particular provisions in the Constitution. It is not otherwise to be supposed that the Constitution could intend to enable the representatives of the people to substitute their *will* to that of their constituents. It is far more rational to suppose that the courts were designed to be an intermediate body between the people and the legislature in order, among other things, to keep the latter within the limits assigned to their authority. The interpretation of the laws is the proper and peculiar province of the courts. A constitution is in fact, and must be regarded by the judges as, a fundamental law. It therefore belongs to them to ascertain its meaning as well as the meaning of any particular act proceeding from the legislative body. If there should happen to be an irreconcilable variance between the two, that which has the superior obligation and validity ought, of course; to be preferred; or, in other words, the Constitution ought to be preferred to the *statute,* the intention of the people to the intention of their agents.

Nor does this conclusion by any means suppose a superiority 13 of the judicial to the legislative power. It only supposes that the power of the people is superior to both, and that where the will of the legislature, declared in its statutes, stands in opposition to that of the people, declared in the Constitution, the judges ought to be governed by the latter rather than the former. They ought to regulate their decisions by the fundamental laws rather than by those which are not fundamental.

This exercise of judicial discretion in determining between 14 two contradictory laws is exemplified in a familiar instance. It not uncommonly happens that there are two statutes existing at one time, clashing in whole or in part with each other, and neither of them containing any repealing clause or expression. In such a case, it is the province of the courts to liquidate and fix their meaning and operation. So far as they can, by any fair construction, be reconciled to each other, reason and law conspire to dictate that this should be done; where this is impracticable, it becomes a matter of necessity to give effect to one in exclusion of the other. The rule which has obtained in the courts for determining their relative validity is that the last in order of time shall be preferred to the first. But this is mere rule of construction, not

conclusive—decisive or convincing

statute—a written law passed by a legislative body

derived from any positive law but from the nature and reason of the thing. It is a rule not enjoined upon the courts by legislative provision but adopted by themselves, as consonant to truth and propriety, for the direction of their conduct as interpreters of the law. They thought it reasonable that between the interfering acts of an *equal* authority that which was the last indication of its will, should have the preference.

derivative—as a result of something, such as a power that comes from the Constitution

converse—opposite

15 But in regard to the interfering acts of a superior and subordinate authority of an original and *derivative* power, the nature and reason of the thing indicate the *converse* of that rule as proper to be followed. They teach us that the prior act of a superior ought to be preferred to the subsequent act of an inferior and subordinate authority; and that, accordingly, whenever a particular statute contravenes the Constitution, it will be the duty of the judicial *tribunals* to adhere to the latter and disregard the former.

tribunal—a court of justice or a hearing by a court

repugnancy—inconsistency or contradiction; dislike

adjudication—decision or judgment

16 It can be of no weight to say that the courts, on the pretence of a *repugnancy,* may substitute their own pleasure to the constitutional intentions of the legislature. This might as well happen in the case of two contradictory statutes; or it might as well happen in every *adjudication* upon any single statute. The courts must declare the sense of the law; and if they should be disposed to exercise WILL instead of JUDGMENT, the consequence would equally be the substitution of their pleasure to that of the legislative body. The observation, if it proved any thing, would prove that there ought to be no judges distinct from that body.

[On the independence and the tenure of judges]

bulwark—protection or defense

encroachment—intrusion or violation

17 If, then, the courts of justice are to be considered as the *bulwarks* of a limited Constitution against legislative *encroachments,* this consideration will afford a strong argument for the permanent tenure of judicial offices, since nothing will contribute so much as this to that independent spirit in the judges which must be essential to the faithful performance of so *arduous* a duty.

arduous—difficult; demanding

18 This independence of the judges is equally requisite to guard the Constitution and the rights of individuals from the effects of those ill humors which the arts of designing men, or the influence of particular conjunctures, sometimes disseminate among the people themselves, and which, though they speedily give place to better information, and more deliberate reflection, have a tendency, in the meantime, to occasion dangerous innovations in the government,

and serious oppressions of the minor party in the community. Though I trust the friends of the proposed Constitution will never concur with its enemies in questioning that fundamental principle of republican government which admits the right of the people to alter or abolish the established Constitution whenever they find it inconsistent with their happiness; yet it is not to be inferred from this principle that the representatives of the people, whenever a momentary inclination happens to lay hold of a majority of their constituents incompatible with the provisions in the existing Constitution would, on that account, be justifiable in a violation of those provisions; or that the courts would be under a greater obligation to connive at infractions in this shape than when they had proceeded wholly from the *cabals* of the representative body. Until the people have, by some solemn and authoritative act, *annulled* or changed the established form, it is binding upon themselves collectively, as well as individually; and no presumption, or even knowledge of their sentiments, can warrant their representatives in a departure from it prior to such an act. But it is easy to see that it would require an uncommon portion of *fortitude* in the judges to do their duty as faithful guardians of the Constitution, where legislative invasions of it had been instigated by the major voice of the community.

cabal—factions; secret political groups

annulled—canceled; invalidated

fortitude—strength; courage

But it is not with a view to infractions of the Constitution only that the independence of the judges may be an essential safeguard against the effects of occasional ill humors in the society. These sometimes extend no farther than to the injury of the private rights of particular classes of citizens, by unjust and partial laws. Here also the firmness of the judicial magistracy is of vast importance in mitigating the severity and confining the operation of such laws. It not only serves to moderate the immediate mischiefs of those which may have been passed but it operates as a check upon the legislative body in passing them; who, perceiving that obstacles to the success of an iniquitous intention are to be expected from the *scruples* of the courts, are in a manner compelled, by the very motives of the injustice they meditate, to qualify their attempts. This is a circumstance calculated to have more influence upon the character of our governments than but few may be aware of. The benefits of the integrity and moderation of the judiciary have already been felt in more states than one; and though they may have displeased those whose sinister expectations they may have disappointed, they must have commanded the esteem and applause of all the virtuous and disinterested.

19

scruples—principles and ethics

Considerate men of every description ought to prize whatever will tend to beget or fortify that temper in the courts; as no man can be sure that he may not be tomorrow the victim of a spirit of injustice, by which he may be a gainer today. And every man must now feel that the inevitable tendency of such a spirit is to sap the foundations of public and private confidence and to introduce in its stead universal distrust and distress.

20   That inflexible and uniform adherence to the rights of the Constitution, and of individuals, which we perceive to be indispensable in the courts of justice, can certainly not be expected from judges who hold their offices by a temporary commission. *Periodical* appointments, however regulated, or by whomsoever made, would in some way or other, be fatal to their necessary independence. If the power of making them was committed either to the executive or legislature there would be danger of an improper complaisance to the branch which possessed it; if to both, there would be an unwillingness to hazard the displeasure of either; if to the people, or to persons chosen by them for the special purpose, there would be too great a disposition to consult popularity to justify a reliance that nothing would be consulted but the Constitution and the laws.

periodical—here, the meaning is "for a certain period of time"

21   There is yet a further and a weighty reason for the permanency of the judicial offices which is deducible from the nature of the qualifications they require. It has been frequently remarked with great propriety that a *voluminous* code of laws is one of the inconveniences necessarily connected with the advantages of a free government. To avoid an arbitrary discretion in the courts, it is indispensable that they should be bound down by strict rules and precedents which serve to define and point out their duty in every particular case that comes before them; and it will readily be conceived from the variety of controversies which grow out of the folly and wickedness of mankind that the records of those precedents must unavoidably swell to a very considerable bulk and must demand long and laborious study to acquire a competent knowledge of them. Hence it is that there can be but few men in the society who will have sufficient skill in the laws to qualify them for the stations of judges. And making the proper deductions for the ordinary depravity of human nature, the number must be still smaller of those who unite the requisite integrity with the requisite knowledge. These considerations apprise us that the government can have no great option between fit characters; and that a

voluminous—large

temporary duration in office which would naturally discourage such characters from quitting a *lucrative* line of practice to accept a seat on the bench would have a tendency to throw the administration of justice into hands less able and less well qualified to conduct it with utility and dignity. In the present circumstances of this country and in those in which it is likely to be for a long time to come, the disadvantages on this score would be greater than they may at first sight appear; but it must be confessed that they are far inferior to those which present themselves under the other aspects of the subject.

lucrative—profitable

Upon the whole, there can be no room to doubt that the convention acted wisely in copying from the models of those constitutions which have established *good behavior* as the tenure of their judicial offices, in point of duration; and that so far from being blamable on this account, their plan would have been inexcusably defective if it had wanted this important feature of good government. The experience of Great Britain affords an illustrious comment on the excellence of the institution.

22

Impact of *Federalist* No. 78

Hamilton wrote *Federalist* numbers 78–83 on topics relating to the judicial branch. Some of those essays cover the appointment and removal of judges, jurisdiction of the courts, and powers and scope of the judiciary.

In the AP® U.S. Government and Politics course description, *Federalist* No. 78 is placed in Unit 2, Interactions Among the Branches of Government. In *Federalist* No. 78, Hamilton establishes the importance of having an independent judiciary with lifetime tenure for federal judges based on "good behavior." *Federalist* No. 78 argues for judicial review and the supremacy of the Constitution over statutory law.

Specifically, the curriculum requires you to use *Federalist* No. 78, alongside Article III of the Constitution and *Marbury v. Madison* (1803), to explain the principle of judicial review and how it checks the power of the executive and legislative branches of government and state governments.

Article III of the Constitution creates the federal judicial branch, describes the jurisdiction of the federal courts, and deals with the crime of treason. Judicial review is not mentioned in the Constitution, and *Marbury v. Madison* was the landmark U.S. Supreme Court case that established the principle of judicial review. In subsequent cases, the Court also established its authority to strike down state laws found to be in violation of the Constitution. *Marbury v. Madison* is one of the most important decisions in constitutional law.

▦ Check for Understanding

1. Describe what Hamilton argued were the necessary components to the judicial structure. (Paragraphs 3–6)
2. Explain why Hamilton claims the judicial department is the least powerful branch of government. (Paragraph 7)
3. Describe Hamilton's position regarding the power of the judiciary to declare void any legislative acts that were contrary to the Constitution. (Paragraphs 10–11)
4. Explain why Hamilton considers the independence of the judiciary to be a vital component of constitutional government. (Paragraph 18)
5. Explain why consistency in decision making is so important in the federal judiciary and how the life term of federal judges contributes to this consistency. (Paragraphs 21–22)

▦ Critical Thinking Question

The primary goal of life tenure is to insulate the officeholder from external pressures and create an independent judiciary. Once appointed by the president and confirmed by the Senate, federal judges have life tenure "during good behavior." The life tenure of federal judges is a unique feature of the federal judiciary. Other countries and state governments rely on term limits, a mandatory retirement age, or both. Should Supreme Court Justices serve for limited terms, or do you agree with Hamilton? Explain the reasons for your opinion.

Letter from Birmingham Jail

Dr. Martin Luther King, Jr.

▉ Focus on *Letter from Birmingham Jail*

Originally written on the margins of a newspaper while Dr. King was in a jail cell, this 1963 essay is now considered a classic civil-rights text. In this text, Dr. King draws on the principle of natural law to explain the goals and tactics of the southern civil rights movement, and expresses his disappointment at the passiveness of the "white moderate." The letter was sent to a group of white ministers who had been critical of Dr. King's willingness to break laws. As a letter written by a minister to other ministers, it is full of theological references, but Dr. King also makes many connections to American political principles and traditions. The letter helped white Americans more broadly understand what life was like for black Americans under Jim Crow, and it continues to serve as an inspiration to civil-rights groups today.

▉ Overview of *Letter from Birmingham Jail*

In this letter, Dr. Martin Luther King, Jr.:

- describes the purpose and tactics of the southern civil-rights movement.
- explains the urgency of the need for societal change regarding Jim Crow laws.
- describes the difference between just and unjust laws, drawing on the principle of natural law.
- describes the difference between the southern civil-rights movement and the actions of black nationalists.
- explains how the civil-rights movement relates to the development of U.S. political culture and religious traditions.

▉ Reader Alert!

This is overall an engaging document, and as the only required document written in the twentieth century, this letter is much easier to read than some of the other foundational documents. However, there are still many religious or historic references that may be unfamiliar. Think through how and why Dr. King draws on these references—but do not get stuck trying to understand the origin of every reference and metaphor. Make connections between the social and political forces at work in 1963 when this letter was written and movements and tactics used by civil-rights groups today.

[On the work that the civil-rights movement was doing in Birmingham]

My Dear Fellow Clergymen:

1   While confined here in the Birmingham city jail, I came across your recent statement calling my present activities "unwise and untimely." Seldom do I pause to answer criticism of my work and ideas. If I sought to answer all the criticisms that cross my desk, my secretaries would have little time for anything other than such correspondence in the course of the day, and I would have no time for constructive work. But since I feel that you are men of genuine good will and that your criticisms are sincerely set forth, I want to try to answer your statement in what I hope will be patient and reasonable terms.

2   I think I should indicate why I am here in Birmingham, since you have been influenced by the view which argues against "outsiders coming in." I have the honor of serving as president of the Southern Christian Leadership Conference, an organization operating in every southern state, with headquarters in Atlanta, Georgia. We have some eighty-five affiliated organizations across the South, and one of them is the Alabama Christian Movement for Human Rights. Frequently we share staff, educational, and financial resources with our affiliates. Several months ago the affiliate here in Birmingham asked us to be on call to engage in a nonviolent direct-action program if such were deemed necessary. We readily consented, and when the hour came we lived up to our promise. So I, along with several members of my staff, am here because I was invited here. I am here because I have organizational ties here.

3   Moreover, I am *cognizant* of the interrelatedness of all communities and states. I cannot sit idly by in Atlanta and not be concerned about what happens in Birmingham. Injustice anywhere is a threat to justice everywhere. We are caught in an inescapable network of mutuality, tied in a single garment of destiny. Whatever affects one directly, affects all indirectly. Never again can we afford to live with the narrow, provincial "outside agitator" idea. Anyone who lives inside the United States can never be considered an outsider anywhere within its bounds.

4   You deplore the demonstrations taking place in Birmingham. But your statement, I am sorry to say, fails to express a similar concern for the conditions that brought about the demonstrations.

The SCLC rose to prominence with the Montgomery Bus Boycott in the 1950s and developed tactics of nonviolent resistance. The SCLC staged campaigns in various southern cities to create pressure on local government and draw awareness to injustice.

cognizant—aware

I am sure that none of you would want to rest content with the superficial kind of social analysis that deals merely with effects and does not grapple with underlying causes. It is unfortunate that demonstrations are taking place in Birmingham, but it is even more unfortunate that the city's white power structure left the Negro community with no alternative.

Why is it more important to analyze the cause of injustice, instead of focusing on its effects?

[Describing the goals and tactics of the movement]

In any nonviolent campaign there are four basic steps: collection of the facts to determine whether injustices exist; negotiation; self-purification; and direct action. We have gone through all these steps in Birmingham. There can be no gainsaying the fact that racial injustice engulfs this community. Birmingham is probably the most thoroughly segregated city in the United States. Its ugly record of brutality is widely known. Negroes have experienced grossly unjust treatment in the courts. There have been more unsolved bombings of Negro homes and churches in Birmingham than in any other city in the nation. These are the hard, brutal facts of the case. On the basis of these conditions, Negro leaders sought to negotiate with the city fathers. But the latter consistently refused to engage in good-faith negotiation.

Then, last September, came the opportunity to talk with leaders of Birmingham's economic community. In the course of the negotiations, certain promises were made by the merchants—for example, to remove the stores' humiliating racial signs. On the basis of these promises, the Reverend Fred Shuttlesworth and the leaders of the Alabama Christian Movement for Human Rights agreed to a moratorium on all demonstrations. As the weeks and months went by, we realized that we were the victims of a broken promise. A few signs, briefly removed, returned; the others remained.

As in so many past experiences, our hopes had been blasted, and the shadow of deep disappointment settled upon us. We had no alternative except to prepare for direct action, whereby we would present our very bodies as a means of laying our case before the conscience of the local and the national community. Mindful of the difficulties involved, we decided to undertake a process of self-purification. We began a series of workshops on nonviolence, and we repeatedly asked ourselves: "Are you able to

What historical movements inspired Dr. King's nonviolent tactics?

accept blows without retaliating?" "Are you able to endure the ordeal of jail?" We decided to schedule our direct-action program for the Easter season, realizing that except for Christmas, this is the main shopping period of the year. Knowing that a strong economic withdrawal program would be the by-product of direct action, we felt that this would be the best time to bring pressure to bear on the merchants for the needed change.

8   You may well ask, "Why direct action? Why sit-ins, marches, and so forth? Isn't negotiation a better path?" You are quite right in calling for negotiation. Indeed, this is the very purpose of direct action. Nonviolent direct action seeks to create such a crisis and foster such a tension that a community which has constantly refused to negotiate is forced to confront the issue. It seeks so to dramatize the issue that it can no longer be ignored. My citing the creation of tension as part of the work of the nonviolent-resister may sound rather shocking. But I must confess that I am not afraid of the word "tension." I have earnestly opposed violent tension, but there is a type of constructive, nonviolent tension which is necessary for growth. Just as Socrates felt that it was necessary to create a tension in the mind so that individuals could rise from the bondage of myths and half-truths to the unfettered realm of creative analysis and objective appraisal, so must we see the need for nonviolent gadflies to create the kind of tension in society that will help men rise from the dark depths of prejudice and racism to the majestic heights of understanding and brotherhood.

Can you think of modern-day movements that seek to create tension to bring about change?

9   The purpose of our direct-action program is to create a situation so crisis-packed that it will inevitably open the door to negotiation. I therefore concur with you in your call for negotiation. Too long has our beloved Southland been bogged down in a tragic effort to live in monologue rather than dialogue.

What is meant by living in "monologue rather than dialogue," and why do you think Dr. King considers it tragic?

[On time and social progress]

10   One of the basic points in your statement is that the action that I and my associates have taken in Birmingham is untimely. Some have asked: "Why didn't you give the new city administration time to act?" The only answer that I can give to this query is that the new Birmingham administration must be prodded about as much as the outgoing one, before it will act. We are sadly mistaken if we feel that the election of Albert Boutwell as mayor will bring the millennium to Birmingham. While Mr. Boutwell is a much more gentle person than Mr. Connor, they are both segregationists,

dedicated to maintenance of the status quo. I have hoped that Mr. Boutwell will be reasonable enough to see the futility of massive resistance to desegregation. But he will not see this without pressure from devotees of civil rights. My friends, I must say to you that we have not made a single gain in civil rights without determined legal and nonviolent pressure. Lamentably, it is an historical fact that privileged groups seldom give up their privileges voluntarily. Individuals may see the moral light and voluntarily give up their unjust posture, but, as Reinhold Niebuhr has reminded us, groups tend to be more immoral than individuals.

Do you believe that groups are more immoral than individuals? Explain why or why not.

11 We know through painful experience that freedom is never voluntarily given by the oppressor; it must be demanded by the oppressed. Frankly, I have yet to engage in a direct-action campaign that was "well timed" in the view of those who have not suffered unduly from the disease of segregation. For years now I have heard the word "Wait!" It rings in the ear of every Negro with piercing familiarity. This "Wait" has almost always meant "Never." We must come to see, with one of our distinguished jurists, that "justice too long delayed is justice denied."

12 We have waited for more than 340 years for our constitutional and God-given rights. The nations of Asia and Africa are moving with jet-like speed toward gaining political independence, but we still creep at horse-and-buggy pace toward gaining a cup of coffee at a lunch counter. Perhaps it is easy for those who have never felt the stinging darts of segregation to say, "Wait." But when you have seen vicious mobs lynch your mothers and fathers at will and drown your sisters and brothers at whim; when you have seen hate-filled policemen curse, kick, and even kill your black brothers and sisters; when you see the vast majority of your twenty million Negro brothers smothering in an airtight cage of poverty in the midst of an affluent society; when you suddenly find your tongue twisted and your speech stammering as you seek to explain to your six-year-old daughter why she can't go to the public amusement park that has just been advertised on television, and see tears welling up in her eyes when she is told that Funtown is closed to colored children, and see ominous clouds of inferiority beginning to form in her little mental sky, and see her beginning to distort her personality by developing an unconscious bitterness toward white people; when you have to concoct an answer for a five-year-old son who is asking, "Daddy, why do white people treat colored people so mean?" when you take a cross-country drive and find it

necessary to sleep night after night in the uncomfortable corners of your automobile because no motel will accept you; when you are humiliated day in and day out by nagging signs reading "white" and "colored"; when your first name becomes "nigger," your middle name becomes "boy" (however old you are) and your last name becomes "John," and your wife and mother are never given the respected title "Mrs."; when you are harried by day and haunted by night by the fact that you are a Negro, living constantly at tiptoe stance, never quite knowing what to expect next, and are plagued with inner fears and outer resentments; when you are forever fighting a degenerating sense of "nobodiness"—then you will understand why we find it difficult to wait. There comes a time when the cup of endurance runs over, and men are no longer willing to be plunged into the abyss of despair. I hope, sirs, you can understand our legitimate and unavoidable impatience.

[On just and unjust laws]

13 You express a great deal of anxiety over our willingness to break laws. This is certainly a legitimate concern. Since we so diligently urge people to obey the Supreme Court's decision of 1954 outlawing segregation in the public schools, at first glance it may seem rather *paradoxical* for us consciously to break laws. One may well ask: "How can you advocate breaking some laws and obeying others?" The answer lies in the fact that there are two types of laws: just and unjust. I would be the first to advocate obeying just laws. One has not only a legal but a moral responsibility to obey just laws. Conversely, one has a moral responsibility to disobey unjust laws. I would agree with St. Augustine that "an unjust law is no law at all."

14   Now, what is the difference between the two? How does one determine whether a law is just or unjust? A just law is a man-made code that squares with the moral law or the law of God. An unjust law is a code that is out of harmony with the moral law. To put it in the terms of St. Thomas Aquinas: An unjust law is a human law that is not rooted in eternal law and natural law. Any law that uplifts human personality is just. Any law that degrades human personality is unjust. All segregation statutes are unjust because segregation distorts the soul and damages the personality. It gives the segregator a false sense of superiority and the segregated a false sense of inferiority. Segregation, to use the terminology of the Jewish philosopher Martin Buber, substitutes an

What required case is Dr. King referring to here? Why would he urge people to obey the ruling?

paradoxical— self-contradictory

Augustine was a prominent early Christian theologian, considered a Church Father, who continues to influence religious thought.

What democratic principle, most famously described in the Declaration of Independence, does Dr. King invoke in this passage?

"I-it" relationship for an "I-thou" relationship and ends up relegating persons to the status of things. Hence segregation is not only politically, economically, and sociologically unsound, it is morally wrong and sinful. Paul Tillich has said that sin is separation. Is not segregation an existential expression of man's tragic separation, his awful estrangement, his terrible sinfulness? Thus it is that I can urge men to obey the 1954 decision of the Supreme Court, for it is morally right; and I can urge them to disobey segregation ordinances, for they are morally wrong.

Let us consider a more concrete example of just and unjust 15 laws. An unjust law is a code that a numerical or power majority group compels a minority group to obey but does not make binding on itself. This is *difference* made legal. By the same token, a just law is a code that a majority compels a minority to follow and that it is willing to follow itself. This is *sameness* made legal.

Let me give another explanation. A law is unjust if it is 16 inflicted on a minority that, as a result of being denied the right to vote, had no part in enacting or devising the law. Who can say that the legislature of Alabama which set up that state's segregation laws was democratically elected? Throughout Alabama all sorts of devious methods are used to prevent Negroes from becoming registered voters, and there are some counties in which, even though Negroes constitute a majority of the population, not a single Negro is registered. Can any law enacted under such circumstances be considered democratically structured?

Sometimes a law is just on its face and unjust in its applica- 17 tion. For instance, I have been arrested on a charge of parading without a permit. Now, there is nothing wrong in having an ordinance which requires a permit for a parade. But such an ordinance becomes unjust when it is used to maintain segregation and to deny citizens the First-Amendment privilege of peaceful assembly and protest.

I hope you are able to see the distinction I am trying to point 18 out. In no sense do I advocate evading or defying the law, as would the rabid segregationist. That would lead to anarchy. One who breaks an unjust law must do so openly, lovingly, and with a willingness to accept the penalty. I submit that an individual who breaks a law that conscience tells him is unjust, and who willingly accepts the penalty of imprisonment in order to arouse the conscience of the community over its injustice, is in reality expressing the highest respect for law.

Dr. King invokes three prominent theologians. Thomas Aquinas has had much influence in Roman Catholicism. Martin Buber was a Jewish philosopher and theologian, who left Germany to settle in Palestine in 1933. Paul Tillich was a Lutheran theologian, born in Germany, who immigrated to the United States after being dismissed from his position after the rise of the Nazis.

Why it is difficult to reach a consensus about which laws are just or unjust?

In the course of these two paragraphs, Dr. King invokes several figures from history, including the three young men from the biblical Book of Daniel, early Christian martyrs, the Greek philosopher Socrates (who was executed by the state), the Boston Tea Party, resisters to the Nazi movement, and the failed Hungarian Revolution of 1956.

19   Of course, there is nothing new about this kind of civil disobedience. It was evidenced sublimely in the refusal of Shadrach, Meshach, and Abednego to obey the laws of Nebuchadnezzar, on the ground that a higher moral law was at stake. It was practiced superbly by the early Christians, who were willing to face hungry lions and the excruciating pain of chopping blocks rather than submit to certain unjust laws of the Roman Empire. To a degree, academic freedom is a reality today because Socrates practiced civil disobedience. In our own nation, the Boston Tea Party represented a massive act of civil disobedience.

20   We should never forget that everything Adolf Hitler did in Germany was "legal" and everything the Hungarian freedom fighters did in Hungary was "illegal." It was "illegal" to aid and comfort a Jew in Hitler's Germany. Even so, I am sure that, had I lived in Germany at the time, I would have aided and comforted my Jewish brothers. If today I lived in a Communist country where certain principles dear to the Christian faith are suppressed, I would openly advocate disobeying that country's antireligious laws.

[On the question of what it means to be "moderate"]

21   I must make two honest confessions to you, my Christian and Jewish brothers. First, I must confess that over the past few years I have been gravely disappointed with the white moderate. I have almost reached the regrettable conclusion that the Negro's great stumbling block in his stride toward freedom is not the White Citizen's Counciler or the Ku Klux Klanner, but the white moderate, who is more devoted to "order" than to justice; who prefers a negative peace which is the absence of tension to a positive peace which is the presence of justice; who constantly says, "I agree with you in the goal you seek, but I cannot agree with your methods of direct action"; who paternalistically believes he can set the timetable for another man's freedom; who lives by a mythical concept of time and who constantly advises the Negro to wait for a "more convenient season." Shallow understanding from people of good will is more frustrating than absolute misunderstanding from people of ill will. Lukewarm acceptance is much more bewildering than outright rejection.

The Citizens' Councils and the Ku Klux Klan are white-supremacist groups that at times incited violence.

22   I had hoped that the white moderate would understand that law and order exist for the purpose of establishing justice and that when they fail in this purpose they become the dangerously

structured dams that block the flow of social progress. I had hoped that the white moderate would understand that the present tension in the South is a necessary phase of the transition from an obnoxious negative peace, in which the Negro passively accepted his unjust plight, to a substantive and positive peace, in which all men will respect the dignity and worth of human personality. Actually, we who engage in nonviolent direct action are not the creators of tension. We merely bring to the surface the hidden tension that is already alive. We bring it out in the open, where it can be seen and dealt with. Like a boil that can never be cured so long as it is covered up but must be opened with all its ugliness to the natural medicines of air and light, injustice must be exposed, with all the tension its exposure creates, to the light of human conscience and the air of national opinion, before it can be cured.

What does Dr. King mean by a "negative peace"?

[On the causes of violence]

In your statement you assert that our actions, even though peace- 23 ful, must be condemned because they precipitate violence. But is this a logical assertion? Isn't this like condemning a robbed man because his possession of money precipitated the evil act of robbery? Isn't this like condemning Socrates because his unswerving commitment to truth and his philosophical inquiries precipitated the act by the misguided populace in which they made him drink hemlock? Isn't this like condemning Jesus because his unique God-consciousness and never-ceasing devotion to God's will precipitated the evil act of crucifixion? We must come to see that, as the federal courts have consistently affirmed, it is wrong to urge an individual to cease his efforts to gain his basic constitutional rights because the quest may precipitate violence. Society must protect the robbed and punish the robber.

[On the meaning of time and timeliness]

I had also hoped that the white moderate would reject the myth 24 concerning time in relation to the struggle for freedom. I have just received a letter from a white brother in Texas. He writes: "All Christians know that the colored people will receive equal rights eventually, but it is possible that you are in too great a religious hurry. It has taken Christianity almost two thousand years to accomplish what it has. The teachings of Christ take time to come to earth." Such an attitude stems from a tragic misconception of time, from the strangely irrational notion that there is something in the very flow of time that will inevitably cure all ills. Actually, time itself is neutral; it can be used either destructively or constructively. More and more I feel that the people of ill will have used time much more effectively than have the people of good will. We will have to repent in this generation not merely for the hateful words and actions of the bad people, but for the appalling silence of the good people. Human progress never rolls in on wheels of inevitability; it comes through the tireless efforts of men willing to be co-workers with God, and without this hard work, time itself becomes an ally of the forces of social stagnation. We must use time creatively, in the knowledge that the time is always ripe to do right. Now is the time to make real the promise of democracy and transform our pending national elegy into a creative psalm of brotherhood. Now is the time to lift our national policy from the quicksand of racial injustice to the solid rock of human dignity.

[Standing between two forces]

25 You speak of our activity in Birmingham as extreme. At first I was rather disappointed that fellow clergymen would see my non-violent efforts as those of an extremist. I began thinking about the fact that I stand in the middle of two opposing forces in the Negro community. One is a force of complacency, made up in part of Negroes who, as a result of long years of oppression, are so drained of self-respect and a sense of "somebodiness" that they have adjusted to segregation; and in part of a few middle-class Negroes who, because of a degree of academic and economic security and because in some ways they profit by segregation, have become insensitive to the problems of the masses. The other force is one of bitterness and hatred, and it comes perilously close to advocating violence. It is expressed in the various black nationalist groups that are springing up across the nation, the largest and best-known being Elijah Muhammad's Muslim movement. Nourished by the Negro's frustration over the continued existence of racial discrimination, this movement is made up of people who have lost faith in America, who have absolutely repudiated Christianity, and who have concluded that the white man is an incorrigible "devil."

This is the group Malcom X was affiliated with. It advocated self-determination for black Americans and did not pledge a commitment to nonviolence.

26   I have tried to stand between these two forces, saying that we need emulate neither the "do-nothingism" of the complacent nor

the hatred and despair of the black nationalist. For there is the more excellent way of love and nonviolent protest. I am grateful to God that, through the influence of the Negro church, the way of nonviolence became an integral part of our struggle.

If this philosophy had not emerged, by now many streets of 27 the South would, I am convinced, be flowing with blood. And I am further convinced that if our white brothers dismiss as "rabble-rousers" and "outside agitators" those of us who employ nonviolent direct action, and if they refuse to support our nonviolent efforts, millions of Negroes will, out of frustration and despair, seek solace and security in black-nationalist ideologies— a development that would inevitably lead to a frightening racial nightmare.

Oppressed people cannot remain oppressed forever. The 28 yearning for freedom eventually manifests itself, and that is what has happened to the American Negro. Something within has reminded him of his birthright of freedom, and something without has reminded him that it can be gained. Consciously or unconsciously, he has been caught up by the *Zeitgeist*, and with his black brothers of Africa and his brown and yellow brothers of Asia, South America, and the Caribbean, the United States Negro is moving with a sense of great urgency toward the promised land of racial justice. If one recognizes this vital urge that has engulfed the Negro community, one should readily understand why public demonstrations are taking place. The Negro has many pent-up resentments and latent frustrations, and he must release them. So let him march; let him make prayer pilgrimages to the city hall; let him go on freedom rides—and try to understand why he must do so. If his repressed emotions are not released in nonviolent ways, they will seek expression through violence; this is not a threat but a fact of history. So I have not said to my people, "Get rid of your discontent." Rather, I have tried to say that this normal and healthy discontent can be channeled into the creative outlet of nonviolent direct action. And now this approach is being termed extremist.

[An extremist for love]

But though I was initially disappointed at being categorized as 29 an extremist, as I continued to think about the matter I gradually gained a measure of satisfaction from the label. Was not Jesus an extremist for love: "Love your enemies, bless them that curse you,

In addition to moral opposition, why do you think Dr. King believed a commitment to nonviolence was an important tactic for the civil-rights movement?

Zeitgeist—the spirit of the times

do good to them that hate you, and pray for them which despite-fully use you, and persecute you." Was not Amos an extremist for justice: "Let justice roll down like waters and righteousness like an ever-flowing stream." Was not Paul an extremist for the Chris-tian gospel: "I bear in my body the marks of the Lord Jesus." Was not Martin Luther an extremist: "Here I stand; I cannot do oth-erwise, so help me God." And John Bunyan: "I will stay in jail to the end of my days before I make a butchery of my conscience." And Abraham Lincoln: "This nation cannot survive half slave and half free." And Thomas Jefferson: "We hold these truths to be self-evident, that all men are created equal...." So the question is not whether we will be extremists, but what kind of extremists we will be. Will we be extremists for hate or for love? Will we be extremists for the preservation of injustice or for the exten-sion of justice? In that dramatic scene on Calvary's hill three men were crucified. We must never forget that all three were crucified for the same crime—the crime of extremism. Two were extrem-ists for immorality, and thus fell below their environment. The other, Jesus Christ, was an extremist for love, truth, and goodness, and thereby rose above his environment. Perhaps the South, the nation, and the world are in dire need of creative extremists.

> Why does Dr. King align himself with all of these religious and historic "extremists"?

[On disappointment at the behavior of churches]

30 I had hoped that the white moderate would see this need. Per-haps I was too optimistic; perhaps I expected too much. I suppose I should have realized that few members of the oppressor race can understand the deep groans and passionate yearnings of the oppressed race, and still fewer have the vision to see that injustice must be rooted out by strong, persistent, and determined action. I am thankful, however, that some of our white brothers in the South have grasped the meaning of this social revolution and committed themselves to it. They are still all too few in quantity, but they are big in quality. Some—such as Ralph McGill, Lillian Smith, Harry Golden, James McBride Dabbs, Anne Braden, and Sarah Patton Boyle—have written about our struggle in eloquent and prophetic terms. Others have marched with us down name-less streets of the South. They have languished in filthy, roach-infested jails, suffering the abuse and brutality of policemen who view them as "dirty nigger-lovers." Unlike so many of their mod-erate brothers and sisters, they have recognized the urgency of the

> The six names given by Dr. King are of prominent white journalists-activists.

moment and sensed the need for powerful "action" antidotes to combat the disease of segregation.

Let me take note of my other major disappointment. I have been so greatly disappointed with the white church and its leadership. Of course, there are some notable exceptions. I am not unmindful of the fact that each of you has taken some significant stands on this issue. I commend you, Reverend [Earl] Stallings, for your Christian stand on this past Sunday, in welcoming Negroes to your worship service on a nonsegregated basis. I commend the Catholic leaders of this state for integrating Spring Hill College several years ago. 31

Located in Mobile, Alabama, the college was integrated in 1954.

But despite these notable exceptions, I must honestly reiterate that I have been disappointed with the church. I do not say this as one of those negative critics who can always find something wrong with the church. I say this as a minister of the gospel, who loves the church; who was nurtured in its bosom; who has been sustained by its spiritual blessings and who will remain true to it as long as the cord of life shall lengthen. 32

When I was suddenly catapulted into the leadership of the bus protest in Montgomery, Alabama, a few years ago, I felt we would be supported by the white church. I felt that the white ministers, priests, and rabbis of the South would be among our strongest allies. Instead, some have been outright opponents, refusing to understand the freedom movement and misrepresenting its leaders; all too many others have been more cautious than courageous and have remained silent behind the anesthetizing security of stained-glass windows. 33

In spite of my shattered dreams, I came to Birmingham with the hope that the white religious leadership of this community would see the justice of our cause and, with deep moral concern, would serve as the channel through which our just grievances could reach the power structure. I had hoped that each of you would understand. But again I have been disappointed. 34

I have heard numerous southern religious leaders admonish their worshipers to comply with a desegregation decision because it is the law, but I have longed to hear white ministers declare: "Follow this decree because integration is morally right and because the Negro is your brother." In the midst of blatant injustices inflicted upon the Negro, I have watched white church men stand on the sideline and mouth pious irrelevancies and sanctimonious trivialities. In the midst of a mighty struggle to rid 35 our nation of racial and economic injustice, I have heard many ministers say: "Those are social issues, with which the gospel has no real concern." And I have watched many churches commit themselves to a completely otherworldly religion which makes a strange, un-Biblical distinction between body and soul, between the sacred and the secular.

[On the role of the white church]

36 I have traveled the length and breadth of Alabama, Mississippi, and all the other southern states. On sweltering summer days and crisp autumn mornings I have looked at the South's beautiful churches with their lofty spires pointing heavenward. I have beheld the impressive outlines of her massive religious-education buildings. Over and over I have found myself asking: "What kind of people worship here? Who is their God? Where were their voices when the lips of Governor [Ross] Barnett dripped with words of *interposition* and *nullification*? Where were they when Governor [George] Wallace gave a *clarion* call for defiance and hatred? Where were their voices of support when bruised and weary Negro men and women decided to rise from the dark dungeons of complacency to the bright hills of creative protest?"

37   Yes, these questions are still in my mind. In deep disappointment I have wept over the laxity of the church. But be assured that my tears have been tears of love. There can be no deep disappointment where there is not deep love. Yes, I love the church. How could I do otherwise? I am in the rather unique position of being the son, the grandson, and the great-grandson of preachers. Yes, I see the church as the body of Christ. But, oh! How we have blemished and scarred that body through social neglect and through fear of being nonconformists.

38   There was a time when the church was very powerful—in the time when the early Christians rejoiced at being deemed worthy to suffer for what they believed. In those days the church was not merely a thermometer that recorded the ideas and principles of popular opinion; it was a thermostat that transformed the mores of society. Whenever the early Christians entered a town, the people in power became disturbed and immediately sought to convict the Christians for being "disturbers of the peace" and "outside agitators." But the Christians pressed on, in the conviction that they were "a colony of heaven," called to obey God rather than man. Small in number, they were big in commitment. They were

interposition—interference

nullification—rooted in a theory that a state has the right to ignore any federal law that state authorities hold to be inconsistent with the Constitution

clarion—loud and clear, like a sound from a trumpet

too God-intoxicated to be "astronomically intimidated." By their effort and example they brought an end to such ancient evils as infanticide and gladiatorial contests.

Things are different now. So often the contemporary church 39 is a weak, ineffectual voice with an uncertain sound. So often it is an archdefender of the status quo. Far from being disturbed by the presence of the church, the power structure of the average community is consoled by the church's silent—and often even vocal—sanction of things as they are.

But the judgment of God is upon the church as never before. If 40 today's church does not recapture the sacrificial spirit of the early church, it will lose its authenticity, forfeit the loyalty of millions, and be dismissed as an irrelevant social club with no meaning for the twentieth century. Every day I meet young people whose disappointment with the church has turned into outright disgust.

Perhaps I have once again been too optimistic. Is organized 41 religion too inextricably bound to the status quo to save our nation and the world? Perhaps I must turn my faith to the inner spiritual church, the church within the church, as the true *ekklesia* and the hope of the world. But again I am thankful to God that some noble souls from the ranks of organized religion have broken loose from the paralyzing chains of conformity and joined us as active partners in the struggle for freedom. They have left their secure congregations and walked the streets of Albany, Georgia, with us. They have gone down the highways of the South on tortuous rides for freedom. Yes, they have gone to jail with us. Some have been dismissed from their churches, have lost the support of their bishops and fellow ministers. But they have acted in the faith that right defeated is stronger than evil triumphant. Their witness has been the spiritual salt that has preserved the true meaning of the gospel in these troubled times. They have carved a tunnel of hope through the dark mountain of disappointment.

ekklesia—a Greek term, sometimes meaning those called together as a group of people who believe in God

[Optimism about the future]

I hope the church as a whole will meet the challenge of this deci- 42 sive hour. But even if the church does not come to the aid of justice, I have no despair about the future. I have no fear about the outcome of our struggle in Birmingham, even if our motives are at present misunderstood. We will reach the goal of freedom in Birmingham and all over the nation, because the goal of America is freedom. Abused and scorned though we may be, our destiny is

How do an optimistic outlook and a connection with American political values serve the civil-rights movement?

tied up with America's destiny. Before the pilgrims landed at Plymouth, we were here. Before the pen of Jefferson etched the majestic words of the Declaration of Independence across the pages of history, we were here. For more than two centuries our forebears labored in this country without wages: they made cotton king; they built the homes of their masters while suffering gross injustice and shameful humiliation—and yet out of a bottomless vitality they continued to thrive and develop. If the inexpressible cruelties of slavery could not stop us, the opposition we now face will surely fail. We will win our freedom because the sacred heritage of our nation and the eternal will of God are embodied in our echoing demands.

[On the police in Birmingham]

43 Before closing I feel impelled to mention one other point in your statement that has troubled me profoundly. You warmly commended the Birmingham police force for keeping "order" and "preventing violence." I doubt that you would have so warmly commended the police force if you had seen its dogs sinking their teeth into unarmed, nonviolent Negroes. I doubt that you would so quickly commend the policemen if you were to observe their ugly and inhumane treatment of Negroes here in the city jail; if you were to watch them push and curse old Negro women and young Negro girls; if you were to see them slap and kick old Negro men and young boys; if you were to observe them, as they did on two occasions, refuse to give us food because we wanted to sing our grace together. I cannot join you in your praise of the Birmingham police department.

44   It is true that the police have exercised a degree of discipline in handling the demonstrators. In this sense they have conducted themselves rather "nonviolently" in public. But for what purpose? To preserve the evil system of segregation. Over the past few years I have consistently preached that nonviolence demands that the means we use must be as pure as the ends we seek. I have tried to make clear that it is wrong to use immoral means to attain moral ends. But now I must affirm that it is just as wrong, or perhaps even more so, to use moral means to preserve immoral ends. Perhaps Mr. Connor and his policemen have been rather nonviolent in public, as was Chief Pritchett in Albany, Georgia, but they have used the moral means of nonviolence to maintain the immoral end of racial injustice. As T. S. Eliot has said, "The last temptation is the greatest treason: To do the right deed for the wrong reason."

T.S. Eliot,
Anglo-American poet

I wish you had commended the Negro sit-inners and demon- 45
strators of Birmingham for their sublime courage, their willingness to suffer, and their amazing discipline in the midst of great
provocation. One day the South will recognize its real heroes.
They will be the James Merediths, with the noble sense of purpose that enables them to face jeering and hostile mobs, and with
the agonizing loneliness that characterizes the life of the pioneer.
They will be old, oppressed, battered Negro women, symbolized
in a seventy-two-year-old woman in Montgomery, Alabama, who
rose up with a sense of dignity and with her people decided not
to ride segregated buses, and who responded with ungrammatical
profundity to one who inquired about her weariness: "My feets is
tired, but my soul is at rest." They will be the young high school
and college students, the young ministers of the gospel and a host
of their elders, courageously and nonviolently sitting in at lunch
counters and willingly going to jail for conscience' sake. One day
the South will know that when these disinherited children of God
sat down at lunch counters, they were in reality standing up for
what is best in the American dream and for the most sacred values in our Judaeo-Christian heritage, thereby bringing our nation
back to those great wells of democracy which were dug deep by
the founding fathers in their formulation of the Constitution and
the Declaration of Independence.

First African-American student at the University of Mississippi, 1962

In what ways do the civil-rights movement and the actions of nonviolent protesters connect with the values set forth in the Constitution and the Declaration of Independence?

[In Closing]

Never before have I written so long a letter. I'm afraid it is much 46
too long to take your precious time. I can assure you that it would
have been much shorter if I had been writing from a comfortable
desk, but what else can one do when he is alone in a narrow jail
cell, other than write long letters, think long thoughts, and pray
long prayers?

If I have said anything in this letter that overstates the truth 47
and indicates an unreasonable impatience, I beg you to forgive
me. If I have said anything that understates the truth and indicates
my having a patience that allows me to settle for anything less
than brotherhood, I beg God to forgive me.

I hope this letter finds you strong in the faith. I also hope that 48
circumstances will soon make it possible for me to meet each of
you, not as an integrationist or a civil-rights leader but as a fellow clergyman and a Christian brother. Let us all hope that the
dark clouds of racial prejudice will soon pass away and the deep
fog of misunderstanding will be lifted from our fear-drenched

To what extent has Dr. King's vision been realized today? What evidence supports your position?

communities, and in some not too distant tomorrow the radiant stars of love and brotherhood will shine over our great nation with all their scintillating beauty.

49 Yours for the cause of Peace and Brotherhood,
Martin Luther King Jr.

Impact of *Letter from Birmingham Jail* on U.S. law and culture

This document helped explain the realities of segregated life in the U.S. South to white Americans. You will mainly encounter this document in your Unit 3 study of civil rights. You should be able to connect the text to the Fourteenth Amendment's equal protection clause as well as to how new interpretation of the clause in *Brown v. Board of Education* helped spur the civil-rights movement. Likewise, you should be able to discuss specific ways in which the government eventually responded to this letter and the civil-rights movement, most importantly with the passage of the Civil Rights Act (1964) and the Voting Rights Act (1965).

Be prepared to discuss how this document influenced later social movements, as well as how the goals and tactics of the Southern Christian Leadership Conference and other groups (including the NAACP) exemplify successful tactics of interest groups and social movements in bringing about change in policymaking and society—looping back in Unit 5.

Check for Understanding

1. Describe the non-violent tactics of the southern civil-rights movement.
2. Describe the difference between just and unjust laws as laid out by Dr. King. (Paragraphs 13 through 20.)
3. Explain how Dr. King aligns his movement with Christian values as well as American political traditions.
4. Identify the required Supreme Court case mentioned by Dr. King in this letter, and explain how that case relates to the southern civil rights movement.
5. Explain what Dr. King meant about the "timeliness" of social movements. (See paragraph 24.)

Critical Thinking Question

In Letter from Birmingham Jail, Dr. King discusses how social movements create tension to bring about change. Identify a contemporary example of a social movement that seeks to create tension to force political change, and evaluate the success of the contemporary movement.

Required Supreme Court Cases

How to Tackle the Supreme Court Cases

Reading Supreme Court cases is a lot like reading short stories. By their very nature, all of the cases involve very strong legal arguments on both sides, often with competing constitutional claims. Most of the cases are interesting, and you might find yourself very engaged with them.

The required Supreme Court cases offer quite a bit of variety. Some of the Supreme Court cases were written a long time ago. Others are much more recent. So, some of the cases are going to be easier to read than others. Most of the cases contain some formal legal language. All of the cases are common-law decisions that serve as precedent for future cases.

The following strategies are designed to help you tackle the Supreme Court cases. You are not expected to read the full Court decisions, and this document reader contains carefully selected excerpts from the majority and dissenting opinions that will help you focus on the most important aspects of each case.

1. Before you read the case excerpt, get an overview

This document reader contains *Focus on* and *Reader Alert!* sections to give you a preview of each case. You may be able to find plain-English summaries of each case online. Be sure these summaries come from a credible source. Remember that summaries are a tool to help you understand difficult reading, but *they do not replace* reading the excerpts contained in this document reader. This is very important, especially if you want to do well on the AP® Exam, where you will be asked to apply required Supreme Court cases to nonrequired Supreme Court cases. If you don't fully understand the facts, issue, decision, reasoning, and impact of each of the required Supreme Court cases, you will struggle on the exam.

2. Pay attention to the facts

The facts section explains which parties are involved in the case and how the case ended up in court. Make sure you understand the facts, because the AP® Exam requires you to explain how the facts of the required case are similar to or different from the facts of a nonrequired case. For example, the case of *Engel v. Vitale* (1962) involved state-sponsored prayer in a public school. Suppose you were asked to apply *Engel v. Vitale* to a different case involving a holiday display in front of a government building, with Santa, a Christmas tree, a manger, and Rudolph. The cases are alike because both displays are state-sponsored and involve religion (a prayer in the *Engel* case and a manger in the example), but the cases differ because the holiday display does not target minors, is voluntary, and contains secular elements (Santa, a Christmas tree, and Rudolph).

3. Understand the issue and the constitutional clause involved in the case

The issue is the legal question the Supreme Court was asked to resolve, often whether or not an action or law violates a *specific clause* in the Constitution. For example, the issue in *Engel v. Vitale* is whether state-sponsored prayer in a public school violates the establishment clause of the First Amendment. Be specific. Your answer will be too vague if it just refers to the First Amendment, which protects several civil liberties.

4. Pay attention to the logic set forth in the majority and dissenting opinions

Each Supreme Court case excerpt is broken into sections and paragraphs, with headings to help you understand the Court's logic. Pay attention to these headings, because they are designed to help you understand how the logic of each decision is structured. You are encouraged to take notes to help you interact with and remember each argument. The document reader defines difficult and unusual terms, including Latin phrases often used in Supreme Court decisions. Pay attention to these definitions as you read, because you may encounter them again in the multiple-choice section or SCOTUS free-response question on the AP® Exam.

5. Focus on the impact

Supreme Court cases are important because they serve as precedent for future cases. Focus on the impact of each case. For example, the impact of *Engel v. Vitale* was that public schools are no longer allowed to officially endorse religious practices, such as daily prayer over the loudspeaker. This doesn't mean students can't pray in public school if they conduct the prayer independently from school officials. It's important to remember the precedent set by the case, as well as the limits of that precedent.

6. Use the Supreme Court case analysis sheet

This document reader contains a court-case analysis template to help you remember the important aspects of each required case, including the facts, issue, decision, reasoning, and impact. (See pages 127 and 129.) Make copies of this worksheet, and fill it out for each case. Store the worksheets where you can easily find them later to help you study for the AP® Exam.

How to Turn the Template into Worksheets

Do not mark up the template here in the document reader. There are fifteen required cases, so you should make fifteen copies of the template instead. You have two options:

1. Make fifteen photocopies of the template here in the book on page 129.
2. Download the file from the textbook site and print out fifteen copies.
    The Supreme Court case analysis template can be found at:

    highschool.bfwpub.com/AmGov1e

Supreme Court Case Analysis

Directions: Fill out this worksheet for each of the required Supreme Court cases, retain them, and use them to review for the AP® Exam.

Name of the case:

Year decided:

Facts (who did what, and how the case ended up in court):

Issue (In the form of a question, the legal question the Supreme Court is asked to resolve, often whether or not an action or law violates a *specific clause* in the Constitution):

Decision (who won):

Majority Decision Reasoning (explanation *why* the majority of justices reached the decision):

Dissenting Opinion Reasoning (explanation of why the dissenting judges disagree with the majority):

Impact of the case (why the precedent is important):

McCulloch v. Maryland

Focus on *McCulloch v. Maryland* (1819)

One of the main arguments in the early republic was over the scope of the implied powers of the national government, specifically Congress. On one side of the debate were those who believed that the Constitution should be applied literally (a theory known as strict constructionism). This would mean that Congress could only exercise the powers that are explicitly listed in the Constitution. On the other side of the argument were those who believed in the doctrine of implied powers (also known as loose constructionism). Loose constructionists believe that Congress should exercise powers beyond those enumerated in the Constitution, as long as those powers were implied by an enumerated power. In *McCulloch v. Maryland* (17 U.S. 316), the Supreme Court found that the implied powers doctrine was constitutional. Using the supremacy and the necessary and proper clauses, the Supreme Court ruled that Congress had the power to charter a national bank and that the state of Maryland could not tax that bank.

Reader Alert!

The Court's decision in *McCulloch v. Maryland* was part of a string of decisions (*Marbury v. Madison, Fletcher v. Peck,* and *Gibbons v. Ogden*) handed down by the Marshall Court in the early nineteenth century that defined and expanded national power. This case helps to clarify the application of the supremacy clause and the necessary and proper clause.

Facts of the Case

In 1816, Congress created the Second Bank of the United States after the charter for the first bank expired. Congress did this to help it conduct the business of government, such as collecting taxes. The bank was headquartered in Philadelphia. In 1817, a branch was opened in Baltimore, Maryland. In response, the state legislature of Maryland passed a tax of $15,000 a year on the bank's Baltimore branch in an effort to drive it out of business. A cashier at the bank, James McCulloch, refused to pay the tax. The Maryland Court of Appeals ruled that the bank was unconstitutional. McCulloch appealed to the Supreme Court.

Issue

There were two issues that the Supreme Court had to address in this case. First, does Congress have the authority to charter a bank? And if it does, can a state tax the bank?

■ Holding/Decision

In a unanimous decision, the Court ruled that Congress does have the right to create a bank because it is necessary for Congress to carry out its enumerated powers. (17 U.S. 316.) The Court also ruled that a state could not tax an institution of the national government because the laws of Congress are superior to the laws of the individual states.

Excerpt from Majority Opinion

[On the ability of Congress to incorporate a bank, which is the first question]

1   The first question made in the cause is—has Congress power to incorporate a bank?

[On Maryland's argument]

2   In discussing this question, the counsel for the State of Maryland have deemed it of some importance, in the construction of the Constitution, to consider that instrument not as emanating from the people, but as the act of sovereign and independent States. The powers of the General Government, it has been said, are delegated by the States, who alone are truly sovereign, and must be exercised in subordination to the States, who alone possess supreme dominion.

What argument does the state of Maryland make about the creation of the Constitution?

[Chief Justice Marshall's argument about the source of the Constitution]

3   But the instrument, when it came from their hands, was a mere proposal, without obligation or pretensions to it. It was reported to the then existing Congress of the United States with a request that it might

What argument did Chief Justice Marshall make against Maryland's assertion about the creation of the Constitution?

4   "be submitted to a convention of delegates, chosen in each State by the people thereof, under the recommendation of its legislature, for their assent and ratification."

5   This mode of proceeding was adopted, and by the convention, by Congress, and by the State legislatures, the instrument was submitted to the people. They acted upon it in the only manner in which they can act safely, effectively and wisely, on such a subject—by assembling in convention.... But the measures they adopt do not, on that account, cease to be the measures of the people themselves, or become the measures of the State governments.

From these conventions the Constitution derives its whole 6 authority. The government proceeds directly from the people; is "ordained and established" in the name of the people, and is declared to be ordained,

"in order to form a more perfect union, establish justice, 7 insure domestic tranquillity, and secure the blessings of liberty to themselves and to their posterity."

[On the meaning of the doctrine of implied powers]

Among the enumerated powers, we do not find that of establish- 8 ing a bank or creating a corporation. But there is no phrase in the instrument which, like the Articles of Confederation, excludes incidental or implied powers and which requires that everything granted shall be expressly and minutely described. ... The men who drew and adopted this amendment had experienced the embarrassments resulting from the insertion of this word in the Articles of Confederation, and probably omitted it to avoid those embarrassments. A Constitution, to contain an accurate detail of all the subdivisions of which its great powers will admit, and of all the means by which they may be carried into execution, would partake of the *prolixity* of a legal code, and could scarcely be embraced by the human mind. It would probably never be understood by the public. Its nature, therefore, requires that only its great outlines should be marked, its important objects designated, and the minor ingredients which compose those objects be deduced from the nature of the objects themselves. That this idea was entertained by the framers of the American Constitution is not only to be inferred from the nature of the instrument, but from the language. Why else were some of the limitations found in the 9th section of the 1st article introduced? It is also in some degree warranted by their having omitted to use any restrictive term which might prevent its receiving a fair and just interpretation. In considering this question, then, we must never forget that it is *a Constitution* we are expounding.

Although, among the enumerated powers of Government, we 9 do not find the word "bank" or "incorporation," we find the great powers, to lay and collect taxes; to borrow money; to regulate commerce; to declare and conduct a war; and to raise and support armies and navies.... But it may with great reason be contended that a Government intrusted with such ample powers, on the due

According to Chief Justice Marshall, what key provision differentiates the Constitution and the Articles of Confederation when it comes to the idea of implied powers? Why did the Framers include the provision in question?

prolixity—long-winded, having too much detail

Chief Justice Marshall points out that the Constitution contains the necessary and proper clause, which was not a part of the Articles of Confederation.

Which enumerated powers imply Congress's right to charter a bank?

execution of which the happiness and prosperity of the Nation so vitally depends, must also be intrusted with ample means for their execution. The power being given, it is the interest of the Nation to facilitate its execution. It can never be their interest, and cannot be presumed to have been their intention, to clog and embarrass its execution by withholding the most appropriate means. ... The *exigencies* of the Nation may require that the treasure raised in the north should be transported to the south that raised in the east, conveyed to the west, or that this order should be reversed. Is that construction of the Constitution to be preferred which would render these operations difficult, hazardous and expensive? Can we adopt that construction (unless the words imperiously require it) which would *impute* to the framers of that instrument, when granting these powers for the public good, the intention of impeding their exercise, by withholding a choice of means?

[On the purpose of the necessary and proper clause]

10 But the Constitution of the United States has not left the right of Congress to employ the necessary means for the execution of the powers conferred on the Government to general reasoning. To its enumeration of powers is added that of making

11 "all laws which shall be necessary and proper for carrying into execution the foregoing powers, and all other powers vested by this Constitution in the Government of the United States or in any department thereof."

12 But the argument on which most reliance is placed is drawn from that peculiar language of this clause. Congress is not empowered by it to make all laws which may have relation to the powers conferred on the Government, but such only as may be "necessary and proper" for carrying them into execution. The word "necessary" is considered as controlling the whole sentence, and as limiting the right to pass laws for the execution of the granted powers to such as are indispensable, and without which the power would be *nugatory*. That it excludes the choice of means, and leaves to Congress in each case that only which is most direct and simple.

13 Is it true that this is the sense in which the word "necessary" is always used? Does it always import an absolute physical necessity so strong that one thing to which another may be termed necessary cannot exist without that other? We think it

exigencies—urgent demands or needs

impute—represent as undesirable; attribute

How would implied powers help Congress carry out its enumerated powers?

nugatory—of no value or importance

Describe the two definitions of the word *necessary*. How is Chief Justice Marshall's definition important to upholding the constitutionality of the bank?

does not. If reference be had to its use in the common affairs of the world or in approved authors, we find that it frequently imports no more than that one thing is convenient, or useful, or essential to another. To employ the means necessary to an end is generally understood as employing any means calculated to produce the end, and not as being confined to those single means without which the end would be entirely unattainable. ... The word "necessary" is of this description. It has not a fixed character peculiar to itself. It admits of all degrees of comparison, and is often connected with other words which increase or diminish the impression the mind receives of the urgency it imports. A thing may be necessary, very necessary, absolutely or indispensably necessary. To no mind would the same idea be conveyed by these several phrases...This word, then, like others, is used in various senses, and, in its construction, the subject, the context, the intention of the person using them are all to be taken into view.

This provision is made in a Constitution intended to endure 14 for ages to come, and consequently to be adapted to the various crises of human affairs. To have prescribed the means by which Government should, in all future time, execute its powers would have been to change entirely the character of the instrument and give it the properties of a legal code. It would have been an unwise attempt to provide by immutable rules for exigencies which, if foreseen at all, must have been seen dimly, and which can be best provided for as they occur. To have declared that the best means shall not be used, but those alone without which the power given would be nugatory, would have been to deprive the legislature of the capacity to avail itself of experience, to exercise its reason, and to accommodate its legislation to circumstances.

How does the necessary and proper clause ensure that the Constitution will endure in the future?

What is the difference between a legal code and a constitution?

[On Maryland's power to tax the branch of the bank, which is the second question]

2. Whether the State of Maryland may, without violating the Constitution, tax that branch? 15

The sovereignty of a State extends to everything which exists 16 by its own authority or is introduced by its permission, but does it extend to those means which are employed by Congress to carry

How are the sources of power for a state and Congress different?

How does this difference in source of power make the laws of Congress supreme?

into execution powers conferred on that body by the people of the United States? We think it demonstrable that it does not. Those powers are not given by the people of a single State. They are given by the people of the United States, to a Government whose laws, made in pursuance of the Constitution, are declared to be supreme. Consequently, the people of a single State cannot confer a sovereignty which will extend over them.

What does Chief Justice Marshall mean by, "The power to tax involves the power to destroy"?

Ultimately, what argument does Chief Justice Marshall make in regard to Maryland's right to tax the bank?

17   That the power to tax involves the power to destroy; that the power to destroy may defeat and render useless the power to create; that there is a plain repugnance in conferring on one Government a power to control the constitutional measures of another, which other, with respect to those very measures, is declared to be supreme over that which exerts the control, are propositions not to be denied.

[On national supremacy, the bank, and Maryland's argument]

18   The Court has bestowed on this subject its most deliberate consideration. The result is a conviction that the States have no power, by taxation or otherwise, to retard, impede, burden, or in any manner control the operations of the constitutional laws enacted by Congress to carry into execution the powers vested in the General Government. This is, we think, the unavoidable consequence of that supremacy which the Constitution has declared.

What constitutional clause does Chief Justice Marshall allude to?

19   We are unanimously of opinion that the law passed by the Legislature of Maryland, imposing a tax on the Bank of the United States is unconstitutional and void.

Impact of *McCulloch v. Maryland* on national power

McCulloch v. Maryland was the landmark case that created the implied powers doctrine. The idea that the national government, and specifically Congress, can exercise powers not specifically listed in the Constitution to assist in carrying out its enumerated powers fundamentally altered the power of the national government and the relationship between the national government and the states. Today, much of the policy that Congress creates and has carried out—everything from drug prohibition, health care, and road building—can be traced to the implied powers doctrine.

Check for Understanding

1. Identify the constitutional clause used by Chief Justice Marshall to uphold Congress's ability to create a bank.
2. Explain how the opinion in *McCulloch v. Maryland* defines the word "necessary."
3. Identify the constitutional clause used by Chief Justice Marshall to deny Maryland's ability to tax the bank.
4. Explain why the use of implied powers is important to the relationship between the national and state governments.
5. Describe one policy area in which Congress has used the implied powers doctrine to expand its power relative to the states.

SCOTUS Practice Question

In the early nineteenth century, Thomas Gibbons operated a steamboat business along the Hudson River between New York and New Jersey under a federal license. Aaron Ogden, a former business partner of Gibbons, started a competing steamboat company under a license from the state of New York. Gibbons sued Ogden, arguing that his license from Congress gave him a monopoly. Ogden received a court order to prevent Gibbons from operating his steamboat line. The State of New York dismissed Gibbons's claim against Ogden. Gibbons then appealed his decision.

In 1824, in the case *Gibbons v. Ogden*, the Supreme Court ruled unanimously in favor of Gibbons who held the federal license, restoring his right to operate his steamboat line. Chief Justice John Marshall wrote, in part, "The laws of New York granting to Robert R. Livingston and Robert Fulton the exclusive right of navigating the waters of that State with steamboats are in collision with the acts of Congress regulating the coasting trade, which, being made in pursuance of the Constitution..."

Based on the information above, respond to parts A, B, and C.

A. Identify the common constitutional clause used by the Supreme Court to reach its decisions in both *McCulloch v. Maryland* (1819) and *Gibbons v. Ogden* (1824).

B. Explain how the facts of *McCulloch v. Maryland* (1819) and the facts of *Gibbons v. Ogden* (1824) led to a similar holding in both cases.

C. Describe an action that Congress could take in response to the ruling in *Gibbons v. Ogden* (1824) to prevent future lawsuits arising from competing state and federal contracts.

United States v. Lopez

Focus on *United States v. Lopez* (1995)

United States v. Lopez, 514 U.S. 549 (1995), is generally considered to be a turning point in the Supreme Court's interpretation of federalism. This case reaffirms the rights of the states under the Tenth Amendment and restricts Congress's power to pass legislation under the commerce clause to those laws that have a "substantial effect" on interstate commerce. This case reverses a trend in which Congress increasingly encroached on state powers by broadly interpreting congressional power under the commerce clause.

Reader Alert!

In *United States v. Lopez*, the Supreme Court interpreted the commerce clause more narrowly than in the past, reasserting the power of the states under the Tenth Amendment. Although this case is about a student who brought a gun to school, the case does not have any impact on Second Amendment rights, because it does not address the right to own a firearm. Instead, this is a federalism case, which focuses on whether the states or the national government has the power to pass regulations banning firearms in school zones.

Facts of the Case

In the Gun Free School Zones Act of 1990, Congress made it a federal offense "for any individual knowingly to possess a firearm at a place that the individual knows, or has reasonable cause to believe, is a school zone."

On March 10, 1992, respondent, who was then a 12th grade student, arrived at Edison High School in San Antonio, Texas, carrying a concealed .38 caliber handgun and five bullets. Acting upon an anonymous tip, school authorities confronted respondent, who admitted that he was carrying the weapon. He was arrested and charged under Texas law with firearm possession on school premises. The next day, the state charges were dismissed after federal agents charged respondent with violating the Gun Free School Zones Act of 1990.

On appeal, respondent challenged his conviction based on his claim that [The Gun Free School Zones Act] exceeded Congress's power to legislate under the Commerce Clause. [514 U.S. 549.]

▓ Issue

Did Congress exceed its authority under the commerce clause in passing the Gun Free School Zones Act of 1990?

▓ Holding/Decision

The Supreme Court ruled in favor of Lopez. (515 U.S. 549.)

Excerpt from Majority Opinion

[Overview of federalism]

1   Chief Justice Rehnquist delivered the opinion of the Court.

Why does the majority opinion begin with a review of the principle of federalism?

2   We start with first principles. The Constitution creates a Federal Government of enumerated powers. See U. S. Const., Art. I, §8. As James Madison wrote, "[t]he powers delegated by the proposed Constitution to the federal government are few and defined. Those which are to remain in the State governments are numerous and indefinite." The Federalist No. 45, pp. 292–293 (C. Rossiter ed. 1961). This constitutionally mandated division of authority "was adopted by the Framers to ensure protection of our fundamental liberties." *Gregory* v. *Ashcroft*, 501 U.S. 452, 458 (1991) (internal quotation marks omitted). "Just as the separation and independence of the coordinate branches of the Federal Government serves to prevent the accumulation of excessive power in any one branch, a healthy balance of power between the States and the Federal Government will reduce the risk of tyranny and abuse from either front." *Ibid.*

[On the dangers of expanding congressional power under the commerce clause]

How does the majority opinion use precedent to define the limits of the commerce clause?

3   In *Jones & Laughlin Steel*, the Court warned that the scope of the interstate commerce power "must be considered in the light of our dual system of government and may not be extended so as to embrace effects upon interstate commerce so indirect and remote that to embrace them, in view of our complex society, would effectually obliterate the distinction between what is national and what is local and create a completely centralized government." 301 U. S., at 37.

[On the act's lack of effect on commerce]

[The Gun Free School Zone Act] is a criminal statute that by its 4
terms has nothing to do with "commerce" or any sort of economic
enterprise, however broadly one might define those terms. [The
Gun Free School Zone Act] is not an essential part of a larger
regulation of economic activity, in which the regulatory scheme
could be undercut unless the intrastate activity were regulated. It
cannot, therefore, be sustained under our cases upholding regulations of activities that arise out of or are connected with a commercial transaction, which viewed in the aggregate, substantially
affects interstate commerce.

We pause to consider the implications of the Government's 5
arguments. The Government admits, under its "costs of crime"
reasoning, that Congress could regulate not only all violent crime,
but all activities that might lead to violent crime, regardless of how
tenuously they relate to interstate commerce. See Tr. of Oral Arg.
8-9. Similarly, under the Government's "national productivity"
reasoning, Congress could regulate any activity that it found was
related to the economic productivity of individual citizens: family
law (including marriage, divorce, and child custody), for example.
Under the theories that the Government presents in support of
[The Gun Free School Zones Act], it is difficult to perceive any
limitation on federal power, even in areas such as criminal law
enforcement or education where States historically have been sovereign. Thus, if we were to accept the Government's arguments,
we are hard pressed to posit any activity by an individual that
Congress is without power to regulate.

[On protecting state powers]

To uphold the Government's contentions here, we would have to 6
pile inference upon inference in a manner that would *bid fair* to
convert congressional authority under the Commerce Clause to
a general police power of the sort retained by the States. Admittedly, some of our prior cases have taken long steps down that
road, giving great deference to congressional action. The broad
language in these opinions has suggested the possibility of additional expansion, but we decline here to proceed any further. To
do so would require us to conclude that the Constitution's enumeration of powers does not presuppose something not enumerated, cf. *Gibbons* v. *Ogden*, ... at 195, and that there never will

According to the majority opinion, what was the main purpose of the Gun Free School Zone Act?

How does the majority opinion use a "slippery slope" argument as part of its reasoning?

bid fair—likely

How does the Court deal with previous precedents that expanded congres-sional power under the commerce clause?

be a distinction between what is truly national and what is truly local, cf. *Jones & Laughlin Steel, supra,* at 30. This we are unwilling to do.

7   For the foregoing reasons the judgment of the Court of Appeals is *Affirmed.*

Excerpt from Dissenting Opinion

8   Justice Breyer, with whom Justice Stevens, Justice Souter, and Justice Ginsburg join, dissenting.

9   The issue in this case is whether the Commerce Clause authorizes Congress to enact a statute that makes it a crime to possess a gun in, or near, a school. In my view, the statute falls well within the scope of the commerce power as this Court has understood that power over the last half century.

[How guns in schools undermine education]

10   For one thing, reports, hearings, and other readily available literature make clear that the problem of guns in and around schools is widespread and extremely serious. These materials report, for example, that four percent of American high school students (and six percent of inner city high school students) carry a gun to school at least occasionally, Centers for Disease Control 2342; Sheley, McGee, & Wright 679; that 12 percent of urban high school students have had guns fired at them, *ibid.;* that 20 percent of those students have been threatened with guns, *ibid.;* and that, in any 6 month period, several hundred thousand schoolchildren are victims of violent crimes in or near their schools, U. S. Dept. of Justice 1 (1989); House Select Committee Hearing 15 (1989). And, they report that this widespread violence in schools throughout the Nation significantly interferes with the quality of education in those schools. See, *e.g.,* House Judiciary Committee Hearing 44 (1990) (linking school violence to dropout rate); U. S. Dept. of Health 118-119 (1978) (school violence victims suffer academically); compare U. S. Dept. of Justice 1 (1991) (gun violence worst in inner city schools), with National Center 47 (dropout rates highest in inner cities). Based on reports such as these, Congress obviously could have thought that guns and learning are mutually exclusive. Senate Labor and Human

How does the dissenting opinion use statistics to support its argument that guns in school undermine education in the nation?

Resources Committee Hearing 39 (1993); U. S. Dept. of Health 118, 123-124 (1978). And, Congress could therefore have found a substantial educational problem—teachers unable to teach, students unable to learn—and concluded that guns near schools contribute substantially to the size and scope of that problem.

[On the impact of education on interstate commerce]

Having found that guns in schools significantly undermine the quality of education in our Nation's classrooms, Congress could also have found, given the effect of education upon interstate and foreign commerce, that gun related violence in and around schools is a commercial, as well as a human, problem. Education, although far more than a matter of economics, has long been *inextricably* intertwined with the Nation's economy.

Increasing global competition also has made primary and secondary education economically more important. The portion of the American economy attributable to international trade nearly tripled between 1950 and 1980, and more than 70 percent of American made goods now compete with imports. Marshall 205; Marshall & Tucker 33. Yet, lagging worker productivity has contributed to negative trade balances and to real hourly compensation that has fallen below wages in 10 other industrialized nations. See National Center 57; Handbook of Labor Statistics 561, 576 (1989); Neef & Kask 28, 31. At least some significant part of this serious productivity problem is attributable to students who emerge from classrooms without the reading or mathematical skills necessary to compete with their European or Asian counterparts, Finally, there is evidence that, today more than ever, many firms base their location decisions upon the presence, or absence, of a work force with a basic education. See MacCormack, Newman, & Rosenfield 73; Coffee 296. Scholars on the subject report, for example, that today, "[h]igh speed communication and transportation make it possible to produce most products and services anywhere in the world," National Center 38; that "[m]odern machinery and production methods can therefore be combined with low wage workers to drive costs down," *ibid.*; that managers can perform "'back office functions anywhere in the world now,'" and say that if they "'can't get enough skilled workers here'" they will "'move the skilled jobs out of the country,'" *id.*, at 41; with the consequence that "rich countries need better education and

11 | How does this paragraph serve as a transition connecting education and commerce?

inextricably—in a way that cannot be separated

12 | How does the dissenting opinion use statistics to support its argument that education impacts commerce?

retraining, to reduce the supply of unskilled workers and to equip them with the skills they require for tomorrow's jobs," Survey of Global Economy 37. In light of this increased importance of education to individual firms, it is no surprise that half of the Nation's manufacturers have become involved with setting standards and shaping curricula for local schools, Maturi 65–68, that 88 percent think this kind of involvement is important, *id.*, at 68, that more than 20 States have recently passed educational reforms to attract new business, Overman 61–62, and that business magazines have begun to rank cities according to the quality of their schools, see Boyle 24.

How does the dissenting opinion use a "slippery slope" argument as part of its reasoning?

How does the dissenting opinion set a different standard for determining Congress's power under the commerce clause than the majority opinion?

13 Businesses are less likely to locate in communities where violence plagues the classroom. Families will hesitate to move to neighborhoods where students carry guns instead of books. Congress expressly found in 1994 that "parents may decline to send their children to school" in certain areas "due to concern about violent crime and gun violence." ... And (to look at the matter in the most narrowly commercial manner), interstate publishers therefore will sell fewer books and other firms will sell fewer school supplies where the threat of violence disrupts learning. Most importantly, like the local racial discrimination at issue in *McClung* and *Daniel*, the local instances here, taken together and considered as a whole, create a problem that causes serious human and social harm, but also has nationally significant economic dimensions.

[Using a rational-basis test]

14 Upholding this legislation would do no more than simply recognize that Congress had a "rational basis" for finding a significant connection between guns in or near schools and (through their effect on education) the interstate and foreign commerce they threaten. For these reasons, I would reverse the judgment of the Court of Appeals. Respectfully, I dissent.

Impact of *United States v. Lopez* **on federalism**

The AP® U.S. Government and Politics curriculum specifically requires you to understand how *United States v. Lopez* impacted the balance of power between the national government and the states.

United States v. Lopez is generally seen as a turning point in defining the powers of Congress under the interstate commerce clause. Earlier decisions, like the required Supreme Court case of *McCulloch v. Maryland* (1819) and the nonrequired cases of *Gibbons v. Ogden* (1824) and *Heart of Atlanta Motel v. United States* (1964), expanded Congress's power relative to the states.

Partly as a result of the *Lopez* decision and subsequent cases that restricted Congress's power relative to the states, federalism continues to be a vibrant topic in United States government and politics. As discussed in Chapter 3, many states have reasserted their power to make laws over a wide range of policy areas, such as the legalization of marijuana.

Check for Understanding

1. Identify the two constitutional clauses that the Supreme Court interpreted in *United States v. Lopez*.
2. Describe the standard set by the majority opinion for determining whether or not an activity falls within Congress's power to regulate interstate commerce.
3. Describe the standard proposed by the dissenting opinion for determining whether or not an activity falls within Congress's power to regulate interstate commerce.
4. Describe the impact of the Court's decision in *United States v. Lopez* on the relationship between the national government and the states.
5. Explain how Congress can extend its influence beyond its enumerated powers through the use of grants-in-aid.

SCOTUS Practice Question

In 1994, Christy Brzonkala, a student at Virginia Polytechnic Institute (Virginia Tech), alleged that she had been raped by Antonio Morrison and James Crawford, both students and varsity football players at Virginia Tech. In 1995, Brzonkala filed a complaint against Morrison and Crawford under Virginia Tech's sexual assault policy. A hearing board found Morrison guilty of sexual assault and suspended him from Virginia Tech for two semesters. Brzonkala sued Morrison, Crawford, and Virginia Tech in federal district court, alleging that Morrison's and Crawford's attack violated the Violence Against Women Act of 1994 (42 U.S.C. § 13981), which provides a federal civil remedy to victims of gender-motivated violence.

In a 5-4 opinion, the Supreme Court held that Congress lacked the authority to enact the Violence Against Women Act of 1994. Chief Justice Rehnquist wrote the majority decision which states that "under our federal system that remedy must be provided by the Commonwealth of Virginia, and not by the United States."

A. Identify the constitutional clause that is common to both *United States v. Morrison* (2000) and *United States v. Lopez* (1995).

B. Based on the constitutional clause identified in part A, explain why the facts of *United States v. Morrison* led to a similar holding as the holding in *United States v. Lopez*.

C. Describe one way in which Congress could influence state policies regarding domestic violence.

Marbury v. Madison

Focus on *Marbury v. Madison* (1803)

Marbury v. Madison (5 U.S. (1 Cranch) 137) definitively establishes judicial review—the Supreme Court's most important power. The Supreme Court's power to interpret the Constitution, and, as such, strike down the actions of Congress, the president, and the states if those actions are deemed unconstitutional, is derived from the majority opinion in this case. Judicial review was not a "formal" power explicitly granted in the Constitution, but Chief Justice John Marshall drew on *Federalist* No. 78 (another required reading) in arguing for the Court's role in interpreting the Judiciary Act of 1801, finding it to be inconsistent with Article III of the Constitution, which structures the judiciary.

Reader Alert!

The facts of this case are somewhat complicated, and it's important not to get bogged down in what happened to William Marbury. It is better to focus only briefly on the political context of the case stemming from the election of 1800 (John Adams versus Thomas Jefferson) and then to put more effort into how this ruling changed the role of the Court in the political system, especially how the judiciary relates to the other institutions of government. This case made the judiciary a coequal branch of government.

Facts of the Case

Before leaving office after his defeat in the election of 1800, President Adams worked with Congress to pass the Judiciary Act of 1801, creating new courts and many more judges and justices of the peace. Because the Act was regarded mainly as an attempt to frustrate the incoming Jefferson administration, the new Secretary of State under Jefferson, James Madison, refused to deliver commissions to the new appointees. A group of these appointees, including William Marbury, petitioned for a writ of mandamus to compel the delivery of the commissions. A writ of mandamus is an official order from a court to a lower government official directing them to fulfill their official duties.

Issue

Do the plaintiffs have the right to petition for their commissions in court? Does the Supreme Court have the authority to order the delivery of commissions? Does the Supreme Court have the authority to overturn acts of Congress that violate the Constitution?

Holding/Decision

William Marbury was entitled to receive his commission (5 U.S. 167–168), yet the Court could not compel the secretary of state to deliver it. Because Section 13 of the Judiciary Act of 1801 was declared to be in conflict with Article III of the Constitution (5 U.S. 176), it was therefore struck down by the Supreme Court. This established the principle of judicial review (5 U.S. 178).

Excerpt from Majority Opinion

1 Mr. Chief Justice MARSHALL delivered the opinion of the Court.

[Determining whether or not Marbury has "standing" in this suit]

In what ways does this statement reflect Marshall's understanding of the goal and intent of separation of powers and checks and balances?

2 Mr. Marbury, then, since his commission was signed by the President and sealed by the Secretary of State, was appointed, and as the law creating the office gave the officer a right to hold for five years independent of the Executive, the appointment was not revocable, but vested in the officer legal rights which are protected by the laws of his country.

[Establishing that Marbury has a right to his commission and pivoting to the second question: the legal remedy]

violative—breaking or failing to comply with

vested—secured or assigned to a person

3 To withhold the commission, therefore, is an act deemed by the Court not warranted by law, but *violative* of a *vested* legal right.

4   This brings us to the second inquiry, which is:

5   2. If he has a right, and that right has been violated, do the laws of his country afford him a remedy?

What does the statement tell us about Justice Marshall's judicial philosophy and his view of the role of the Court in our political system?

6   The very essence of civil liberty certainly consists in the right of every individual to claim the protection of the laws whenever he receives an injury. One of the first duties of government is to afford that protection. In Great Britain, the King himself is sued in the respectful form of a petition, and he never fails to comply with the judgment of his court.

[On the legal remedy and how it can be applied to Marbury's case]

It follows, then, that the question whether the legality of an act of ⁊ the head of a department be examinable in a court of justice or not must always depend on the nature of that act.

If some acts be examinable and others not, there must be some ₈ rule of law to guide the Court in the exercise of its jurisdiction.

In some instances, there may be difficulty in applying the rule ₉ to particular cases; but there cannot, it is believed, be much difficulty in laying down the rule.

By the Constitution of the United States, the President is 10 invested with certain important political powers, in the exercise of which he is to use his own discretion, and is accountable only to his country in his political character and to his own conscience. To aid him in the performance of these duties, he is authorized to appoint certain officers, who act by his authority and in conformity with his orders.

[On the division of powers in the federal government]

In such cases, their acts are his acts; and whatever opinion may be 11 entertained of the manner in which executive discretion may be used, still there exists, and can exist, no power to control that discretion. The subjects are political. They respect the nation, not individual rights, and, being entrusted to the Executive, the decision of the Executive is conclusive. The application of this remark will be perceived by adverting to the act of Congress for establishing the Department of Foreign Affairs. This officer, as his duties were prescribed by that act, is to conform precisely to the will of the President. He is the mere organ by whom that will is communicated. The acts of such an officer, as an officer, can never be examinable by the Courts.

But when the Legislature proceeds to impose on that officer 12 other duties; when he is directed peremptorily to perform certain acts; when the rights of individuals are dependent on the performance of those acts; he is so far the officer of the law, is amenable to the laws for his conduct, and cannot at his discretion, sport away the vested rights of others.

The conclusion from this reasoning is that, where the heads 13 of departments are the political or confidential agents of the

What is Marshall's viewpoint about the power of an executive to order officials to carry out his wishes?

What is Marshall asserting about the role of Congress?

How does this passage describe the formal presidential role of chief executive?

Executive, merely to execute the will of the President, or rather to act in cases in which the Executive possesses a constitutional or legal discretion, nothing can be more perfectly clear than that their acts are only politically examinable. But where a specific duty is assigned by law, and individual rights depend upon the performance of that duty, it seems equally clear that the individual who considers himself injured has a right to resort to the laws of his country for a remedy.

14   If this be the rule, let us inquire how it applies to the case under the consideration of the Court.

[Turning to the case's third legal question]

15 This, then, is a plain case of a mandamus, either to deliver the commission or a copy of it from the record, and it only remains to be inquired:

16   whether it can issue from this court.

[How the Constitution frames the power and role of the Supreme Court]

17 The Constitution vests the whole judicial power of the United States in one Supreme Court, and such inferior courts as Congress shall, from time to time, ordain and establish. This power is expressly extended to all cases arising under the laws of the United States; and consequently, in some form, may be exercised over the present case, because the right claimed is given by a law of the United States.

18   In the distribution of this power. it is declared that

19   "The Supreme Court shall have original jurisdiction in all cases affecting ambassadors, other public ministers and *consuls*, and those in which a state shall be a party. In all other cases, the Supreme Court shall have appellate jurisdiction."

consul—an official appointed to live in a foreign city and to represent the government's interests there

20   It has been insisted at the bar, that, as the original grant of jurisdiction to the Supreme and inferior courts is general, and the clause assigning original jurisdiction to the Supreme Court contains no negative or restrictive words, the power remains to the Legislature to assign original jurisdiction to that Court in other cases than those specified in the article which has been recited, provided those cases belong to the judicial power of the United States.

If it had been intended to leave it in the discretion of the Leg- 21
islature to apportion the judicial power between the Supreme and
inferior courts according to the will of that body, it would certainly have been useless to have proceeded further than to have
defined the judicial power and the tribunals in which it should be
vested. The subsequent part of the section is mere *surplusage*—
is entirely without meaning—if such is to be the construction. If
Congress remains at liberty to give this court appellate jurisdiction where the Constitution has declared their jurisdiction shall
be original, and original jurisdiction where the Constitution has
declared it shall be appellate, the distribution of jurisdiction made
in the Constitution, is form without substance.

> *surplusage*—a useless and irrelevant statement

Affirmative words are often, in their operation, negative of 22
other *objects* than those affirmed, and, in this case, a negative or
exclusive sense must be given to them or they have no operation
at all.

> *object*—a purpose, goal, or objective

It cannot be presumed that any clause in the Constitution is 23
intended to be without effect, and therefore such construction is
inadmissible unless the words require it.

> What is Marshall's viewpoint about how language in the Constitution should be interpreted?

[Ensuring the Constitution is followed when enacting legislation]

The question whether an act repugnant to the Constitution can 24
become the law of the land is a question deeply interesting to the
United States, but, happily, not of an intricacy proportioned to its
interest. It seems only necessary to recognise certain principles,
supposed to have been long and well established, to decide it.

That the people have an original right to establish for their 25
future government such principles as, in their opinion, shall most
conduce to their own happiness is the basis on which the whole
American fabric has been erected. The exercise of this original right
is a very great exertion; nor can it nor ought it to be frequently
repeated. The principles, therefore, so established are deemed
fundamental. And as the authority from which they proceed, is
supreme, and can seldom act, they are designed to be permanent.

> *conduce*—help to bring about; lead to

This original and supreme will organizes the government and 26
assigns to different departments their respective powers. It may
either stop here or establish certain limits not to be *transcended*
by those departments.

> *transcend*—go beyond

Why does Marshall emphasize that the Constitution both defines and limits the powers of Congress?

How does Marshall distinguish limited and unlimited powers—and their effects?

What are the two alternative views of the role of the Constitution that Marshall addresses?

Why is it important to establish that the Constitution is more important than ordinary federal law?

27   The Government of the United States is of the latter description. The powers of the Legislature are defined and limited; and that those limits may not be mistaken or forgotten, the Constitution is written. To what purpose are powers limited, and to what purpose is that limitation committed to writing, if these limits may at any time be passed by those intended to be restrained? The distinction between a government with limited and unlimited powers is abolished if those limits do not confine the persons on whom they are imposed, and if acts prohibited and acts allowed are of equal obligation. It is a proposition too plain to be contested that the Constitution controls any legislative act repugnant to it, or that the Legislature may alter the Constitution by an ordinary act.

28   Between these alternatives there is no middle ground. The Constitution is either a superior, paramount law, unchangeable by ordinary means, or it is on a level with ordinary legislative acts, and, like other acts, is alterable when the legislature shall please to alter it.

29   If the former part of the alternative be true, then a legislative act contrary to the Constitution is not law; if the latter part be true, then written Constitutions are absurd attempts on the part of the people to limit a power in its own nature illimitable.

30   Certainly all those who have framed written Constitutions contemplate them as forming the fundamental and paramount law of the nation, and consequently the theory of every such government must be that an act of the Legislature repugnant to the Constitution is void.

[Making the case for judicial review]

31   This theory is essentially attached to a written Constitution, and is consequently to be considered by this Court as one of the fundamental principles of our society. It is not, therefore, to be lost sight of in the further consideration of this subject.

32   If an act of the Legislature repugnant to the Constitution is void, does it, notwithstanding its invalidity, bind the Courts and oblige them to give it effect? Or, in other words, though it be not law, does it constitute a rule as operative as if it was a law? This would be to overthrow in fact what was established in theory, and would seem, at first view, an absurdity too gross to be insisted on. It shall, however, receive a more attentive consideration.

It is emphatically the *province* and duty of the Judicial Department to say what the law is. Those who apply the rule to particular cases must, of necessity, expound and interpret that rule. If two laws conflict with each other, the Courts must decide on the operation of each.

So, if a law be in opposition to the Constitution, if both the law and the Constitution apply to a particular case, so that the Court must either decide that case conformably to the law, disregarding the Constitution, or conformably to the Constitution, disregarding the law, the Court must determine which of these conflicting rules governs the case. This is of the very essence of judicial duty.

If, then, the Courts are to regard the Constitution, and the Constitution is superior to any ordinary act of the Legislature, the Constitution, and not such ordinary act, must govern the case to which they both apply.

Those, then, who *controvert* the principle that the Constitution is to be considered in court as a paramount law are reduced to the necessity of maintaining that courts must close their eyes on the Constitution, and see only the law.

[Ensuring the Constitution has meaning]

This doctrine would subvert the very foundation of all written Constitutions. It would declare that an act which, according to the principles and theory of our government, is entirely void, is yet, in practice, completely obligatory. It would declare that, if the Legislature shall do what is expressly forbidden, such act, notwithstanding the express prohibition, is in reality *effectual*. It would be giving to the Legislature a practical and real omnipotence with the same breath which professes to restrict their powers within narrow limits. It is prescribing limits, and declaring that those limits may be passed at pleasure.

That it thus reduces to nothing what we have deemed the greatest improvement on political institutions—a written Constitution, would of itself be sufficient, in America where written Constitutions have been viewed with so much reverence, for rejecting the construction. But the peculiar expressions of the Constitution of the United States furnish additional arguments in favour of its rejection.

Margin notes:

33 *province*—area of responsibility

35 To what extent are you convinced by Marshall's argument that courts must determine whether acts of the legislature are constitutional, given that judicial review is never mentioned in the Constitution?

controvert—dispute; deny the truth of

37 Why would it be contradictory to allow Congress to pass laws that go against the Constitution?

effectual—producing its intended result

38 Why is a written Constitution "the greatest improvement on political institutions"?

39   The judicial power of the United States is extended to all cases arising under the Constitution.

In this part of the decision, Marshall emphasizes the Constitution's importance in establishing the rule of law by mentioning unfair laws such as bills of attainder, insisting that the Constitution requires rules of evidence.

40   There are many other parts of the Constitution which serve to illustrate this subject.

41   From these and many other selections which might be made, it is apparent that the framers of the Constitution contemplated that instrument as a rule for the government of courts, as well as of the Legislature.

42   Why otherwise does it direct the judges to take an oath to support it? This oath certainly applies in an especial manner to their conduct in their official character. How immoral to impose it on them if they were to be used as the instruments, and the knowing instruments, for violating what they swear to support!

[Concluding the argument for judicial review]

Describe an alternate perspective to Marshall's view that the role of the judiciary is to interpret the Constitution.

43   Thus, the particular phraseology of the Constitution of the United States confirms and strengthens the principle, supposed to be essential to all written Constitutions, that a law repugnant to the Constitution is void, and that courts, as well as other departments, are bound by that instrument.

44   The rule must be discharged.

Impact of *Marbury v. Madison* on the federal judiciary

Marbury v. Madison transformed the role of the Supreme Court in the judicial system, making it much more powerful. Some scholars wonder if the justices would have been granted life tenure by the framers of the Constitution had the framers anticipated how much power the justices would be granting themselves with this decision. The AP® U.S. Government and Politics course curriculum stresses the independence of the Supreme Court and the emergence of judicial review as a "powerful practice." It also mentions ongoing debate about the legitimacy of the Supreme Court's power.

Disciplinary Practice 2 is Supreme Court comparison. Throughout the course, you will practice comparing required cases to a nonrequired case. You will be given information about the nonrequired case. In a sense, *Marbury v. Madison* serves as a meaningful precedent for most of the cases that followed it, because it established judicial review, now practiced in many of the cases involving the Court's appellate jurisdiction.

Students should also be prepared to talk about how this case affected the balance of power in the federal government. The Supreme Court may overturn important policies passed by Congress, executive actions, and state legislation. Today, many voters make their choice for president based on the ability to appoint Supreme Court justices above any other issue. It is the power bestowed on the Court by *this* judicial decision that has made control of the Court such a prominent and partisan issue in politics today.

Check for Understanding

1. Describe Chief Justice Marshall's argument for establishing the power of judicial review. (See paragraphs 31 through 36.)
2. Describe what Article III of the Constitution says concerning the establishment and powers of the Supreme Court. (See paragraphs 17 through 21.)
3. Explain why Marshall believes the Judiciary Act must be struck down. (Paragraph 34.)
4. Describe Marshall's view of the role and powers of the executive branch.
5. Explain why the power of judicial review makes the courts coequal with Congress and the president.

SCOTUS Practice Question

Congress passed the Migratory Bird Treaty Act of 1918 to enforce a treaty made with Great Britain. When a U.S. game warden attempted to enforce the act, the state of Missouri sued, arguing that Congress lacked any formal power to regulate bird hunting, and that the Migratory Bird Treaty Act violated the Tenth Amendment guaranteeing reserved powers to the states for anything not enumerated in the Constitution.

In *Missouri v. Holland* (1920), the Court ruled 7-2 that Congress did in fact have the power to pass an act enforcing the Migratory Bird Treaty. The holding reasoned that under the supremacy clause, treaties are rendered the "supreme law of the land," overriding state laws.

A. Identify the constitutional clause that is common to both *Marbury v. Madison* (1803) and *Missouri v. Holland* (1920).

B. Based on the constitutional clause identified in part A, explain why the facts of *Marbury v. Madison* led to a similar holding in *Missouri v. Holland*.

C. Describe an action Congress might take to limit the role of the federal courts in making new policies or in shaping policymaking.

Engel v. Vitale

Focus on *Engel v. Vitale* (1962)

The case of *Engel v. Vitale,* 370 U.S. 421 (1962), centers on the First Amendment's establishment clause and the application of this clause in public school. This case outlawed the practice of school-sanctioned or teacher-led prayer in public school, even if the prayer is non-denominational and/or students may remain silent. In a 6-1 decision, the Court held that a prayer led or organized by public school teachers breached the constitutional "wall of separation" between church and state. Teachers or school leaders are representative of the government because they work in public institutions funded by taxpayers. Since this ruling, other cases have sought to determine whether or when the practice or presence of religion and taxpayer-funded schooling can be compatible.

Reader Alert!

This case did not "ban prayer in schools." The constitutional issue arises with teacher-led or school-sanctioned prayer. Students may still pray in school—to forbid student prayer would be a violation of the free exercise clause, the other protection of freedom of religion in the First Amendment. According to the Court's ruling, though, even voluntary prayer can at times be deemed coercive. Consider your own experiences or understanding of the relationship between religion and public school. Can public schools decorate for religious holidays? Are religious student groups permitted to meet on campus? Do school teams say a prayer before a game? Thinking about examples will help you to understand the impact of the case, as well as the differences between the application of the free exercise clause and the establishment clause.

Facts of the Case

The respondent Board of Education of Union Free School District No. 9, New Hyde Park, New York, acting in its official capacity under state law, directed the School District's principal to cause the following prayer to be said aloud by each class in the presence of a teacher at the beginning of each school day:

"Almighty God, we acknowledge our dependence upon Thee, and we beg Thy blessings upon us, our parents, our teachers and our Country."

...Shortly after the practice of reciting the Regents' prayer was adopted by the School District, the parents of ten pupils brought this action in a New York State Court insisting that use of this official prayer in the public schools was contrary to the beliefs, religions, or religious practices of both themselves and their children. Among other things, these parents challenged the constitutionality of both the state law authorizing the School District to direct the use of prayer in public schools and the School District's regulation ordering the recitation of this particular prayer on the ground that these actions of official governmental agencies violate that part of the First Amendment of the Federal Constitution which commands that "Congress shall make no law respecting an establishment of religion"—a command which was "made applicable to the State of New York by the Fourteenth Amendment of the said Constitution." The New York Court of Appeals, over the dissents of Judges Dye and Fuld, sustained an order of the lower state courts which had upheld the power of New York to use the Regents' prayer as a part of the daily procedures of its public schools so long as the schools did not compel any pupil to join in the prayer over his or his parents' objection. (370 U.S. 422, 424.)

The "regents" referred to are the New York Board of Regents, which is a body that sets standards for the public and private schools in the state of New York.

Issue

Is a voluntary, school-organized daily prayer in a public school setting a violation of the establishment clause of the First Amendment?

Holding/Decision

The state cannot organize prayer in public school, even if the prayer is non-denominational and students are given options for non-participation.

Excerpt from Majority Opinion

1 MR. JUSTICE BLACK delivered the opinion of the Court.

[On prayer and "spiritual heritage"]

Based on your understanding of the founding principles of the United States, do you believe religion is part of American political traditions?

2 The Board of Regents as *amicus curiae*, the respondents, and intervenors all concede the religious nature of prayer, but seek to distinguish this prayer because it is based on our spiritual heritage. ...

[On government programs and religious belief]

3 The petitioners contend, among other things, that the state laws requiring or permitting use of the Regents' prayer must be struck down as a violation of the Establishment Clause because that

prayer was composed by governmental officials as a part of a governmental program to further religious beliefs. For this reason, petitioners argue, the State's use of the Regents' prayer in its public school system breaches the constitutional wall of separation between Church and State. We agree with that contention, since we think that the constitutional prohibition against laws respecting an establishment of religion must at least mean that, in this country, it is no part of the business of government to compose official prayers for any group of the American people to recite as a part of a religious program carried on by government.

Why are schools and school officials synonymous with "government" in this instance?

[Seeking religious freedom]

It is a matter of history that this very practice of establishing governmentally composed prayers for religious services was one of the reasons which caused many of our early colonists to leave England and seek religious freedom in America.

4 Why does the majority opinion refer to colonial history?

[On the dangers of a union of church and state]

By the time of the adoption of the Constitution, our history shows that there was a widespread awareness among many Americans of the dangers of a union of Church and State. These people knew, some of them from bitter personal experience, that one of the greatest dangers to the freedom of the individual to worship in his own way lay in the Government's placing its official stamp of approval upon one particular kind of prayer or one particular form of religious services. They knew the anguish, hardship and bitter strife that could come when zealous religious groups struggled with one another to obtain the Government's stamp of approval from each King, Queen, or Protector that came to temporary power. The Constitution was intended to avert a part of this danger by leaving the government of this country in the hands of the people, rather than in the hands of any monarch. But this safeguard was not enough. Our Founders were no more willing to let the content of their prayers and their privilege of praying whenever they pleased be influenced by the ballot box than they were to let these vital matters of personal conscience depend upon the succession of monarchs. The First Amendment was added to the Constitution to stand as a guarantee that neither the power nor the prestige of the Federal Government would be used to control, support or influence the kinds of prayer the American people can say—that the people's religions must not

5

be subjected to the pressures of government for change each time a new political administration is elected to office. Under that Amendment's prohibition against governmental establishment of religion, as reinforced by the provisions of the Fourteenth Amendment, government in this country, be it state or federal, is without power to prescribe by law any particular form of prayer which is to be used as an official prayer in carrying on any program of governmentally sponsored religious activity.

[On protecting both government and religion]

6   There can be no doubt that New York's state prayer program officially establishes the religious beliefs embodied in the Regents' prayer. The respondents' argument to the contrary, which is largely based upon the contention that the Regents' prayer is "*nondenominational*" and the fact that the program, as modified and approved by state courts, does not require all pupils to recite the prayer, but permits those who wish to do so to remain silent or be excused from the room, ignores the essential nature of the program's constitutional defects. Neither the fact that the prayer may be denominationally neutral nor the fact that its observance on the part of the students is voluntary can serve to free it from the limitations of the Establishment Clause, as it might from the Free Exercise Clause, of the First Amendment, both of which are operative against the States by virtue of the Fourteenth Amendment. Although these two clauses may, in certain instances, overlap, they forbid two quite different kinds of governmental encroachment upon religious freedom. The Establishment Clause, unlike the Free Exercise Clause, does not depend upon any showing of direct governmental compulsion and is violated by the enactment of laws which establish an official religion whether those laws operate directly to coerce nonobserving individuals or not. This is not to say, of course, that laws officially prescribing a particular form of religious worship do not involve coercion of such individuals. When the power, prestige and financial support of government is placed behind a particular religious belief, the indirect coercive pressure upon religious minorities to conform to the prevailing officially approved religion is plain. But the purposes underlying the Establishment Clause go much further

nondenominational— not associated with a particular religious group

How are the clauses of the First Amendment related? And how do they relate to the Fourteenth Amendment?

Describe the Court's reasoning that state-sponsored prayer results in coercion.

than that. Its first and most immediate purpose rested on the belief that a union of government and religion tends to destroy government and to degrade religion. The history of governmentally established religion, both in England and in this country, showed that whenever government had allied itself with one particular form of religion, the inevitable result had been that it had incurred the hatred, disrespect and even contempt of those who held contrary beliefs. That same history showed that many people had lost their respect for any religion that had relied upon the support of government to spread its faith. The Establishment Clause thus stands as an expression of principle on the part of the Founders of our Constitution that religion is too personal, too sacred, too holy, to permit its "unhallowed perversion" by a civil magistrate. Another purpose of the Establishment Clause rested upon an awareness of the historical fact that governmentally established religions and religious persecutions go hand in hand.

Describe the arguments that "a union of government and religion tends to destroy government and to degrade religion."

[On a governmental endorsement of prayer]

It is true that New York's establishment of its Regents' prayer as an officially approved religious doctrine of that State does not amount to a total establishment of one particular religious *sect* to the exclusion of all others—that, indeed, the governmental endorsement of that prayer seems relatively insignificant when compared to the governmental encroachments upon religion which were commonplace 200 years ago. To those who may subscribe to the view that, because the Regents' official prayer is so brief and general there can be no danger to religious freedom in its governmental establishment, however, it may be appropriate to say in the words of James Madison, the author of the First Amendment:

7

sect—a particular religious group

> "[I]t is proper to take alarm at the first experiment on our liberties. … Who does not see that the same authority which can establish Christianity, in exclusion of all other Religions, may establish with the same ease any particular sect of Christians, in exclusion of all other Sects? That the same authority which can force a citizen to contribute three *pence* only of his property for the support of any one establishment may force him to conform to any other establishment in all cases whatsoever?"

8

pence—pennies

9   The judgment of the Court of Appeals of New York is reversed, and the cause remanded for further proceedings not inconsistent with this opinion.

10   *Reversed and remanded.*

Excerpt from Dissenting Opinion

11   MR. JUSTICE STEWART, dissenting.

12   A local school board in New York has provided that those pupils who wish to do so may join in a brief prayer at the beginning of each school day, acknowledging their dependence upon God and asking His blessing upon them and upon their parents, their teachers, and their country. The Court today decides that, in permitting this brief nondenominational prayer, the school board has violated the Constitution of the United States. I think this decision is wrong.

[Denying an opportunity]

Describe the comparison Justice Stewart is making between *West Virginia v. Barnette* and this case.

13   The Court does not hold, nor could it, that New York has interfered with the free exercise of anybody's religion. For the state courts have made clear that those who object to reciting the prayer must be entirely free of any compulsion to do so, including any "embarrassments and pressures." *Cf. West Virginia State Board of Education v. Barnette,* 319 U. S. 624. But the Court says that, in permitting school children to say this simple prayer, the New York authorities have established "an official religion."

14   With all respect, I think the Court has misapplied a great constitutional principle. I cannot see how an "official religion" is established by letting those who want to say a prayer say it. On the contrary, I think that to deny the wish of these school children to join in reciting this prayer is to deny them the opportunity of sharing in the spiritual heritage of our Nation.

[On religious traditions]

15   What is relevant to the issue here is not the history of an established church in sixteenth century England or in eighteenth century America, but the history of the religious traditions of our people, reflected in countless practices of the institutions and officials of our government.

[On traditions of religious practice in government]

At the opening of each day's Session of this Court we stand, while one of our officials invokes the protection of God. Since the days of John Marshall, our Crier has said, "God save the United States and this Honorable Court." Both the Senate and the House of Representatives open their daily Sessions with prayer. Each of our Presidents, from George Washington to John F. Kennedy, has, upon assuming his Office, asked the protection and help of God.

In 1954, Congress added a phrase to the Pledge of Allegiance to the Flag so that it now contains the words "one Nation *under* God, indivisible, with liberty and justice for all." In 1952, Congress enacted legislation calling upon the President each year to proclaim a National Day of Prayer. Since 1865, the words "IN GOD WE TRUST" have been impressed on our coins.

Countless similar examples could be listed, but there is no need to belabor the obvious. It was all summed up by this Court just ten years ago in a single sentence: "We are a religious people whose institutions presuppose a Supreme Being." *Zorach v. Clauson*, 343 U. S. 306, 343 U. S. 313.

16 | Do you believe the examples cited here are a violation of the establishment clause? Or are they proof of a religious tradition that is central to American political culture?

17

18

■ Impact of *Engel v. Vitale* on the legal relation of church and state

This case impacted many public schools across the country that included organized prayer as part of the school day. The case was one flashpoint in a broader culture war over American values in the past several decades.

Subsequent cases have sought to further define the boundaries of the establishment clause, seeking to determine whether the presence of religion in a school setting constituted "excessive entanglement" between church and state. Other cases have focused on public funding for religious schools or for a religious purpose.

■ Check for Understanding

1. Describe the difference between the establishment clause and the free exercise clause.
2. Explain how both the First Amendment and the Fourteenth Amendment were invoked in this case.
3. Based on this ruling, explain whether or not it would be constitutionally permissible for a group of Christian athletes to gather for a prayer after a game if not organized by their coach.

4. Explain why religious schools are allowed to begin each school day with an organized prayer.
5. Explain whether or not you believe this case strikes the correct balance between preventing "coercive" religious practice and allowing for religious freedom for students in school.

SCOTUS Practice Question

Both Pennsylvania and Rhode Island passed laws that provided funding to private, religious schools. In Pennsylvania, the funding went toward teachers' salaries, textbooks, and instructional materials for secular subjects. In Rhode Island, the funding supplemented elementary teachers' salaries. A group of taxpayers challenged the laws in both states as unconstitutional, and the Pennsylvania case went to the Supreme Court as *Lemon v. Kurtzman* (1971).

The Supreme Court struck down both state laws, arguing that the funding constituted "excessive entanglement" between church and state.

A. Identify the constitutional clause that is common to both *Lemon v. Kurtzman* (1971) and *Engel v. Vitale* (1962).
B. Based on the constitutional clause listed in part A, explain why the facts of *Lemon v. Kurtzman* led to a holding similar to the holding in *Engel v. Vitale*.
C. Describe one way in which Congress could influence policies concerning schools and religious practices.

Wisconsin v. Yoder

Focus on *Wisconsin v. Yoder* (1972)

The First Amendment's free exercise clause protects the right of individuals to exercise their religious beliefs. In *Wisconsin v. Yoder,* 406 U.S. 205 (1972), members of a religious group, the Amish, argued that their religion forbade formal education for their children beyond eighth grade. When the Amish declined to send their children to school after the eighth grade, they violated the state of Wisconsin's compulsory school attendance law, which required education through the age of sixteen. In this case, the Supreme Court had to rule on whether the First Amendment allowed the Amish to refuse to follow the compulsory education law.

Facts of the Case

Members of the Old Order Amish and the Conservative Amish Mennonite Church in Green County, Wisconsin, were convicted of violating Wisconsin's compulsory school attendance law (requiring a child's school attendance until age sixteen) by declining to send their children to public or private school after they had graduated from the eighth grade. The Amish claimed the compulsory attendance law violated their First Amendment rights and argued that their children's attendance at high school, public or private, was contrary to their religion and way of life. The evidence showed that respondents sincerely believed that attendance at a high school endangered their own salvation and that of their children. The Amish provided vocational education to their children designed to prepare them for life in an isolated rural Amish community and claimed that Wisconsin's law violated their rights under the free exercise clause of the First Amendment, made applicable to the states by the Fourteenth Amendment.

The state of Wisconsin argued that the compulsory school attendance until age sixteen was reasonable exercise of governmental power and that the state has the responsibility for educating its citizens. The state further argued that it had a compelling interest in educating all citizens through age sixteen to benefit the larger society and that this interest overrode the arguments of the Amish. The state of Wisconsin argued that the final years of high school prepare students for employment and civic participation and that if the Amish chose to leave the community they would need to have a proper education to be successful. Mandatory school laws apply to everyone regardless of religion.

The state supreme court sustained the claim of the Amish that application of the compulsory school attendance law violated their rights under the free exercise clause of the First Amendment, made applicable to the states by the Fourteenth Amendment, and the state appealed.

Issues

Did Wisconsin's requirement that all parents send their children to school at least until the age of sixteen violate the free exercise clause of the First Amendment by criminalizing the conduct of Amish parents who refused to send their children to school after eighth grade for religious reasons?

Decision

The Supreme Court ruled unanimously in favor of Yoder (the Amish), reasoning that an individual's interests in the free exercise of religion under the First Amendment outweighed the State's interests in compelling school attendance beyond the eighth grade. Justice Burger delivered the opinion and Justice Douglas dissented in part.

The Supreme Court ruled that the free exercise clause of the First Amendment, as incorporated by the Fourteenth Amendment, prevented the state of Wisconsin from compelling the Amish to send their children to formal secondary school beyond the age of fourteen. The Court ruled that the family's religious beliefs and practices outweighed the state's interests in making the children attend school beyond eighth grade because it would interfere with well-established deeply held religious convictions of the Amish.

Reader Alert!

The court sided with the Amish, but at the same time, the Court recognized that the state has an interest in universal education.

Excerpt from Majority Opinion

1　MR. CHIEF JUSTICE BURGER delivered the opinion of the Court.

[Considering the beliefs and practices of the Amish]

Justice Burger in the majority opinion refers to the "sincerely held" religious beliefs of the Amish. Why do you think it was important to refer to the beliefs as "sincere"?

2　The trial testimony showed that respondents believed, in accordance with the tenets of Old Order Amish communities generally, that their children's attendance at high school, public or private, was contrary to the Amish religion and way of life. They believed that, by sending their children to high school, they would not only expose themselves to the danger of the censure of the church community, but, as found by the county court, also endanger their own salvation and that of their children. The State *stipulated* that respondents' religious beliefs were sincere.

In support of their position, respondents presented as expert witnesses scholars on religion and education whose testimony is uncontradicted. They expressed their opinions on the relationship of the Amish belief concerning school attendance to the more general tenets of their religion, and described the impact that compulsory high school attendance could have on the continued survival of Amish communities as they exist in the United States today. The history of the Amish *sect* was given in some detail, beginning with the Swiss Anabaptists of the 16th century, who rejected institutionalized churches and sought to return to the early, simple, Christian life deemphasizing material success, rejecting the competitive spirit, and seeking to insulate themselves from the modern world. As a result of their common heritage, Old Order Amish communities today are characterized by a fundamental belief that salvation requires life in a church community separate and apart from the world and worldly influence. This concept of life aloof from the world and its values is central to their faith.

A related feature of Old Order Amish communities is their devotion to a life in harmony with nature and the soil, as exemplified by the simple life of the early Christian era that continued in America during much of our early national life. Amish beliefs require members of the community to make their living by farming or closely related activities. Broadly speaking, the Old Order Amish religion pervades and determines the entire mode of life of its adherents. Their conduct is regulated in great detail by the *Ordnung*, or rules, of the church community. Adult baptism, which occurs in late adolescence, is the time at which Amish young people voluntarily undertake heavy obligations, not unlike the Bar Mitzvah of the Jews, to abide by the rules of the church community.

[On the objections of the Amish to continuing education at high school]

Amish objection to formal education beyond the eighth grade is firmly grounded in these central religious concepts. They object to the high school, and higher education generally, because the values they teach are in marked variance with Amish values and the Amish way of life; they view secondary school education as an impermissible exposure of their children to a "worldly" influence

stipulate—(in legal writing), to clarify, specify, or agree

Why does the opinion describe the history of the Amish?

sect—a religious group, sometimes one outside the mainstream

in conflict with their beliefs. The high school tends to emphasize intellectual and scientific accomplishments, self-distinction, competitiveness, worldly success, and social life with other students. Amish society emphasizes informal "learning through doing;" a life of "goodness," rather than a life of intellect; wisdom, rather than technical knowledge; community welfare, rather than competition; and separation from, rather than integration with, contemporary worldly society.

6   Formal high school education beyond the eighth grade is contrary to Amish beliefs not only because it places Amish children in an environment hostile to Amish beliefs, with increasing emphasis on competition in class work and sports and with pressure to conform to the styles, manners, and ways of the peer group, but also because it takes them away from their community, physically and emotionally, during the crucial and formative adolescent period of life. During this period, the children must acquire Amish attitudes favoring manual work and self-reliance and the specific skills needed to perform the adult role of an Amish farmer or housewife. They must learn to enjoy physical labor. Once a child has learned basic reading, writing, and elementary mathematics, these traits, skills, and attitudes admittedly fall within the category of those best learned through example and "doing," rather than in a classroom. And, at this time in life, the Amish child must also grow in his faith and his relationship to the Amish community if he is to be prepared to accept the heavy obligations imposed by adult baptism. In short, high school attendance with teachers who are not of the Amish faith—and may even be hostile to it— interposes a serious barrier to the integration of the Amish child into the Amish religious community.

Excerpt from Dissenting Opinion

Note: The vote in favor of the Amish on this case was unanimous. Justice Douglas dissented in part, 406 U. S. 241, arguing that the ruling upholds a parent's right to free exercise but that a child who wishes to attend public school in conflict with the wishes of his parents should not be prevented from doing so.

scruple—an unwillingness to do something seen as morally wrong

7   I agree with the Court that the religious *scruples* of the Amish are opposed to the education of their children beyond the grade schools, yet I disagree with the Court's conclusion that the matter

is within the dispensation of parents alone. The Court's analysis assumes that the only interests at stake in the case are those of the Amish parents, on the one hand, and those of the State, on the other. The difficulty with this approach is that, despite the Court's claim, the parents are seeking to vindicate not only their own free exercise claims, but also those of their high-school-age children.

It is argued that the right of the Amish children to religious freedom is not presented by the facts of the case, as the issue before the Court involves only the Amish parents' religious freedom to defy a state criminal statute imposing upon them an affirmative duty to cause their children to attend high school. 8

First, respondents' motion to dismiss in the trial court expressly asserts not only the religious liberty of the adults, but also that of the children, as a defense to the prosecutions. It is, of course, beyond question that the parents have standing as defendants in a criminal prosecution to assert the religious interests of their children as a defense. Although the lower courts and a majority of this Court assume an identity of interest between parent and child, it is clear that they have treated the religious interest of the child as a factor in the analysis. 9

...If the parents in this case are allowed a religious exemption, the inevitable effect is to impose the parents' notions of religious duty upon their children. Where the child is mature enough to express potentially conflicting desires, it would be an invasion of the child's rights to permit such an imposition without canvassing his views. As in *Prince v. Massachusetts,* 321 U. S. 158, it is an imposition resulting from this very litigation. As the child has no other effective forum, it is in this litigation that his rights should be considered. And if an Amish child desires to attend high school, and is mature enough to have that desire respected, the State may well be able to override the parents' religiously motivated objections. 10

> What is Justice Douglas's main reason for dissenting? On what grounds does he agree with the majority?

▮ **Impact of** *Wisconsin v. Yoder* **on the First Amendment**

The AP® U.S. Government and Politics curriculum specifically requires you to understand how a majority of the Court in *Wisconsin v. Yoder* interpreted the free exercise clause to protect the free exercise rights of the Amish. The curriculum requires an understanding of how the free exercise clause creates a balancing act between majoritarian religious practice and the right of individual free exercise. The Court had to consider whether, in this circumstance, the Amish were asking for a reasonable accommodation of their religious beliefs under the umbrella of free exercise of religion. The beliefs of the Amish were considered sincere. The Amish have practiced their religion since the sixteenth century and the basic principles have remained stable. It is unclear whether other religious groups requesting similar exemptions from the laws will be accommodated.

Check for Understanding

1. Describe the most important facts in this case.
2. Explain how the Court interpreted the free exercise clause in *Wisconsin v. Yoder*.
3. Describe the Court's reasoning for the holding that the free exercise clause protected the Amish in this case.
4. Explain whether or not you believe all citizens have the right, under *Wisconsin v. Yoder*, to opt their children out of school after eighth grade.
5. Explain how the Court's decision in *Wisconsin v. Yoder* demonstrates a balance between religious liberty and other important societal values.

SCOTUS Practice Question

Walter "Billy" Gobitas, a ten-year old elementary school student in 1935, was asked to salute the flag while reciting the Pledge of Allegiance but refused. Gobitas was a member of the Jehovah's Witnesses denomination, which does not allow saluting anything but God. As a member of the Jehovah's Witnesses, he believed that saluting the flag was akin to idol worship and a violation of the commandments. Gobitas was expelled. Gobitas argued that the school policy requiring him to salute the flag violated the First Amendment's guarantee of religious freedom. In 1940, the Supreme Court ruled in favor of the school, arguing that the government could require respect for the flag and that the Pledge of Allegiance is a symbol of national unity. The Court held that parents, not the schools, are children's main religious instructors and that the pledge would not interfere with the upbringing of children. (And note that the name of the case misspells the Gobitas family name, which sometimes happens.)

A. Identify the constitutional clause that is common to both *Wisconsin v. Yoder* (1972) and *Minersville School District v. Gobitis* (1940).
B. Based on the constitutional clause identified in part A, explain why the facts of *Minersville School District v. Gobitis* led to a similar holding as the facts of *Wisconsin v. Yoder*.
C. Describe one way a state could limit the impact of the ruling in either *Wisconsin v. Yoder* or *Minersville School District v. Gobitis*.

Tinker v. Des Moines Independent Community School District

Focus on *Tinker v. Des Moines Independent Community School District* (1969)

Tinker v. Des Moines Independent Community School District, 393 U.S. 503, is generally considered a landmark case with a major impact on many other court rulings concerning the rights of students to free-speech. The case established a precedent in favor of students' free-speech rights in schools under the First and Fourteenth Amendments. Mary Beth Tinker continues to work as an advocate for preserving "democratized speech," often speaking to student groups across the country.

Reader Alert!

In *Tinker v. Des Moines Independent Community School District,* the Supreme Court held that the First Amendment applied to public schools and that school officials could not censor student speech unless it disrupted the educational process. The decision affirmed the protections of symbolic speech. In deciding this case, the Court looked at precedent from numerous cases, including *West Virginia State Board of Education v. Barnette* (1943). In *West Virginia State Board of Education v. Barnette,* the Supreme Court ruled that a mandatory salute to the flag was unconstitutional. The Court determined that a salute to the flag was a form of speech because it was a way to communicate ideas. The Court held that, in most cases, the government could not require people to express ideas that they disagree with. *Tinker v. Des Moines Independent Community School District* remains an important precedent-setting case because it affirmed the protections of symbolic speech. Five justices agreed with the majority opinion. Two justices concurred. Two justices dissented.

Facts of the Case

In December 1965, a group of adults and students in Des Moines, Iowa, held a meeting in the home of Christopher Eckhardt to plan a two-week public display of their support for a truce in the Vietnam war. The students planned to wear two-inch-wide black armbands to school during the holiday season. The school district learned of the plan, and two days before the planned protest, the district created a policy that any student who wore a black armband to school would be asked to remove it. If the student refused, the student would be suspended from school and sent home.

John Tinker, 15 years old, and Christopher Eckhardt, 16 years old, attended high schools in Des Moines, Iowa. Mary Beth Tinker, John's sister, was a 13-year-old student in junior high school. Mary Beth Tinker and Christopher Eckhardt wore their armbands to their schools and were sent home. The following day, John Tinker wore his armband to school and was also sent home. Hope and Paul Tinker wore armbands to their elementary school but received no penalty. The three older students were suspended for the duration of the protest based on their armbands.

Through their parents, the students, who were below the legal age to file suit, sued the school district for violating the students' right of expression and sought an injunction to prevent the school district from disciplining the students. The district court dismissed the case and held that the school district's actions were reasonable to uphold school discipline. The U.S. Court of Appeals for the Eighth Circuit affirmed the decision without opinion.

Issue

Do the First and Fourteenth Amendments permit officials of state-supported public schools to prohibit students from wearing symbols of political views within school premises where the symbols are not disruptive of school discipline?

Holding/Decision

The Supreme Court ruled in favor of the Tinkers, 7–2. "First Amendment rights, applied in light of the special characteristics of the school environment, are available to teachers and students. It can hardly be argued that either students or teachers shed their constitutional rights to freedom of speech or expression at the schoolhouse gate...." (393 U.S. at 506.) First Amendment protections extend to students in public schools, and educational authorities who want to censor speech must show that permitting the speech would significantly interfere with the discipline required for the school to function.

Excerpt from Majority Opinion

1   MR. JUSTICE FORTAS delivered the opinion of the Court.

[On the history of students' First Amendment rights]

2   The District Court recognized that the wearing of an armband for the purpose of expressing certain views is the type of symbolic act

that is within the Free Speech Clause of the First Amendment. ...
As we shall discuss, the wearing of armbands in the circumstances
of this case was entirely divorced from actually or potentially disruptive conduct by those participating in it. It was closely *akin* to
"pure speech" which, we have repeatedly held, is entitled to *comprehensive* protection under the First Amendment.

akin—similar

pure speech—written
and spoken words

comprehensive—
complete

First Amendment rights, applied in light of the special characteristics of the school environment, are available to teachers
and students. It can hardly be argued that either students or
teachers shed their constitutional rights to freedom of speech
or expression at the schoolhouse gate. This has been the unmistakable holding of this Court for almost 50 years. In *Meyer v.
Nebraska*, 262 U. S. 390 (1923), and *Bartels v. Iowa*, 262 U. S.
404 (1923), this Court, in opinions by Mr. Justice McReynolds,
held that the Due Process Clause of the Fourteenth Amendment
prevents States from forbidding the teaching of a foreign language to young students. Statutes to this effect, the Court held,
unconstitutionally interfere with the liberty of teacher, student,
and parent.

3

Which clause of the
First Amendment
protects wearing an
armband?

In *West Virginia v. Barnette,* ... this Court held that, under
the First Amendment, the student in public school may not be
compelled to salute the flag. Speaking through Mr. Justice Jackson, the Court said:

4

> The Fourteenth Amendment, as now applied to the States, pro-
> tects the citizen against the State itself and all of its creatures—
> Boards of Education not excepted. These have, of course, import-
> ant, delicate, and highly discretionary functions, but none that
> they may not perform within the limits of the Bill of Rights. That
> they are educating the young for citizenship is reason for scru-
> pulous protection of Constitutional freedoms of the individual,
> if we are not to strangle the free mind at its source and teach
> youth to discount important principles of our government as
> mere platitudes.

5

Why is the
Fourteenth Amend-
ment applicable in
this case?

On the other hand, the Court has repeatedly emphasized the
need for affirming the comprehensive authority of the States and
of school officials, consistent with fundamental constitutional
safeguards, to prescribe and control conduct in the schools....
Our problem lies in the area where students in the exercise of
First Amendment rights collide with the rules of the school
authorities.

6

Why was the
wearing of armbands
considered a form of
speech?

[On the events and policies in this case]

7   The problem posed by the present case does not relate to regulation of the length of skirts or the type of clothing, to hair style, or deportment. ... It does not concern aggressive, disruptive action or even group demonstrations. Our problem involves direct, primary First Amendment rights akin to "pure speech."

8   The school officials banned and sought to punish petitioners for a silent, passive expression of opinion, unaccompanied by any disorder or disturbance on the part of petitioners. There is here no evidence whatever of petitioners' interference, actual or nascent, with the schools' work or of collision with the rights of other students to be secure and to be let alone. Accordingly, this case does not concern speech or action that intrudes upon the work of the schools or the rights of other students.

9   The District Court concluded that the action of the school authorities was reasonable because it was based upon their fear of a disturbance from the wearing of the armbands. But, in our *undifferentiated—not specific* system, *undifferentiated* fear or apprehension of disturbance is not enough to overcome the right to freedom of expression. Any departure from absolute regimentation may cause trouble. Any variation from the majority's opinion may inspire fear. Any word spoken, in class, in the lunchroom, or on the campus, that deviates from the views of another person may start an argument or cause a disturbance. But our Constitution says we must take this risk, *Terminiello v. Chicago*, 337 U. S. 1 (1949); and our history says that it is this sort of hazardous freedom—this kind of openness— that is the basis of our national strength and of the independence and vigor of Americans who grow up and live in this relatively *disputatious—fond of arguing* permissive, often *disputatious*, society.

undifferentiated—not specific

disputatious—fond of arguing

[On the school district's legal burden]

What did schools have to prove for the policy to be upheld?

10   In order for the State in the person of school officials to justify prohibition of a particular expression of opinion, it must be able to show that its action was caused by something more than a mere desire to avoid the discomfort and unpleasantness that always accompany an unpopular viewpoint. Certainly where there is no finding and no showing that engaging in the forbidden conduct *materially—significantly* would "*materially* and substantially interfere with the requirements of appropriate discipline in the operation of the school," the prohibition cannot be sustained.

materially—significantly

In the present case, the District Court made no such finding, 11 and our independent examination of the record fails to yield evidence that the school authorities had reason to anticipate that the wearing of the armbands would substantially interfere with the work of the school or *impinge* upon the rights of other students. Even an official memorandum prepared after the suspension that listed the reasons for the ban on wearing the armbands made no reference to the anticipation of such disruption.

impinge—have an impact, especially a negative one

On the contrary, the action of the school authorities appears 12 to have been based upon an urgent wish to avoid the controversy which might result from the expression, even by the silent symbol of armbands, of opposition to this Nation's part in the conflagration in Vietnam.

What reason does the majority cite for the school's policy about armbands?

It is also relevant that the school authorities did not *purport* 13 to prohibit the wearing of all symbols of political or controversial significance. The record shows that students in some of the schools wore buttons relating to national political campaigns, and some even wore the Iron Cross, traditionally a symbol of Nazism. The order prohibiting the wearing of armbands did not extend to these. Instead, a particular symbol—black armbands worn to exhibit opposition to this Nation's involvement in Vietnam—was singled out for prohibition. Clearly, the prohibition of expression of one particular opinion, at least without evidence that it is necessary to avoid material and substantial interference with schoolwork or discipline, is not constitutionally permissible.

purport—intend

[On public schools and free speech]

In our system, state-operated schools may not be enclaves of 14 totalitarianism. School officials do not possess absolute authority over their students. Students in school, as well as out of school, are "persons" under our Constitution. They are possessed of fundamental rights which the State must respect, just as they themselves must respect their obligations to the State. In our system, students may not be regarded as closed-circuit recipients of only that which the State chooses to communicate. They may not be confined to the expression of those sentiments that are officially approved. In the absence of a specific showing of constitutionally valid reasons to regulate their speech, students are entitled to freedom of expression of their views.

A student's rights, therefore, do not embrace merely the 15 classroom hours. When he is in the cafeteria, or on the playing field, or on the campus during the authorized hours, he may express his opinions, even on controversial subjects like the conflict in Vietnam, if he does so without "materially and substantially interfer[ing] with the requirements of appropriate discipline in the operation of the school" and without colliding with the rights of others. ... But conduct by the student, in class or out of it, which for any reason—whether it stems from time, place, or type of behavior—materially disrupts classwork or involves substantial disorder or invasion of the rights of others is, of course, not immunized by the constitutional guarantee of freedom of speech.

> According to the majority, when can schools limit free speech for students?

> Why do students possess fundamental rights that all levels of government must respect?

16   Under our Constitution, free speech is not a right that is given only to be so circumscribed that it exists in principle, but not in fact. Freedom of expression would not truly exist if the right could be exercised only in an area that a benevolent government has provided as a safe haven for crackpots. The Constitution says that Congress (and the States) may not *abridge* the right to free speech. This provision means what it says. We properly read it to permit reasonable regulation of speech-connected activities in carefully restricted circumstances. But we do not confine the permissible exercise of First Amendment rights to a telephone booth or the four corners of a pamphlet, or to supervised and ordained discussion in a school classroom.

> *abridge*—reduce or lessen

Excerpt from Dissenting Opinion

17   MR. JUSTICE BLACK, dissenting.

[On limits on free speech]

18   While I have always believed that, under the First and Fourteenth Amendments, neither the State nor the Federal Government has any authority to regulate or censor the content of speech, I have never believed that any person has a right to give speeches or engage in demonstrations where he pleases and when he pleases. This Court has already rejected such a notion. In *Cox v. Louisiana*, 379 U. S. 536, 554 (1965), for example, the Court clearly stated that the rights of free speech and assembly "do not mean that everyone with opinions or beliefs to express may address a group at any public place and at any time."

[On public schools and free speech]

I deny, therefore, that it has been the "unmistakable holding of
this Court for almost 50 years" that "students" and "teachers"
take with them into the "schoolhouse gate" constitutional rights
to "freedom of speech or expression." Even *Meyer* did not hold
that. It makes no reference to "symbolic speech" at all; what it
did was to strike down as "unreasonable," and therefore unconstitutional, a Nebraska law barring the teaching of the German
language before the children reached the eighth grade. One can
well agree with Mr. Justice Holmes and Mr. Justice Sutherland,
as I do, that such a law was no more unreasonable than it would
be to bar the teaching of Latin and Greek to pupils who have
not reached the eighth grade. In fact, I think the majority's reason for invalidating the Nebraska law was that it did not like
it, or, in legal jargon, that it "shocked the Court's conscience,"
"offended its sense of justice," or was "contrary to fundamental
concepts of the English-speaking world," as the Court has sometimes said.... The truth is that a teacher of kindergarten, grammar
school, or high school pupils no more carries into a school with
him a complete right to freedom of speech and expression than
an anti-Catholic or anti-Semite carries with him a complete freedom of speech and religion into a Catholic church or Jewish syn-
agogue. Nor does a person carry with him into the United States
Senate or House, or into the Supreme Court, or any other court,
a complete constitutional right to go into those places contrary
to their rules and speak his mind on any subject he pleases. It is a
myth to say that any person has a constitutional right to say what
he pleases, where he pleases, and when he pleases. Our Court has
decided precisely the opposite.

19 | What argument does Justice Black use about the difference between speech protected in the First Amendment and symbolic speech?

Why did Justice Black believe that there should be some limitations on free-speech protec-tions under the First Amendment?

[On the purpose of the public schools]

In my view, teachers in state-controlled public schools are hired
to teach there. Although Mr. Justice McReynolds may have intimated to the contrary in *Meyer v. Nebraska,* ... certainly a teacher
is not paid to go into school and teach subjects the State does
not hire him to teach as a part of its selected curriculum. Nor are
public school students sent to the schools at public expense to
broadcast political or any other views to educate and inform the
public. The original idea of schools, which I do not believe is yet

20

abandoned as worthless or out of date, was that children had not yet reached the point of experience and wisdom which enabled them to teach all of their elders.

[On the authority of the local schools]

In a separate dissent, Justice Harlan argued that "... school officials should be accorded the widest authority in maintaining discipline and good order in their institutions."

21 Here, the Court should accord Iowa educational institutions the same right to determine for themselves to what extent free expression should be allowed in its schools as it accorded Mississippi with reference to freedom of assembly. But even if the record were silent as to protests against the Vietnam war distracting students from their assigned class work, members of this Court, like all other citizens, know, without being told, that the disputes over the wisdom of the Vietnam war have disrupted and divided this country as few other issues ever have. Of course, students, like other people, cannot concentrate on lesser issues when black armbands are being ostentatiously displayed in their presence to call attention to the wounded and dead of the war, some of the wounded and the dead being their friends and neighbors. It was, of course, to distract the attention of other students that some students insisted up to the very point of their own suspension from school that they were determined to sit in school with their symbolic armbands.

Why are schools not the proper setting for protest?

What evidence exists that wearing the armbands was disruptive?

What duty do schools have to students?

22 Change has been said to be truly the law of life, but sometimes the old and the tried and true are worth holding. The schools of this Nation have undoubtedly contributed to giving us tranquility and to making us a more law-abiding people. Uncontrolled and uncontrollable liberty is an enemy to domestic peace. We cannot close our eyes to the fact that some of the country's greatest problems are crimes committed by the youth, too many of school age. School discipline, like parental discipline, is an integral and important part of training our children to be good citizens—to be better citizens. Here a very small number of students have crisply and summarily refused to obey a school order designed to give pupils who want to learn the opportunity to do so.

23 I wish, therefore, wholly to disclaim any purpose on my part to hold that the Federal Constitution compels the teachers, parents, and elected school officials to surrender control of the American public school system to public school students. I dissent.

Impact of *Tinker v. Des Moines Independent Community School District* on freedom of speech

Tinker v. Des Moines Independent Community School District established that the First Amendment protects the free-speech rights of students, even when their views might be controversial or violate school policy. One of the most quoted passages from the majority opinion sums up the Court's holding, "It can hardly be argued that either students or teachers shed their constitutional rights to freedom of speech or expression at the schoolhouse gate...."

Although the *Tinker* ruling guaranteed free-speech rights for students, it does not give students unlimited free speech. School districts have a right to place limits on certain types of expression. One example is the case of Matthew Fraser, who was suspended from high school after delivering a speech containing vulgar and sexually provocative language. The Court sided with the school in finding that it had every right to find this language offensive in a public setting (*Bethel School District v. Fraser*, 1986). More recently, in *Morse v. Frederick* (2007), the Court upheld the school's suspension of Joseph Frederick, who held up a banner promoting marijuana use that read "Bong Hits 4 Jesus," at a school-sponsored event.

Check for Understanding

1. Define symbolic speech.
2. Explain how the Fourteenth Amendment applies to *Tinker v. Des Moines Independent Community School District*.
3. Explain why the majority opinion supported the students' rights to free speech.
4. Explain why free speech for students is not absolute.
5. Explain why it is important for students to be able to express their political beliefs in school, even when those beliefs are controversial.

SCOTUS Practice Question

Joseph Frederick, a senior at Juneau-Douglas High School, displayed a banner reading "Bong Hits 4 Jesus" during the Olympic Torch Relay in 2002 through Juneau, Alaska. Although the event took place off school grounds, student attendance at this event was part of a school-sponsored activity. The school's principal, Deborah Morse, instructed Frederick to put away the banner, because she was concerned it could be interpreted as promoting marijuana use. Established school policy prohibited students from displaying drug-related messages at school events. Frederick refused, and Morse confiscated the banner and later suspended him. The suspension was upheld by the school superintendent and school board "because his banner appeared to advocate illegal drug use in violation of school policy."

In *Morse v. Frederick* (2007), the Supreme Court held that school officials may prohibit students from displaying messages that promote illegal drug use. The majority opinion stated that the school officials did not violate Frederick's First Amendment rights. First, the Court held that the "school speech" doctrine should apply since the "event occurred during normal school hours ... sanctioned by Principal Morse 'as an approved social event or class trip'" and that "social events and class trips are subject to district rules for student conduct." Second, the Court found that the sign was "reasonably viewed as promoting illegal drug use" and "Congress has declared that part of a school's job is educating students about the dangers of illegal drug use ... provided billions of dollars to support state and local drug-prevention programs."

A. Identify the constitutional clause that is common to both *Morse v. Frederick* (2007) and *Tinker v. Des Moines Independent Community School District* (1969).

B. Based on the constitutional clause identified in part A, explain why the facts of *Tinker v. Des Moines Independent Community School District* led to a different holding from the holding in *Morse v. Frederick*.

C. Describe an action Congress could take to limit the effects of *Morse v. Frederick*.

New York Times Co. v. United States

Focus on New York Times Co. v. United States (1971)

New York Times Co. v. United States (403 U.S. 713) involves a decision by two newspapers, the New York Times and Washington Post, to print illegally leaked, classified documents about U.S. involvement in the Vietnam War. The conflict over the documents created a First Amendment battle between the executive branch and two of the most respected newspapers in the country.

Reader Alert!

In New York Times Co. v. United States, the Supreme Court issued a per curiam opinion, an opinion from the Court as a whole. This is often done when each justice on the Court wishes to write his or her own opinion concerning the outcome of the case. The per curiam opinion is a brief, unsigned statement of the holding. Six justices voted with the majority, each writing a concurrence. Justices Hugo Black, William O. Douglas, William Brennan, Potter Stewart, Byron White, and Thurgood Marshall each delivered a separate concurring opinion. Three justices dissented, with each justice writing a separate dissent. They were Chief Justice Warren Burger, Justice Harry Blackmun, and Justice John Marshall Harlan.

Facts of the Case

Military analyst Daniel Ellsberg secretly copied more than 7,000 pages of classified Department of Defense documents revealing the history of the government's actions in the Vietnam War and exposing in detail the government's misleading statements to the public concerning U.S. involvement in the war. Since the American people were deeply divided on the question of U.S. involvement in the war, Ellsberg believed that Americans needed to know that the government had not been truthful and decided to make the "Pentagon Papers" public, giving copies to the New York Times and Washington Post. The New York Times began printing excerpts from the documents on June 13, 1971.

The Nixon administration immediately obtained a court order preventing the New York Times from printing more of the documents, arguing that publishing the material threatened national security. A U.S. court of appeals in New York issued a temporary injunction that directed the New York Times not to publish the documents. The Washington Post then began printing excerpts as well. The government sought another injunction, but this time, it was refused. Both cases were appealed to the Supreme Court. The New York Times argued that prior restraint (censoring the documents before they were published) violated freedom of the press under the First Amendment. The president argued that prior restraint was necessary to protect national security. The two cases of the *New York Times* and *Washington Post* were decided together.

Issue

Did the government meet the heavy burden of showing justification for prior restraint of the *New York Times* and *Washington Post* to prevent the publication of classified documents in violation of the First Amendment?

Holding/Decision

The Court ruled 6-3 in *New York Times Co. v. United States* that the prior restraint to prevent the publication of the "Pentagon Papers" was unconstitutional.

Excerpt from Majority Opinion

per curiam—a brief unsigned decision of the court

prior restraint—pre-publication censorship

presumption—belief

Why did the Court hold that prior restraint was unconstitutional in this decision?

1   *PER CURIAM*

2   We granted certiorari in these cases in which the United States seeks to enjoin the New York Times and the Washington Post from publishing the contents of a classified study entitled "History of U.S. Decision-Making Process on Viet Nam Policy."

3   "Any system of *prior restraints* of expression comes to this Court bearing a heavy *presumption* against its constitutional validity."... The Government "thus carries a heavy burden of showing justification for the imposition of such a restraint."... The District Court for the Southern District of New York, in the *New York Times* case, and the District Court for the District of Columbia and the Court of Appeals for the District of Columbia Circuit, in the *Washington Post* case, held that the Government had not met that burden. We agree.

Excerpts from Concurring Opinions

[Concurrence by Justice Black]

4   MR. JUSTICE BLACK, with whom MR. JUSTICE DOUGLAS joins, concurring.

5   I adhere to the view that the Government's case against the Washington Post should have been dismissed, and that the

injunction against the New York Times should have been vacated without oral argument when the cases were first presented to this Court. I believe that every moment's continuance of the injunctions against these newspapers amounts to a flagrant, indefensible, and continuing violation of the First Amendment.

Our Government was launched in 1789 with the adoption of the Constitution. The Bill of Rights, including the First Amendment, followed in 1791. Now, for the first time in the 182 years since the founding of the Republic, the federal courts are asked to hold that the First Amendment does not mean what it says, but rather means that the Government can halt the publication of current news of vital importance to the people of this country.

6

[On the purpose of the First Amendment]

In seeking *injunctions* against these newspapers, and in its presentation to the Court, the Executive Branch seems to have forgotten the essential purpose and history of the First Amendment. When the Constitution was adopted, many people strongly opposed it because the document contained no Bill of Rights to safeguard certain basic freedoms. They especially feared that the new powers granted to a central government might be interpreted to permit the government to curtail freedom of religion, press, assembly, and speech. In response to an overwhelming public clamor, James Madison offered a series of amendments to satisfy citizens that these great liberties would remain safe and beyond the power of government to abridge. Madison proposed what later became the First Amendment in three parts, two of which are set out below, and one of which proclaimed:

7

injunction—judicial orders that prohibit a person from beginning or continuing an action or that compel a person to carry out a certain act

> "The people shall not be deprived or abridged of their right to speak, to write, or to publish their sentiments, and the freedom of the press, as one of the *great bulwarks of liberty, shall be inviolable.*"

8

What amendment did Justice Black cite as important in keeping an informed representative government?

(Emphasis added.)

[On the branches of government and the First Amendment]

The amendments were offered to curtail and restrict the general powers granted to the Executive, Legislative, and Judicial Branches two years before in the original Constitution. The Bill of Rights changed the original Constitution into a new charter under which no branch of government could abridge the people's

9

freedoms of press, speech, religion, and assembly. Yet the Solicitor General argues and some members of the Court appear to agree that the general powers of the Government adopted in the original Constitution should be interpreted to limit and restrict the specific and emphatic guarantees of the Bill of Rights adopted later. I can imagine no greater perversion of history. Madison and the other Framers of the First Amendment, able men that they were, wrote in language they earnestly believed could never be misunderstood: "Congress shall make no law ... abridging the freedom ... of the press. ..." Both the history and language of the First Amendment support the view that the press must be left free to publish news, whatever the source, without censorship, injunctions, or prior restraints.

10   In the First Amendment, the Founding Fathers gave the free press the protection it must have to fulfill its essential role in our democracy. The press was to serve the governed, not the governors. The Government's power to censor the press was abolished so that the press would remain forever free to censure the Government. The press was protected so that it could bare the secrets of government and inform the people. Only a free and unrestrained press can effectively expose deception in government. And paramount among the responsibilities of a free press is the duty to prevent any part of the government from deceiving the people and sending them off to distant lands to die of foreign fevers and foreign shot and shell. In my view, far from deserving condemnation for their courageous reporting, the New York Times, the Washington Post, and other newspapers should be commended for serving the purpose that the Founding Fathers saw so clearly. In revealing the workings of government that led to the Vietnam war, the newspapers nobly did precisely that which the Founders hoped and trusted they would do.

11   The Government's case here is based on *premises* entirely different from those that guided the Framers of the First Amendment.

12   And the Government argues in its brief that, in spite of the First Amendment,

13   "[t]he authority of the Executive Department to protect the nation against publication of information whose disclosure would endanger the national security stems from two interrelated sources: the constitutional power of the President over the conduct of foreign affairs and his authority as Commander-in-Chief."

According to Justice Black, what is the essential role of the press in a democracy?

Why was the government prohibited from censoring the press?

premise—a statement that is the basis for a work or hypothesis

In other words, we are asked to hold that, despite the First 14
Amendment's emphatic command, the Executive Branch, the
Congress, and the Judiciary can make laws enjoining publication
of current news and abridging freedom of the press in the name
of "national security." The Government does not even attempt
to rely on any act of Congress. Instead, it makes the bold and
dangerously far-reaching contention that the courts should take
it upon themselves to "make" a law abridging freedom of the
press in the name of equity, presidential power and national
security, even when the representatives of the people in Congress have adhered to the command of the First Amendment and
refused to make such a law.... To find that the President has
"*inherent* power" to halt the publication of news by resort to
the courts would wipe out the First Amendment and destroy the
fundamental liberty and security of the very people the Government hopes to make "secure." No one can read the history of
the adoption of the First Amendment without being convinced
beyond any doubt that it was injunctions like those sought here
that Madison and his collaborators intended to outlaw in this
Nation for all time.

inherent—
fundamental, vested
as a right or privilege

The word "security" is a broad, vague generality whose con- 15
tours should not be invoked to abrogate the fundamental law
embodied in the First Amendment. The guarding of military and
diplomatic secrets at the expense of informed representative government provides no real security for our Republic.

[Justice Douglas, adding his own concurrence]

MR. JUSTICE DOUGLAS, with whom MR. JUSTICE BLACK 16
joins, concurring.

While I join the opinion of the Court, I believe it necessary to 17
express my views more fully.

It should be noted at the *outset* that the First Amendment 18
provides that "Congress shall male no law ... *abridging* the freedom of speech, or of the press." That leaves, in my view, no room
for governmental restraint on the press.

outset—beginning
abridge—to reduce,
lessen, shorten

There is, moreover, no statute barring the publication by the 19
press of the material which the Times and the Post seek to use.

So any power that the Government possesses must come from 20
its "inherent power."

21   The Government says that it has inherent powers to go into court and obtain an injunction to protect the national interest, which, in this case, is alleged to be national security.

22   *Near v. Minnesota,…*, repudiated that expansive doctrine in no uncertain terms.

23   The dominant purpose of the First Amendment was to prohibit the widespread practice of governmental suppression of embarrassing information. It is common knowledge that the First Amendment was adopted against the widespread use of the common law of *seditious* libel to punish the dissemination of material that is embarrassing to the powers-that-be…. The present cases will, I think, go down in history as the most dramatic illustration of that principle. A debate of large proportions goes on in the Nation over our posture in Vietnam. That debate *antedated* the disclosure of the contents of the present documents. The latter are highly relevant to the debate in progress.

24   Secrecy in government is fundamentally anti-democratic, perpetuating bureaucratic errors. Open debate and discussion of public issues are vital to our national health. On public questions, there should be "uninhibited, robust, and wide-open" debate.

seditious—inciting a rebellion

antedate—to precede in time

Excerpts from Dissenting Opinion

25 MR. CHIEF JUSTICE BURGER, dissenting.

[First Amendment not absolute]

26 So clear are the constitutional limitations on prior restraint against expression that, from the time of *Near v. Minnesota*, 283 U. S. 697 (1931), until recently in *Organization for a Better Austin v. Keefe*, 402 U. S. 415 (1971), we have had little occasion to be concerned with cases involving prior restraints against news reporting on matters of public interest. There is, therefore, little variation among the members of the Court in terms of resistance to prior restraints against publication. Adherence to this basic constitutional principle, however, does not make these cases simple. In these cases, the imperative of a free and unfettered press comes into collision with another imperative, the effective functioning of a complex modern government, and, specifically, the effective exercise of certain constitutional powers of the Executive. Only those who view the First Amendment as an *absolute* in all

absolute—total, unlimited, unrestricted

circumstances—a view I respect, but reject—can find such cases as these to be simple or easy.

[Placing too many limitations on the fact-finders]

These cases are not simple for another and more immediate reason. We do not know the facts of the cases. No District Judge knew all the facts. No Court of Appeals judge knew all the facts. No member of this Court knows all the facts.

    Why are we in this posture, in which only those judges to whom the First Amendment is absolute and permits of no restraint in any circumstances or for any reason, are really in a position to act?

[On the perils of judging in haste]

I suggest we are in this posture because these cases have been conducted in *unseemly* haste. MR. JUSTICE HARLAN covers the chronology of events demonstrating the hectic pressures under which these cases have been processed, and I need not restate them. The prompt setting of these cases reflects our universal abhorrence of prior restraint. But prompt judicial action does not mean unjudicial haste.

    The newspapers make a *derivative* claim under the First Amendment; they denominate this right as the public "right to know"; by implication, the Times asserts a sole trusteeship of that right by virtue of its journalistic "scoop." The right is asserted as an absolute. Of course, the First Amendment right itself is not an absolute, as Justice Holmes so long ago pointed out in his *aphorism* concerning the right to shout "fire" in a crowded theater if there was no fire. There are other exceptions, some of which Chief Justice Hughes mentioned by way of example in *Near v. Minnesota*. There are no doubt other exceptions no one has had occasion to describe or discuss. Conceivably, such exceptions may be lurking in these cases and, would have been flushed had they been properly considered in the trial courts, free from unwarranted deadlines and frenetic pressures. An issue of this importance should be tried and heard in a judicial atmosphere conducive to thoughtful, reflective deliberation, especially when haste, in terms of hours, is *unwarranted* in light of the long period the Times, by its own choice, deferred publication.

27

28

29

unseemly—
inappropriate,
undignified

30

derivative—flowing
from, obtained from
another source

aphorism—
observation that
contains a general
truth

unwarranted—not
called for; unnecessary

31   It is not disputed that the Times has had unauthorized possession of the documents for three to four months, during which it has had its expert analysts studying them, presumably digesting them and preparing the material for publication. During all of this time, the Times, presumably in its capacity as trustee of the public's "right to know," has held up publication for purposes it considered proper, and thus public knowledge was delayed. No doubt this was for a good reason; the analysis of 7,000 pages of complex material drawn from a vastly greater volume of material would inevitably take time, and the writing of good news stories takes time. But why should the United States Government, from whom this information was illegally acquired by someone, along with all the counsel, trial judges, and appellate judges be placed under needless pressure?

Why does Chief Justice Burger believe the decision to allow publication of the documents was made in haste?

32   The consequence of all this melancholy series of events is that we literally do not know what we are acting on. As I see it, we have been forced to deal with litigation concerning rights of great magnitude without an adequate record, and surely without time for adequate treatment either in the prior proceedings or in this Court.

33   We all crave speedier judicial processes, but, when judges are pressured, as in these cases, the result is a parody of the judicial function.

34   As noted elsewhere, the Times conducted its analysis of the 47 volumes of Government documents over a period of several months, and did so with a degree of security that a government might envy. Such security was essential, of course, to protect the enterprise from others. Meanwhile, the Times has copyrighted its material, and there were strong intimations in the oral argument that the Times contemplated *enjoining* its use by any other publisher in violation of its copyright. Paradoxically, this would afford it a protection, analogous to prior restraint, against all others—a protection the Times denies the Government of the United States.

enjoin—to prohibit by law, to issue an injunction

35   Interestingly, the Times explained its refusal to allow the Government to examine its own *purloined* documents by saying in substance this might compromise its sources and informants! The Times thus asserts a right to guard the secrecy of *its* sources while denying that the Government of the United States has that power.

purloin—to make off with, to steal, to heist

36   With respect to the question of inherent power of the Executive to classify papers, records, and documents as secret, or

otherwise unavailable for public exposure, and to secure aid of the courts for enforcement, there may be an analogy with respect to this Court. No statute gives this Court express power to establish and enforce the utmost security measures for the secrecy of our deliberations and records. Yet I have little doubt as to the inherent power of the Court to protect the confidentiality of its internal operations by whatever judicial measures may be required.

[Justice Harlan, adding further to the dissent]

37

MR. JUSTICE HARLAN, with whom THE CHIEF JUSTICE and MR. JUSTICE BLACKMUN join, dissenting.

These cases forcefully call to mind the wise admonition of Mr. 38 Justice Holmes, dissenting in *Northern Securities Co. v. United States*, … (1904):

> "Great cases, like hard cases, make bad law. For great cases are 39 called great not by reason of their real importance in shaping the law of the future, but because of some accident of immediate over-whelming interest which appeals to the feelings and distorts the judgment. These immediate interests exercise a kind of *hydraulic pressure* which makes what previously was clear seem doubtful, and before which even well settled principles of law will bend."

hydraulic pressure— here, meaning the distorting effect of outside pressure on a material

With all respect, I consider that the Court has been almost 40 irresponsibly feverish in dealing with these cases.

[On being too rushed to judgment]

Forced as I am to reach the merits of these cases, I dissent from the 41 opinion and judgments of the Court. Within the severe limitations imposed by the time constraints under which I have been required to operate, I can only state my reasons in telescoped form, even though, in different circumstances, I would have felt constrained to deal with the cases in the fuller sweep indicated above.

It is a sufficient basis for affirming the Court of Appeals for 42 the Second Circuit in the *Times* litigation to observe that its order must rest on the conclusion that, because of the time elements the Government had not been given an adequate opportunity to present its case to the District Court. At the least this conclusion was not an abuse of discretion.

[On the judiciary's proper role in relation to the executive]

43　In the *Post* litigation, the Government had more time to prepare; this was apparently the basis for the refusal of the Court of Appeals for the District of Columbia Circuit on rehearing to conform its judgment to that of the Second Circuit. But I think there is another and more fundamental reason why this judgment cannot stand—a reason which also furnishes an additional ground for not reinstating the judgment of the District Court in the *Times* litigation, set aside by the Court of Appeals. It is plain to me that the scope of the judicial function in passing upon the activities of the Executive Branch of the Government in the field of foreign affairs is very narrowly restricted.

44　From this constitutional primacy in the field of foreign affairs, it seems to me that certain conclusions necessarily follow. Some of these were stated concisely by President Washington, declining the request of the House of Representatives for the papers leading up to the negotiation of the Jay Treaty:

impolitic—unwise, not careful in one's judgments

pernicious—likely to do harm or have a harmful effect

45　"The nature of foreign negotiations requires caution, and their success must often depend on secrecy; and even when brought to a conclusion, a full disclosure of all the measures, demands, or eventual concessions which may have been proposed or contemplated would be extremely *impolitic*; for this might have a *pernicious* influence on future negotiations, or produce immediate inconveniences, perhaps danger and mischief, in relation to other powers."

What concerns does Justice Harlan express in his dissent about constitutional relations of the branches of government?

46　The power to evaluate the "pernicious influence" of premature disclosure is not, however, lodged in the Executive alone. I agree that, in performance of its duty to protect the values of the First Amendment against political pressures, the judiciary must review the initial Executive determination to the point of satisfying itself that the subject matter of the dispute does lie within the proper compass of the President's foreign relations power.

47　Even if there is some room for the judiciary to override the executive determination, it is plain that the scope of review must be exceedingly narrow. I can see no indication in the opinions of either the District Court or the Court of Appeals in the *Post* litigation that the conclusions of the Executive were given even the deference owing to an administrative agency, much less that owing to a co-equal branch of the Government operating within the field of its constitutional prerogative.

Impact of *New York Times Co. v. United States* on freedom of the press

The AP® U.S. Government and Politics curriculum specifically requires you to understand the extent to which the Supreme Court's interpretation of the First Amendment reflects a commitment to individual liberty.

New York Times Co. v. United States is seen as bolstering freedom of the press and establishing a "heavy presumption against prior restraint" even in cases involving national security. The Supreme Court expanded freedom of expression by placing a heavy burden on the U.S. government before it is allowed to censor the press. Earlier decisions, like the nonrequired Supreme Court case of *Near v. Minnesota* (1931) established protections of the press from prior restraint. More recent decisions have continued to support those protections.

Check for Understanding

1. Describe the Pentagon Papers.
2. Describe why the Founders provided freedom of the press in the First Amendment. (Refer to paragraphs 6 through 10.)
3. Describe the standard the government must meet before it is allowed to censor something prior to publication. (See paragraphs 26, 30, and 31.)
4. Explain why the government sought to prevent publication of the Pentagon Papers by the *New York Times* and the *Washington Post*.
5. Explain why the Court found the use of prior restraint unconstitutional.

SCOTUS Practice Question

In October 1975, the police found that several members of a local family had been murdered. A suspect was immediately detained by law enforcement and taken into custody. The crime attracted widespread media coverage, and both the prosecutor and defense attorney pursued an order restraining press coverage of the murders to discourage the potential prejudicial effect on a future jury. State District Judge Stuart granted an order restraining members of the press from publishing or broadcasting certain aspects of the trial. The Nebraska Supreme Court approved a modified version of the restraining order. The Nebraska Press Association sought review of the order in the U.S. Supreme Court.

In *Nebraska Press Association v. Stuart* (1976), the Supreme Court, in a unanimous decision, agreed with the trial judge that the case would generate "intense and pervasive pretrial publicity." However, as Chief Justice Burger wrote, "prior restraints on speech and publication are the most serious and least tolerable infringement on First Amendment Rights" and that the lower courts should have considered a less restrictive way to protect the rights of the defendant.

A. Identify the constitutional provision that is common to both *Nebraska Press Association v. Stuart* (1976) and *New York Times Co. v. United States* (1971).

B. Based on the constitutional provision identified in part A, explain why the facts of *New York Times Co. v. United States* led to a similar holding in *Nebraska Press Association v. Stuart*.

C. Explain how the holding in *Nebraska Press Association v. Stuart* could potentially make an impact on campaigns or elections in the United States.

Schenck v. United States

Focus on *Schenck v. United States* (1919)

Schenck v. United States, 249 U.S. 47, is generally considered important for establishing the "clear and present danger" standard for determining if and under what circumstances government may constitutionally limit an individual's right to freedom of speech under the First Amendment. The Supreme Court held in a unanimous opinion that in certain contexts, words may create a "clear and present danger" that Congress may constitutionally prohibit. Greater restrictions on free speech are allowed during wartime than would be allowed during peacetime because new and greater dangers are present when the country is at war. While the ruling in *Schenck v. United States* has since been revised, making it more difficult for the government to limit speech, *Schenck* is still significant for creating a standard for balancing freedom of speech and the needs of the government in free-speech challenges.

Reader Alert!

In *Schenck v. United States*, the Supreme Court determined that free-speech rights under the First Amendment are not limitless and that the context of the speech determines the limits. The Court upheld the Espionage Act of 1917 and affirmed Charles Schenck's conviction because Schenck's speech had created a clear and present danger of disobedience and defiance of the draft during wartime.

Justice Holmes, in the majority opinion uses the example of "a man falsely shouting fire in a theatre and causing a panic." This phrase has often been reworded to "shouting fire in a crowded theater" and used to describe speech or actions made for the main purpose of creating unnecessary panic.

Facts of the Case

During the World War I, Congress passed the Espionage Act of 1917, forbidding conduct undermining the war effort, including conduct that would "obstruct the recruiting or enlistment service."

> Whoever, when the United States is at war, ... shall willfully cause or attempt to cause insubordination, disloyalty, mutiny, refusal of duty, in the military or naval forces of the United States, or shall willfully obstruct the recruiting or enlistment service of the United States, to the injury of the service or of the United States, shall be punished by a fine of not more than $10,000 or imprisonment for not more than twenty years, or both.
>
> [Espionage Act, Section 3, 40 Stat. 219]

Charles Schenck, General Secretary of the Socialist Party, distributed 15,000 leaflets declaring that the draft violated the Thirteenth Amendment's prohibition against involuntary servitude and urged draftees to resist the draft through peaceful actions. Schenck was charged with violating the Espionage Act of 1917.

Schenck was convicted of violating the Espionage Act and appealed. Schenck challenged his conviction on First Amendment grounds. His case went to the Supreme Court, which had to consider if freedom of speech is an absolute right and, if not, under what circumstances it may be limited in wartime.

Issue

Did Schenck's conviction under the Espionage Act for criticizing the draft violate his First Amendment right to freedom of speech?

Holding/Decision

The Supreme Court ruled unanimously in favor of the United States. (249 U.S. 47)

Excerpt from Majority Opinion

1   MR. JUSTICE HOLMES delivered the opinion of the court.

[On the charges and the admission of evidence]

What crimes does the majority opinion accuse Schenck of committing?

insubordination— disobeying of orders

overt— done openly, not hidden

pursuance— furtherance, carrying out of an action or plan

2   This is an indictment in three counts. The first charges a conspiracy to violate the Espionage Act of June 15, 1917, c. 30, § 3, 40 Stat. 217, 219, by causing and attempting to cause *insubordination*, &c., in the military and naval forces of the United States, and to obstruct the recruiting and enlistment service of the United States, when the United States was at war with the German Empire, to-wit, that the defendants willfully conspired to have printed and circulated to men who had been called and accepted for military service under the Act of May 18, 1917, a document set forth and alleged to be calculated to cause such insubordination and obstruction. The count alleges *overt* acts in *pursuance* of the conspiracy, ending in the distribution of the document set forth. The second count alleges a conspiracy to commit an offence against the United States, to-wit, to use the mails for the transmission of matter declared to be nonmailable by Title XII, § 2 of the Act

of June 15, 1917, to-wit, the above mentioned document, with an *averment* of the same overt acts. The third count charges an unlawful use of the mails for the transmission of the same matter and otherwise as above. The defendants were found guilty on all the counts. They set up the First Amendment to the Constitution forbidding Congress to make any law abridging the freedom of speech, or of the press, and bringing the case here on that ground have argued some other points also of which we must dispose.

It is argued that the evidence, if admissible, was not sufficient to prove that the defendant Schenck was concerned in sending the documents. According to the testimony, Schenck said he was general secretary of the Socialist party, and had charge of the Socialist headquarters from which the documents were sent. ... Schenck personally attended to the printing. On August 20, the general secretary's report said "Obtained new leaflets from printer and started work addressing envelopes" &c., and there was a resolve that Comrade Schenck be allowed $125 for sending leaflets through the mail. He said that he had about fifteen or sixteen thousand printed. ... Without going into confirmatory details that were proved, no reasonable man could doubt that the defendant Schenck was largely instrumental in sending the circulars about. ... The argument as to the sufficiency of the evidence that the defendants conspired to send the documents only impairs the seriousness of the real defence.

It is objected that the documentary evidence was not admissible because obtained upon a search warrant, valid so far as appears. The contrary is established. ... The search warrant did not issue against the defendant, but against the Socialist headquarters at 1326 Arch Street, and it would seem that the documents technically were not even in the defendants' possession. ... Notwithstanding some protest in argument, the notion that evidence even directly proceeding from the defendant in a criminal proceeding is excluded in all cases by the Fifth Amendment is plainly unsound.

[What was in the disputed document]

The document in question, upon its first printed side, recited the first section of the Thirteenth Amendment, said that the idea embodied in it was violated by the Conscription Act, and that a *conscript* is little better than a convict. In impassioned language, it *intimated* that conscription was despotism in its worst form, and a monstrous wrong against humanity in the interest of Wall Street's

---

averment— confirmation by the defendants

What arguments did Schenck use to defend his actions?

3

Why is Schenck held responsible for the incriminating documents?

How does Justice Holmes refute the argument that Schenck is not responsible for the documents?

4 How did the majority opinion address Schenck's arguments regarding the search warrant?

5 Why did Schenck use the Thirteenth Amendment to justify ignoring the draft?

conscript—draftee or recruit

intimate—to imply or state

chosen few. It said "Do not submit to intimidation," but in form, at least, confined itself to peaceful measures such as a petition for the repeal of the act. The other and later printed side of the sheet was headed "Assert Your Rights." It stated reasons for alleging that anyone violated the Constitution when he refused to recognize "your right to assert your opposition to the draft," and went on

6   "If you do not assert and support your rights, you are helping to deny or disparage rights which it is the solemn duty of all citizens and residents of the United States to retain."

["A clear and present danger"]

What does Holmes mean by "ordinary times"?

7   We admit that, in many places and in ordinary times, the defendants, in saying all that was said in the circular, would have been within their constitutional rights. But the character of every act depends upon the circumstances in which it is done. ... The most stringent protection of free speech would not protect a man in falsely shouting fire in a theatre and causing a panic. It does not even protect a man from an injunction against uttering words that may have all the effect of force. ... The question in every case is whether the words used are used in such circumstances and are of such a nature as to create a clear and present danger that they will bring about the substantive evils that Congress has a right to prevent. It is a question of proximity and degree. When a nation is at war, many things that might be said in time of peace are such a hindrance to its effort that their utterance will not be endured so long as men fight, and that no Court could regard them as protected by any constitutional right. It seems to be admitted that, if an actual obstruction of the recruiting service were proved, liability for words that produced that effect might be enforced. The statute of 1917, in § 4, punishes conspiracies to obstruct, as well as actual obstruction. If the act (speaking, or circulating a paper), its tendency, and the intent with which it is done are the same, we perceive no ground for saying that success alone warrants making the act a crime.

Why would yelling fire in a crowed theater and causing a panic not be protected free speech?

What does the majority mean by a "clear and present danger"?

What crimes does the Espionage Act punish?

Impact of *Schenck v. United States* on First Amendment protections of freedom of speech

The AP® U.S. Government and Politics curriculum specifically requires you to understand how *Schenck v. United States* impacted the interpretation of freedom of speech under the First Amendment. *Schenck v. United States* is noteworthy for defining the "clear and present danger" test that the courts have used in other cases brought to punish inflammatory speech under both the Espionage Act and similar state laws.

In *Schenck v. United States*, the Court held that some types of speech do not merit constitutional protections. Statements that "create a clear and present danger" of producing a harm that Congress is authorized to prevent fall in that category of unprotected speech. Just as "free speech would not protect a man in falsely shouting fire in a theatre and causing a panic," the Constitution does not protect efforts to encourage the criminal act of resisting the draft during a time of war.

The "clear and present danger" test would last for another fifty years. In the 1969 case of *Brandenburg v. Ohio*, the Court replaced it with the "imminent lawless action" test. This new test specified that the government could only limit speech that incites *imminent* (about-to-happen) unlawful action. This test is still applied by the Court today in free-speech cases involving encouragement of violence.

Check for Understanding

1. Describe the two amendments to the U.S. Constitution that Schenck cited in support of his actions.
2. Describe Schenck's major argument.
3. Describe the standard imposed by the majority opinion on determining if free speech should be protected or if free speech may be limited.
4. Explain why the Court allowed restrictions on freedom of speech during wartime.
5. Explain how the impact of the Court's decision in *Schenck v. United States* affects the First Amendment's protection of freedom of speech.

SCOTUS Practice Question

Clarence Brandenburg, a leader of the Ku Klux Klan in Ohio, made a speech at a Klan rally in 1964. Portions of the rally were filmed by a television station invited by Brandenburg to cover the rally. Participants of the rally were shown in robes and hoods, some carrying guns, as they burned a cross and made speeches. The speeches called for taking revenge against African Americans and Jews and for a march on Washington, criticizing the president, Congress, and the Supreme Court for conspiring with non-whites against whites. Brandenburg was charged with advocating violence under an Ohio criminal syndicalism law that made it illegal to advocate "crime, sabotage, violence, or unlawful methods of terrorism as a means of accomplishing industrial or political reform." The law also made "voluntarily assembling with any society, group, or assemblage of persons formed to teach or advocate the doctrines of criminal syndicalism." Brandenburg was convicted, fined $1,000, and sentenced to one to ten years in prison. His conviction was affirmed by a state appellate court and dismissed by the Ohio State Supreme Court.

The U.S. Supreme Court held that the Ohio law violated Brandenburg's right to free speech, reversing Brandenburg's conviction. The Court used a two-pronged test to evaluate whether or not the government may limit speech: (1) speech can be prohibited if it is "directed at inciting or producing imminent lawless action" and (2) it is "likely to incite or produce such action." The Ohio criminal syndicalism act made it illegal to advocate and teach political principles, ignoring whether or not that advocacy or teaching would actually incite imminent lawless action. The Court held that the Ohio law was overly broad and therefore unconstitutional.

A. Identify the constitutional provision that is common to both *Brandenburg v. Ohio* (1969) and *Schenck v. United States* (1919).

B. Based on the constitutional provision identified in part A, explain why the facts of *Schenck v. United States* led to a different holding from the holding in *Brandenburg v. Ohio*.

C. Describe an action that a member of Congress who is unhappy with the Court's decision in *Brandenburg v. Ohio* could take to limit the impact of that decision.

Gideon v. Wainwright

Focus on *Gideon v. Wainwright* (1963)

Before the 1960s, and *Gideon v. Wainwright,* 372 U.S. 335 (1963), it was common for individuals accused of crimes to be tried without a lawyer if they could not afford one. This is because states were not required to provide legal counsel at taxpayers' expense, except in cases involving the death penalty. While the Sixth Amendment of the U.S. Constitution guarantees the right of an attorney, this guarantee had been interpreted to apply to only federal cases or state cases with special circumstances. In *Betts v. Brady* (1942), the Court held that in state criminal trials, a defendant is ordinarily not entitled to have an attorney provided at the state's expense, although defendants must be granted an attorney in special circumstances, such as illiteracy or incompetence.

Facts of the Case

Clarence Earl Gideon was tried in a Florida court without an attorney for petty theft. Gideon could not afford an attorney. He requested that an attorney be appointed, but his request was denied. Florida state law at the time provided defendants with lawyers only in cases involving capital punishment. The charge against Gideon was petty larceny, so his crime did not qualify. Gideon did not have any special circumstances, as outlined in *Betts v. Brady,* that would have required that an attorney be appointed on his behalf.

Gideon participated in his own defense at trial. He did a poor job defending himself and was found guilty of larceny as well as breaking and entering. While in prison, Gideon read law books and prepared a petition for habeas corpus (arguing that he had been imprisoned illegally due to being tried without a lawyer) with the state of Florida. His habeas corpus appeal was denied. He then hand-wrote a petition for a writ of certiorari asking the Supreme Court to hear his case, and certiorari was granted.

Gideon's attorneys argued that the Sixth Amendment's right to an attorney should be incorporated into state law because of the due process clause of the Fourteenth Amendment. The due process clause of the Fourteenth Amendment has been used to incorporate parts of the Bill of Rights and make them applicable to the states in certain cases.

Issue

Does the Sixth Amendment's right to counsel extend to defendants in state courts without special circumstances?

Holding/Decision

The Court decided unanimously in favor of Gideon, arguing that the right of a defendant in a criminal trial to have the assistance of counsel is a right essential to a fair trial. The petitioner's trial and conviction without counsel violated the Sixth and Fourteenth Amendments.

Reader Alert!

The decision in this case did not make Gideon innocent of the larceny charges. It made the trail without a lawyer invalid. As a result, Gideon had to be retried with a lawyer for the same offense. In this separate trial that occurred after the Supreme Court decision in *Gideon v. Wainwright,* Gideon was tried with a lawyer and found innocent of the charges.

Excerpt from Majority Opinion

1   MR. JUSTICE BLACK delivered the opinion of the Court.

[On Gideon's legal troubles]

2   Petitioner was charged in a Florida state court with having broken and entered a poolroom with intent to commit a misdemeanor. This offense is a felony under Florida law. Appearing in court without funds and without a lawyer, petitioner asked the court to appoint counsel for him, whereupon the following colloquy took place:

3   The COURT: Mr. Gideon, I am sorry, but I cannot appoint Counsel to represent you in this case. Under the laws of the State of Florida, the only time the Court can appoint Counsel to represent a Defendant is when that person is charged with a capital offense. I am sorry, but I will have to deny your request to appoint Counsel to defend you in this case.

4   The DEFENDANT: The United States Supreme Court says I am entitled to be represented by Counsel.

[How the case reached the Supreme Court]

5   Put to trial before a jury, Gideon conducted his defense about as well as could be expected from a layman. He made an opening

statement to the jury, cross-examined the State's witnesses, presented witnesses in his own defense, declined to testify himself, and made a short argument "emphasizing his innocence to the charge contained in the Information filed in this case." The jury returned a verdict of guilty, and petitioner was sentenced to serve five years in the state prison. Later, petitioner filed in the Florida Supreme Court this habeas corpus petition attacking his conviction and sentence on the ground that the trial court's refusal to appoint counsel for him denied him rights "guaranteed by the Constitution and the Bill of Rights by the United States Government." Treating the petition for habeas corpus as properly before it, the State Supreme Court, "upon consideration thereof" but without an opinion, denied all relief. Since 1942, when *Betts v. Brady*... was decided by a divided Court, the problem of a defendant's federal constitutional right to counsel in a state court has been a continuing source of controversy and litigation in both state and federal courts. To give this problem another review here, we granted certiorari. ... Since Gideon was proceeding *in forma pauperis*, we appointed counsel to represent him and requested both sides to discuss in their briefs and oral arguments the following: "Should this Court's holding in *Betts v. Brady*, ..., be reconsidered?"

Why was certiorari granted in Gideon's case?

in forma pauperis— legal term for someone who can proceed to trial but is too poor to pay legal fees

[On the history of the right to counsel and the action of the Fourteenth Amendment]

The Sixth Amendment provides, "In all criminal prosecutions, the accused shall enjoy the right... to have the Assistance of Counsel for his defence." We have construed this to mean that in federal courts counsel must be provided for defendants unable to employ counsel unless the right is competently and intelligently waived. Betts argued that this right is extended to *indigent* defendants in state courts by the Fourteenth Amendment. In response, the Court stated that, while the Sixth Amendment laid down

6

indigent—poor (and unable to pay legal fees)

> no rule for the conduct of the States, the question recurs whether the constraint laid by the Amendment upon the national courts expresses a rule so fundamental and essential to a fair trial, and so, to due process of law, that it is made obligatory upon the States by the Fourteenth Amendment

7

8   On the basis of this historical data the Court concluded that "appointment of counsel is not a fundamental right, essential to a fair trial."

9   We accept *Betts v. Brady's* assumption, based as it was on our prior cases, that a provision of the Bill of Rights which is "fundamental and essential to a fair trial" is made obligatory upon the States by the Fourteenth Amendment. We think the Court in *Betts* was wrong, however, in concluding that the Sixth Amendment's guarantee of counsel is not one of these fundamental rights.

What part of the *Betts* decision does the Court agree with? How does this decision disagree with *Betts*?

10   Several years later, in 1936, the Court reemphasized what it had said about the fundamental nature of the right to counsel in this language:

11   We concluded that certain fundamental rights, safeguarded by the first eight amendments against federal action, were also safeguarded against state action by the due process of law clause of the Fourteenth Amendment, and among them the fundamental right of the accused to the aid of counsel in a criminal prosecution.

11   … And again, in 1938, this Court said:

12   [The assistance of counsel] is one of the safeguards of the Sixth Amendment deemed necessary to insure fundamental human rights of life and liberty.… The Sixth Amendment stands as a constant admonition that, if the constitutional safeguards it provides be lost, justice will not "still be done."

[On the ideal of fair trials for all]

13   Not only these precedents, but also reason and reflection, require us to recognize that, in our *adversary system* of criminal justice, any person *haled* into court, who is too poor to hire a lawyer, cannot be assured a fair trial unless counsel is provided for him. This seems to us to be an obvious truth. Governments, both state and federal, quite properly spend vast sums of money to establish machinery to try defendants accused of crime. Lawyers to prosecute are everywhere deemed essential to protect the public's interest in an orderly society. Similarly, there are few defendants charged with crime, few indeed, who fail to hire the best lawyers they can get to prepare and present their defenses. That government hires lawyers to prosecute and defendants who have the money hire lawyers to defend are the strongest indications of the widespread belief that lawyers in criminal courts are necessities, not luxuries. The right of one charged with crime to counsel may

adversary system—using two opposing attorneys to argue the sides of a case

hale—to force to attend, drag in

not be deemed fundamental and essential to fair trials in some countries, but it is in ours. From the very beginning, our state and national constitutions and laws have laid great emphasis on procedural and substantive safeguards designed to assure fair trials before impartial tribunals in which every defendant stands equal before the law. This noble ideal cannot be realized if the poor man charged with crime has to face his accusers without a lawyer to assist him.

Excerpt from Concurring Opinions

MR. JUSTICE CLARK, concurring in the result.   14

That the Sixth Amendment requires appointment of counsel in "all criminal prosecutions" is clear both from the language of the Amendment and from this Court's interpretation.... It is equally clear from the... cases, all decided after *Betts v. Brady*,..., that the Fourteenth Amendment requires such appointment in all prosecutions for capital crimes. The Court's decision today, then, does no more than erase a distinction which has no basis in logic and an increasingly eroded basis in authority. In *Kinsella v. United States ex rel. Singleton*,... we specifically rejected any constitutional distinction between capital and noncapital offenses as regards congressional power to provide for *court-martial* trials of civilian dependents of armed forces personnel.... Indeed, our opinion there foreshadowed the decision today, as we noted that: 15

court martial—a military court

> Obviously Fourteenth Amendment cases dealing with state action have no application here, but if they did, we believe that to deprive civilian dependents of the safeguards of a jury trial here... would be as invalid under those cases as it would be in cases of a capital nature.   16

MR. JUSTICE HARLAN, concurring.   17

I agree that *Betts v. Brady* should be overruled, but consider it entitled to a more respectful burial than has been accorded, at least on the part of those of us who were not on the Court when that case was decided.   18

How does Justice Harlan then "bury" the *Betts* case in the following paragraphs?

[On extending the right to counsel]

The declaration that the right to appointed counsel in state prosecutions, as established in *Powell v. Alabama*, was not limited to   19 capital cases was, in truth, not a departure from, but an extension of, existing *precedent.*

precedent—earlier related legal decisions

20   The principles declared in *Powell* and in *Betts,* however, have had a troubled journey throughout the years that have followed first the one case and then the other. Even by the time of the *Betts* decision, *dictum* in at least one of the Court's opinions had indicated that there was an absolute right to the services of counsel in the trial of state capital cases. Such dicta continued to appear in subsequent decisions, and any lingering doubts were finally eliminated by the holding of *Hamilton v. Alabama* ...

dictum (plural, *dicta*)—an authoritative but not binding statement in a legal decision

[The fate of the "special circumstances" rule]

Does Justice Harlan consider the precedent of the *Betts* case to be still in effect? How has the definition of "special circumstances" changed?

21   In noncapital cases, the "special circumstances" rule has continued to exist in form while its substance has been substantially and steadily eroded. In the first decade after *Betts,* there were cases in which the Court found special circumstances to be lacking, but usually by a sharply divided vote. However, no such decision has been cited to us, and I have found none, after *Quicksall v. Michigan,* ... decided in 1950. ... The Court has come to recognize, in other words, that the mere existence of a serious criminal charge constituted, in itself, special circumstances requiring the services of counsel at trial. In truth, the *Betts v. Brady* rule is no longer a reality.

22   This evolution, however, appears not to have been fully recognized by many state courts, in this instance charged with the front-line responsibility for the enforcement of constitutional rights. To continue a rule which is honored by this Court only with lip service is not a healthy thing, and, in the long run, will do disservice to the federal system.

How does Justice Harlan interpret the evolution of the "special circumstances" rule?

23   The special circumstances rule has been formally abandoned in capital cases, and the time has now come when it should be similarly abandoned in noncapital cases, at least as to offenses which, as the one involved here, carry the possibility of a substantial prison sentence. (Whether the rule should extend to all criminal cases need not now be decided.) This indeed does no more than to make explicit something that has long since been foreshadowed in our decisions.

Impact of *Gideon v. Wainwright* on the U.S. legal system

This case is important in the AP US® Government and Politics curriculum framework for several reasons. It is an example of the struggle between Liberty and Order (one of the Big Ideas in the course). While the *Gideon* case is well known for assisting the poor in defending themselves in a court of law, it also made it more difficult for the state to prosecute and convict criminals. The idea that Gideon (and others in similar circumstances) deserve a fair trial must be balanced against the need of the state to maintain order. It also provides an example of how protections of the Bill of Rights have been selectively incorporated by the Fourteenth Amendment's due process clause to prevent state infringement of basic liberties.

The case had an enormous impact on how defendants are tried for felonies at the state level, requiring that attorneys for defendants be appointed at taxpayer expense. At the time, the decision was unpopular with some who felt that individuals should have to pay for their own defense and not rely on the state funding. But today, it is a well-established practice in our legal system that individuals are entitled to counsel, and if they cannot afford counsel, one will be appointed at the expense of the state.

Check for Understanding

1. Describe the charges against Gideon, and identify the first court in which he was tried. (Paragraph 2.)
2. Describe the holding in *Betts v. Brady*. (Paragraphs 5 through 9.)
3. Explain why Gideon claimed he had a right to counsel. Explain why the state of Florida denied Gideon counsel. (Paragraphs 2, 3, and 4.)
4. Describe the holding of the Supreme Court in *Gideon v. Wainwright*.
5. Explain why the majority opinion held that the Sixth Amendment requires the state to provide counsel for indigent defendants in felony cases.

SCOTUS Practice Question

Police in Cleveland, Ohio, believed that Dollree Mapp was hiding a fugitive. The police entered Mapp's house without a warrant and searched the home. The police did not find the fugitive but found evidence of other illegal behavior. Mapp was charged and convicted at trial, based partly on the evidence seized by the police without a warrant. Mapp appealed her case to the Supreme Court of Ohio on the basis that the police lacked a warrant to search her home, as required by the Fourth Amendment to the U.S. Constitution. A previous case had decided that the Fourteenth Amendment's due process clause incorporated the Fourth Amendment's requirement that police have a warrant to search a home, but did not forbid the admission of evidence obtained by warrantless searches in state courts.

The Court held that evidence illegally obtained in warrantless searches is inadmissible in court proceedings. This is called the exclusionary rule. The Fourth Amendment was made applicable to the states through the Fourteenth Amendment.

A. Identify the constitutional provision that is common to both *Gideon v. Wainwright* (1963) and *Mapp v. Ohio* (1961).

B. Based on the provision identified in part A, explain how the facts of *Mapp v. Ohio* led to a similar holding as the holding in *Gideon v. Wainwright*. Then describe how the facts of the two cases differed.

C. Explain how both cases have an impact on the principle of federalism.

Roe v. Wade

Focus on *Roe v. Wade* (1973)

Perhaps the most controversial decision of the twentieth century was the Supreme Court's decision in *Roe v. Wade,* 410 U.S. 113 (1973). The Court ruled that a woman's right to an abortion was protected as part of the right to privacy. This decision primarily used *Griswold v. Connecticut* (1965), a case about contraception, as a precedent. In the *Griswold* decision, the Court ruled that the Bill of Rights, specifically the Fourth, Fifth, and Ninth Amendments, along with the Fourteenth Amendment, created an individual right to privacy although it is never explicitly stated in the Constitution. In *Roe,* the Court applied this right to the issue of abortion.

Reader Alert!

The *Roe* decision is perhaps the most controversial Court decision in modern America. Whatever your personal feelings about the issue of abortion, the AP® curriculum framework requires that you understand the facts, issue, rationale, and impact that the *Roe* decision continues to have today on American politics.

Facts of the Case

Jane Roe (which is a pseudonym) sought to abort her pregnancy. However, the state of Texas did not allow abortion unless the pregnancy or the birth process threatened the woman's life. In 1970, Roe sought an injunction from the federal courts to allow her an abortion. The district court struck down the Texas law, yet the court did not issue an injunction against the enforcement of the law, so Roe still could not have an abortion. On appeal, the case eventually reached the Supreme Court.

Issue

The issue before the Court was this: Does the right to privacy, as interpreted by the previous holding in *Griswold v. Connecticut* (1965) and other related cases, protect a woman's right to an abortion? The right to privacy involves the Fourth, Fifth, Ninth, and Fourteenth Amendments.

▦ Holding/Decision

In a 7-2 decision, the Court sided with Jane Roe. The right to privacy does protect access to an abortion. As part of the holding, the Court created a trimester framework to guide state laws on the issue of abortion. The Court held that there was no "compelling state interest" in regulating abortion in the first trimester (a trimester is twelve weeks) of a pregnancy, so states cannot place restrictions on abortions during the first three months of a pregnancy. In the second trimester, state regulation of abortion must focus on safety of the procedure. However, in the third trimester, a state may limit access to an abortion if it so chooses.

Excerpt from Majority Opinion

1   MR. JUSTICE BLACKMUN delivered the opinion of the Court.

2   The principal thrust of appellant's attack on the Texas statutes is that they improperly invade a right, said to be possessed by the pregnant woman, to choose to terminate her pregnancy. Appellant would discover this right in the concept of personal "liberty" embodied in the Fourteenth Amendment's Due Process Clause; or in personal, marital, familial, and sexual privacy said to be protected by the Bill of Rights or its *penumbras*,... or among those rights reserved to the people by the Ninth Amendment, *Griswold v. Connecticut*, 381 U.S. at 486 (Goldberg, J., concurring). Before addressing this claim, we feel it desirable briefly to survey, in several aspects, the history of abortion, for such insight as that history may afford us, and then to examine the state purposes and interests behind the criminal abortion laws.

penumbra—in a legal sense, an implied right found in the Constitution

[On the history of laws criminalizing abortion]

3   It perhaps is not generally appreciated that the restrictive criminal abortion laws in effect in a majority of States today are of relatively recent vintage. Those laws, generally *proscribing* abortion or its attempt at any time during pregnancy except when necessary to preserve the pregnant woman's life, are not of ancient or even of common law origin. Instead, they derive from statutory changes effected, for the most part, in the latter half of the 19th century.

proscribe—to forbid or outlaw

[On the purpose of these laws]

Three reasons have been advanced to explain historically the 4 enactment of criminal abortion laws in the 19th century and to justify their continued existence.

It has been argued occasionally that these laws were the prod- 5 uct of a Victorian social concern to discourage *illicit* sexual conduct. Texas, however, does not advance this justification in the present case, and it appears that no court or commentator has taken the argument seriously. The appellants and *amici* contend, moreover, that this is not a proper state purpose, at all and suggest that, if it were, the Texas statutes are overbroad in protecting it, since the law fails to distinguish between married and unwed mothers.

A second reason is concerned with abortion as a medical pro- 6 cedure. When most criminal abortion laws were first enacted, the procedure was a hazardous one for the woman. This was particularly true prior to the development of *antisepsis*. Antiseptic techniques, of course, were based on discoveries by Lister, Pasteur, and others first announced in 1867, but were not generally accepted and employed until about the turn of the century. Abortion mortality was high. Even after 1900, and perhaps until as late as the development of antibiotics in the 1940's, standard modern techniques such as dilation and curettage were not nearly so safe as they are today. Thus, it has been argued that a State's real concern in enacting a criminal abortion law was to protect the pregnant woman, that is, to restrain her from submitting to a procedure that placed her life in serious jeopardy.

[On the effects of recent scientific and medical advances]

Modern medical techniques have altered this situation. Appellants 7 and various *amici* refer to medical data indicating that abortion in early pregnancy, that is, prior to the end of the first trimester, although not without its risk, is now relatively safe. *Mortality rates* for women undergoing early abortions, where the procedure is legal, appear to be as low as or lower than the rates for normal childbirth. Consequently, any interest of the State in protecting the woman from an inherently hazardous procedure, except when it would be equally dangerous for her to forgo it, has largely disappeared. Of course, important state interests in the areas of health and medical standards do remain.

---

illicit—not accepted, forbidden, or outlawed

amici—a reference to an amicus curiae briefs filed with the Court

Does the state have an interest in discouraging "illicit sexual conduct"? If so, does outlawing abortion achieve this interest?

antisepsis—measures to prevent the spread of disease, including applying antiseptics (antibacterial and antiviral compounds)

How does this paragraph analyze evidence and data regarding the risks to women who seek an abortion?

mortality rate—death rate

[On the state interest in safety of the procedure]

How does this paragraph support the contention that allowing states to continue outlawing abortion would increase the risks to those who seek an abortion?

8   The State has a legitimate interest in seeing to it that abortion, like any other medical procedure, is performed under circumstances that insure maximum safety for the patient. This interest obviously extends at least to the performing physician and his staff, to the facilities involved, to the availability of after-care, and to adequate provision for any complication or emergency that might arise. The prevalence of high mortality rates at illegal "abortion mills" strengthens, rather than weakens, the State's interest in regulating the conditions under which abortions are performed. Moreover, the risk to the woman increases as her pregnancy continues. Thus, the State retains a definite interest in protecting the woman's own health and safety when an abortion is proposed at a late stage of pregnancy.

[On the state's interest in prenatal life]

9   The third reason is the State's interest—some phrase it in terms of duty—in protecting prenatal life. Some of the argument for this justification rests on the theory that a new human life is present from the moment of conception. The State's interest and general obligation to protect life then extends, it is argued, to prenatal life. Only when the life of the pregnant mother herself is at stake, balanced against the life she carries within her, should the interest of the embryo or fetus not prevail. Logically, of course, a legitimate state interest in this area need not stand or fall on acceptance of the belief that life begins at conception or at some other point prior to live birth. In assessing the State's interest, recognition may be given to the less rigid claim that as long as at least potential life is involved, the State may assert interests beyond the protection of the pregnant woman alone.

[On recognition of a right of privacy in the Constitution]

10   The Constitution does not explicitly mention any right of privacy. In a line of decisions, however, going back perhaps as far as *Union Pacific R. Co. v. Botsford*, 141 U.S. 250, 251 (1891), the Court has recognized that a right of personal privacy, or a guarantee of certain areas or zones of privacy, does exist under the Constitution. In varying contexts, the Court or individual Justices have, indeed, found at least the roots of that right in the First Amendment,

Stanley v. Georgia, 394 U.S. 557, 564 (1969); in the Fourth and Fifth Amendments, *Terry v. Ohio*, 392 U.S. 1, 8–9 (1968), *Katz v. United States*, 389 U.S. 347, 350 (1967), *Boyd v. United States*, 116 U.S. 616 (1886), *see Olmstead v. United States*, 277 U.S. 438, 478 (1928) (Brandeis, J., dissenting); in the penumbras of the Bill of Rights, *Griswold v. Connecticut*, 381 U.S. at 484–485; in the Ninth Amendment, *id.* at 486 (Goldberg, J., concurring); or in the concept of liberty guaranteed by the first section of the Fourteenth Amendment, *see Meyer v. Nebraska*, 262 U.S. 390, 399 (1923). These decisions make it clear that only personal rights that can be deemed "fundamental" or "implicit in the concept of ordered liberty," *Palko v. Connecticut*, 302 U.S. 319, 325 (1937), are included in this guarantee of personal privacy. They also make it clear that the right has some extension to activities relating to marriage, *Loving v. Virginia*, 388 U.S. 1, 12 (1967); procreation, *Skinner v. Oklahoma*, 316 U.S. 535, 541–542 (1942); contraception, *Eisenstadt v. Baird*, 405 U.S. at 453–454; *id.* at 460, 463–465 (White, J., concurring in result); family relationships, *Prince v. Massachusetts*, 321 U.S. 158, 166 (1944); and childrearing and education, *Pierce v. Society of Sisters*, 268 U.S. 510, 535 (1925), *Meyer v. Nebraska, supra.*

This right of privacy, whether it be *founded* in the Four- 11 teenth Amendment's concept of personal liberty and restrictions upon state action, as we feel it is, or, as the District Court determined, in the Ninth Amendment's reservation of rights to the people, is broad enough to encompass a woman's decision whether or not to terminate her pregnancy. The detriment that the State would impose upon the pregnant woman by denying this choice altogether is apparent. Specific and direct harm medically diagnosable even in early pregnancy may be involved. Maternity, or additional offspring, may force upon the woman a distressful life and future. Psychological harm may be imminent. Mental and physical health may be *taxed* by child care. There is also the distress, for all concerned, associated with the unwanted child, and there is the problem of bringing a child into a family already unable, psychologically and otherwise, to care for it. In other cases, as in this one, the additional difficulties and continuing stigma of unwed motherhood may be involved. All these are factors the woman and her responsible physician necessarily will consider in consultation.

founded—based

Describe the potential harm that might result from limiting a woman's access to an abortion.

tax—to burden, to make a heavy demand

[Whether the right to an abortion can be absolute]

Explain why the right to privacy is not absolute in regards to abortion, according to Justice Blackmun.

12 On the basis of elements such as these, appellant and some *amici* argue that the woman's right is absolute and that she is entitled to terminate her pregnancy at whatever time, in whatever way, and for whatever reason she alone chooses. With this we do not agree. Appellant's arguments that Texas either has no valid interest at all in regulating the abortion decision, or no interest strong enough to support any limitation upon the woman's sole determination, are unpersuasive. The Court's decisions recognizing a right of privacy also acknowledge that some state regulation in areas protected by that right is appropriate. As noted above, a State may properly assert important interests in safeguarding health, in maintaining medical standards, and in protecting potential life. At some point in pregnancy, these respective interests become sufficiently compelling to sustain regulation of the factors that govern the abortion decision. The privacy right involved, therefore, cannot be said to be absolute. In fact, it is not clear to us that the claim asserted by some *amici* that one has an unlimited right to do with one's body as one pleases bears a close relationship to the right of privacy previously articulated in the Court's decisions. The Court has refused to recognize an unlimited right of this kind in the past.

13 We, therefore, conclude that the right of personal privacy includes the abortion decision, but that this right is not unqualified, and must be considered against important state interests in regulation.

[On compelling interest and permissible regulation]

What kind of restrictions does the Court consider to be permissible when states regulate abortion?

Explain the argument, from a medical standpoint, why the state may not limit access the right to an abortion in the first trimester.

14 With respect to the State's important and legitimate interest in the health of the mother, the "compelling" point, in the light of present medical knowledge, is at approximately the end of the first trimester. This is so because of the now-established medical fact, referred to above … , that, until the end of the first trimester mortality in abortion may be less than mortality in normal childbirth. It follows that, from and after this point, a State may regulate the abortion procedure to the extent that the regulation reasonably relates to the preservation and protection of maternal health. Examples of permissible state regulation in this area are requirements as to

the qualifications of the person who is to perform the abortion; as to the licensure of that person; as to the facility in which the procedure is to be performed, that is, whether it must be a hospital or may be a clinic or some other place of less-than-hospital status; as to the licensing of the facility; and the like.

> Describe the types of regulations states can create in regard to abortion in the second trimester.

With respect to the State's important and legitimate interest 15 in potential life, the "compelling" point is at viability. This is so because the fetus then presumably has the capability of meaningful life outside the mother's womb. State regulation protective of fetal life after viability thus has both logical and biological justifications. If the State is interested in protecting fetal life after viability, it may go so far as to proscribe abortion during that period, except when it is necessary to preserve the life or health of the mother.

> Note the Court's use of the term *viability*, as well as the Court's definition of it.
>
> Describe the standard used that would allow states to outlaw abortion.

Excerpt from Dissenting Opinion

MR. JUSTICE REHNQUIST, dissenting. 16

[On the lack of a right of privacy in this instance]

I have difficulty in concluding, as the Court does, that the right of 17 "privacy" is involved in this case. Texas, by the statute here challenged, bars the performance of a medical abortion by a licensed physician on a plaintiff such as Roe. A transaction resulting in an operation such as this is not "private" in the ordinary usage of that word. Nor is the "privacy" that the Court finds here even a distant relative of the freedom from searches and seizures protected by the Fourth Amendment to the Constitution, which the Court has referred to as embodying a right to privacy.

> Explain why Justice Rehnquist would argue that an abortion is not protected by the right to privacy.

If the Court means by the term "privacy" no more than that 18 the claim of a person to be free from unwanted state regulation of consensual transactions may be a form of "liberty" protected by the Fourteenth Amendment, there is no doubt that similar claims have been upheld in our earlier decisions on the basis of that liberty. I agree with the statement of MR. JUSTICE STEWART in his concurring opinion that the "liberty," against deprivation of which without due process the Fourteenth Amendment protects, embraces more than the rights found in the Bill of Rights. But that liberty is not guaranteed absolutely against deprivation, only against deprivation without due process of law. The test traditionally applied in the area of social and economic legislation is whether or not a law such as that challenged has a rational relation to a valid state objective. *Williamson v. Lee Optical Co.*, 348 U.S. 483, 491 (1955). The Due Process Clause of the Fourteenth Amendment undoubtedly does place a limit, albeit a broad one, on legislative power to enact laws such as this. If the Texas statute were to prohibit an abortion even where the mother's life is in jeopardy, I have little doubt that such a statute would lack a rational relation to a valid state objective under the test stated in *Williamson, supra.* But the Court's sweeping invalidation of any restrictions on abortion during the first trimester is impossible to justify under that standard, and the conscious weighing of competing factors that the Court's opinion apparently substitutes for the established test is far more appropriate to a legislative judgment than to a judicial one.

> A valid or compelling state objective is a standard used to determine if a state action is allowable. The Court has to determine if the state action is so important that it is acceptable to limit individual liberty.

[On judicial "legislation"]

19 As in *Lochner* and similar cases applying *substantive due process* standards to economic and social welfare legislation, the adoption of the compelling state interest standard will inevitably require this Court to examine the legislative policies and pass on the wisdom of these policies in the very process of deciding whether a particular state interest put forward may or may not be "compelling." The decision here to break pregnancy into three distinct terms and to outline the permissible restrictions the State may impose in each one, for example, partakes more of judicial legislation than it does of a determination of the intent of the drafters of the Fourteenth Amendment.

> *substantive due process*—protection of certain basic rights from government interference

> Explain what Justice Rehnquist means by "judicial legislation."

■ **Impact of** *Roe v. Wade* **on U.S. politics and on state law**

The *Roe* decision has been one of, if not the most, divisive Court decisions in recent U.S. history. As a result of the decision, the laws of forty-six states were at least partially invalidated, and abortion is now legal in all states. However, subsequent decisions have permitted greater restrictions on abortions than originally set out in the *Roe* decision.

In addition to the direct impact on abortion legislation, the abortion issue, in many ways, led to the increased political activity by religious conservatives, which has been an important constituency in the Republican Party. Finally, the abortion issue has led to the idea of a litmus test in regards to presidential judicial appointments. Democratic presidents look for judges who will protect access to an abortion, while Republican presidents look for judges that would limit or even eliminate access to abortion.

Check for Understanding

1. Describe three arguments that were used to support laws outlawing abortion. (Paragraphs 4 through 9.)
2. Describe the trimester framework for restricting abortion created by the *Roe* decision. Explain why the Court created this framework. (See paragraph 14.)
3. Explain how the Ninth and Fourteenth Amendments (among others) create a right to privacy.
4. Define due process. Explain how due process is used by the Court to apply the right to privacy in the *Roe* decision.
5. Describe Justice Rehnquist's main reasons for his dissent in the *Roe* decision.

SCOTUS Practice Question

In the late nineteenth century, Connecticut passed a law that banned providing and using contraception. In 1961, a gynecologist from Yale, Dr. C. Lee Buxton, and the executive director of Planned Parenthood, Estelle Griswold, opened a clinic in New Haven, Connecticut for the specific purpose of providing contraception to its patients. Both were arrested and convicted of violating the Connecticut statute that barred the use of contraception. They appealed their conviction, which eventually worked its way to the Supreme Court.

In 1965, the Supreme Court ruled in *Griswold v. Connecticut* that the law outlawing contraception was unconstitutional. In striking down the Connecticut law, Justice Arthur Goldberg in a concurring opinion wrote, "I do agree that the concept of liberty protects those personal rights that are fundamental, and is not confined to the specific terms of the Bill of Rights."

Based on the information above, respond to the following questions.

A. Identify the implied constitutional right common to the decision in both *Griswold v. Connecticut* (1965) and *Roe v. Wade* (1973).
B. Explain how the facts of *Griswold v. Connecticut* (1965) and *Roe v. Wade* (1973) led to a similar holding in both cases.
C. Describe an action that interest groups unhappy with the holding in *Roe v. Wade* (1973) could take to limit its impact.

McDonald v. Chicago

Focus on *McDonald v. Chicago* (2010)

McDonald v. Chicago, 561 U.S. ___ (2010), is the most recent example of an amendment being "incorporated," meaning it applies to the states as well as the federal government. Because the Court can only rule on cases brought before it, the Bill of Rights has been incorporated over time "selectively," beginning with the First Amendment in the 1920s. In the *McDonald* case, the Second Amendment was incorporated for the first time when the city of Chicago's handgun ban was struck down as unconstitutional. The Supreme Court ruled that outright bans by state or local government were not consistent with the Second Amendment, although some gun-control regulations are still permissible. The process of selective incorporation arose from the Court's interpretation of the Fourteenth Amendment, which forbids states from creating laws that deny fundamental rights to their citizens.

Reader Alert!

Selective incorporation is a confusing concept. It helps to recall the history surrounding the passage of the Bill of Rights: The Framers feared overreach at the federal level, not the state level. Then, recall the circumstances after the Civil War when the Fourteenth Amendment was passed: Congress did not trust the southern states to protect the rights of newly freed slaves. The Fourteenth Amendment is the basis for ensuring that protections in the Bill of Rights apply to actions by the states. Through the process of selective incorporation, the Supreme Court has ruled that states are limited in infringing on certain rights, on a case-by-case basis. When evaluating *McDonald v. Chicago*, keep in mind that even though the Court may have looked at the impact of the handgun ban, and the politics surrounding gun control, the key issue for the Court was whether the Second Amendment is a fundamental right, thereby applicable to the due process clause of the Fourteenth Amendment.

Facts of the Case

Otis McDonald, Adam Orlov, Colleen Lawson, and David Lawson were Chicago residents who wanted to keep handguns in their homes for self-defense but were prohibited from doing so by Chicago's firearms laws. Some of the Chicago petitioners had been the targets of threats and violence. A city ordinance then in force, though, provided that "[n]o person shall ... possess ... any firearm unless such person is the holder of a valid registration certificate for such firearm." Chicago's Municipal Code prohibited registration of most handguns, thus effectively banning handgun possession by almost all private citizens in the city. Oak Park, an older suburb that borders Chicago, made it "unlawful for any person to possess ... any firearm," a term that was meant to include "pistols, revolvers, guns and small arms ... commonly known as handguns."

Issue

Is the city of Chicago's handgun ban an unconstitutional violation of the Second Amendment because of the Fourteenth Amendment's due process clause?

Holding/Decision

The Supreme Court ruled in favor of McDonald and the other petitioners. The Second Amendment now applies to state and local government through the doctrine of selective incorporation.

Excerpt from Majority Opinion

[Justice Alito on how precedent cases are related]

Justice Alito announced the judgment of the Court and delivered the opinion of the Court with respect to Parts I, II–A, II–B, II–D, III–A, and III–B, in which The Chief Justice, Justice Scalia, Justice Kennedy, and Justice Thomas join, and an opinion with respect to Parts II–C, IV, and V, in which The Chief Justice, Justice Scalia, and Justice Kennedy join.

Two years ago, in *District of Columbia v. Heller*, 554 U.S. ___ (2008), we held that the Second Amendment protects the right to keep and bear arms for the purpose of self-defense, and we struck down a District of Columbia law that banned the possession of handguns in the home. The city of Chicago (City) and the village of Oak Park, a Chicago suburb, have laws that are similar to the District of Columbia's, but Chicago and Oak Park argue that their laws are constitutional because the Second Amendment has no application to the States. We have previously held that most of the provisions of the Bill of Rights apply with full force to both the Federal Government and the States. Applying the standard that is well established in our case law, we hold that the Second Amendment right is fully applicable to the States.

2 Why did the ruling in *District of Columbia v. Heller* set a precedent that applied to the states?

[On the intent and impact of the Chicago law]

Why is it important to understand the intent and the impact of the handgun law when interpreting the Second Amendment and how it should be applied today?

3   Chicago enacted its handgun ban to protect its residents "from the loss of property and injury or death from firearms." ... The Chicago petitioners and their *amici*, however, argue that the handgun ban has left them vulnerable to criminals. Chicago Police Department statistics, we are told, reveal that the City's handgun murder rate has actually increased since the ban was enacted and that Chicago residents now face one of the highest murder rates in the country and rates of other violent crimes that exceed the average in comparable cities.

[On the outcome that the petitioners are seeking]

4   After our decision in *Heller*, the Chicago petitioners and two groups filed suit against the City in the United States District Court for the Northern District of Illinois. They sought a declaration that the handgun ban and several related Chicago ordinances violate the Second and Fourteenth Amendments to the United States Constitution. Another action challenging the Oak Park law was filed in the same District Court by the National Rifle Association (NRA) and two Oak Park residents. In addition, the NRA and others filed a third action challenging the Chicago ordinances. All three cases were assigned to the same District Judge.

What was the rationale of the lower court in ruling in favor of Chicago and against petitioners?

5   The District Court rejected plaintiffs' argument that the Chicago and Oak Park laws are unconstitutional. ... The court noted that the Seventh Circuit had "squarely upheld the constitutionality of a ban on handguns a quarter century ago,". ... The court observed that a district judge has a "duty to follow established precedent in the Court of Appeals to which he or she is beholden, even though the logic of more recent caselaw may point in a different direction."

Why was the Bill of Rights not "incorporated" all at once?

[Explaining the process of selective incorporation]

6   The Bill of Rights, including the Second Amendment, originally applied only to the Federal Government. In *Barron ex rel. Tiernan v. Mayor of Baltimore*, 7 Pet. 243 (1833), the Court, in an opinion by Chief Justice Marshall, explained that this question was "of

great importance" but "not of much difficulty." ... In less than four pages, the Court firmly rejected the proposition that the first eight Amendments operate as limitations on the States, holding that they apply only to the Federal Government. ... ("[I]t is now settled that those amendments [in the Bill of Rights] do not extend to the states").

The constitutional Amendments adopted in the aftermath of the Civil War fundamentally altered our country's federal system. The provision at issue in this case, §1 of the Fourteenth Amendment, provides, among other things, that a State may not abridge "the privileges or immunities of citizens of the United States" or deprive "any person of life, liberty, or property, without due process of law."

An alternative theory regarding the relationship between the Bill of Rights and §1 of the Fourteenth Amendment was championed by Justice Black. This theory held that §1 of the Fourteenth Amendment totally incorporated all of the provisions of the Bill of Rights. ... As Justice Black noted, the chief congressional proponents of the Fourteenth Amendment espoused the view that the Amendment made the Bill of Rights applicable to the States. ... Nonetheless, the Court never has embraced Justice Black's "total incorporation" theory.

While Justice Black's theory was never adopted, the Court eventually moved in that direction by initiating what has been called a process of "selective incorporation," *i.e.*, the Court began to hold that the Due Process Clause fully incorporates particular rights contained in the first eight Amendments.

[The key legal question about the Second Amendment]

With this framework in mind, we now turn directly to the question whether the Second Amendment right to keep and bear arms is incorporated in the concept of due process. In answering that question, as just explained, we must decide whether the right to keep and bear arms is fundamental to *our* scheme of ordered liberty, *Duncan,* 391 U.S., at 149, or as we have said in a related context, whether this right is "deeply rooted in this Nation's history and tradition," *Washington v. Glucksberg,* 521 U.S. 702, 721 (1997) (internal quotation marks omitted).

Our decision in *Heller* points unmistakably to the answer. Self-defense is a basic right, recognized by many legal systems

7 How did the passage of the Fourteenth Amendment "fundamentally alter our country's federal system"?

8

9 Summarize the Court's argument for using the doctrine of selective incorporation.

10

11 What counterargument could be made to the claim that self-defense as a basic right?

from ancient times to the present day, and in *Heller,* we held that individual self-defense is "the *central component*" of the Second Amendment right.

[On the original meaning and purpose of the Second Amendment]

Explain how this paragraph demonstrates the judicial philosophy of original intent.

12   The right to keep and bear arms was considered no less fundamental by those who drafted and ratified the Bill of Rights. "During the 1788 ratification debates, the fear that the federal government would disarm the people in order to impose rule through a standing army or select militia was pervasive in Antifederalist rhetoric." … Federalists responded, not by arguing that the right was insufficiently important to warrant protection but by contending that the right was adequately protected by the Constitution's assignment of only limited powers to the Federal Government.

[On the purpose of the Fourteenth Amendment]

How has the Fourteenth Amendment been used to expand civil rights and liberties?

13   Today, it is generally accepted that the Fourteenth Amendment was understood to provide a constitutional basis for protecting the rights set out in the Civil Rights Act of 1866.

14   In debating the Fourteenth Amendment, the 39th Congress referred to the right to keep and bear arms as a fundamental right deserving of protection. Senator Samuel Pomeroy described three "indispensable" "safeguards of liberty under our form of Government."

[On respondents' arguments about the intent of the Fourteenth Amendment]

15   Despite all this evidence, municipal respondents contend that Congress, in the years immediately following the Civil War, merely sought to outlaw "discriminatory measures taken against freedmen, which it addressed by adopting a non-discrimination principle" and that even an outright ban on the possession of firearms was regarded as acceptable, "so long as it was not done in a discriminatory manner."

16   Municipal respondents' remaining arguments are at war with our central holding in *Heller*: that the Second Amendment protects a personal right to keep and bear arms for lawful purposes, most notably for self-defense within the home. Municipal

respondents, in effect, ask us to treat the right recognized in *Heller* as a second-class right, subject to an entirely different body of rules than the other Bill of Rights guarantees that we have held to be incorporated into the Due Process Clause.

Municipal respondents maintain that the Second Amendment 17 differs from all of the other provisions of the Bill of Rights because it concerns the right to possess a deadly implement and thus has implications for public safety. ... And they note that there is intense disagreement on the question whether the private possession of guns in the home increases or decreases gun deaths and injuries.

Unless we turn back the clock or adopt a special incorpora- 18 tion test applicable only to the Second Amendment, municipal respondents' argument must be rejected. Under our precedents, if a Bill of Rights guarantee is fundamental from an American perspective, then, unless *stare decisis* counsels otherwise, that guarantee is fully binding on the States and thus *limits* (but by no means eliminates) their ability to devise solutions to social problems that suit local needs and values. As noted by the 38 States that have appeared in this case as *amici* supporting petitioners, "[s]tate and local experimentation with reasonable firearms regulations will continue under the Second Amendment."

It is important to keep in mind that *Heller*, while striking 19 down a law that prohibited the possession of handguns in the home, recognized that the right to keep and bear arms is not "a right to keep and carry any weapon whatsoever in any manner whatsoever and for whatever purpose." ... We made it clear in *Heller* that our holding did not cast doubt on such longstanding regulatory measures as "prohibitions on the possession of firearms by felons and the mentally ill," "laws forbidding the carrying of firearms in sensitive places such as schools and government buildings, or laws imposing conditions and qualifications on the commercial sale of arms."

[On the meaning and purpose of the Second Amendment today]

Municipal respondents argue, finally, that the right to keep and 20 bear arms is unique among the rights set out in the first eight Amendments "because the reason for codifying the Second Amendment (to protect the militia) differs from the purpose (primarily, to use firearms to engage in self-defense) that is claimed to make the

---

Sidebar notes:

To what extent should exemptions for public safety be made when applying the Bill of Rights? What other amendments could be at issue when weighing individual liberty against public safety?

Does this decision help clarify state and. federal control of policymaking on gun regulation, or does this decision create further confusion?

Many proponents of gun control argue that the Second Amendment does not apply to many instances of gun ownership in the twenty-first century, because the framers of the Constitution were mainly concerned with bestowing this right on a "well-regulated militia" to prevent tyranny. In what way is that argument undermined by this passage?

right implicit in the concept of ordered liberty." ... In *Heller*, we recognized that the codification of this right was prompted by fear that the Federal Government would disarm and thus disable the militias, but we rejected the suggestion that the right was valued only as a means of preserving the militias. ... On the contrary, we stressed that the right was also valued because the possession of firearms was thought to be essential for self-defense. As we put it, self-defense was "the *central component* of the right itself." *Ibid.*

21   In *Heller*, we held that the Second Amendment protects the right to possess a handgun in the home for the purpose of self-defense. Unless considerations of *stare decisis* counsel otherwise, a provision of the Bill of Rights that protects a right that is fundamental from an American perspective applies equally to the Federal Government and the States. See *Duncan*, 391 U.S., at 149, and n. 14. We therefore hold that the Due Process Clause of the Fourteenth Amendment incorporates the Second Amendment right recognized in *Heller*. The judgment of the Court of Appeals is reversed, and the case is remanded for further proceedings.

Excerpt from Dissenting Opinion

22   Justice Breyer, with whom Justice Ginsburg and Justice Sotomayor join, dissenting.

23   I can find nothing in the Second Amendment's text, history, or underlying rationale that could warrant characterizing it as "fundamental" insofar as it seeks to protect the keeping and bearing of arms for private self-defense purposes. Nor can I find any justification for interpreting the Constitution as transferring ultimate regulatory authority over the private uses of firearms from democratically elected legislatures to courts or from the States to the Federal Government. I therefore conclude that the Fourteenth Amendment does not "incorporate" the Second Amendment's right "to keep and bear Arms." And I consequently dissent.

[Rejecting the majority's argument about the main meaning of the Second Amendment]

24   The Second Amendment says: "A well regulated Militia, being necessary to the security of a free State, the right of the people to keep and bear Arms, shall not be infringed." Two years ago,

in *District of Columbia v. Heller*, 554 U.S. ___ (2008), the Court rejected the pre-existing judicial consensus that the Second Amendment was primarily concerned with the need to maintain a "well regulated Militia."

The Court based its conclusions almost exclusively upon its reading of history. But the relevant history in *Heller* was far from clear: Four dissenting Justices disagreed with the majority's historical analysis.

[What else besides history should be considered?]

In my view, taking *Heller* as a given, the Fourteenth Amendment does not incorporate the Second Amendment right to keep and bear arms for purposes of private self-defense. Under this Court's precedents, to incorporate the private self-defense right the majority must show that the right is, *e.g.*, "fundamental to the American scheme of justice," ... And this it fails to do. ...

Accordingly, this Court, in considering an incorporation question, has never stated that the historical status of a right is the only relevant consideration. Rather, the Court has either explicitly or implicitly made clear in its opinions that the right in question has remained fundamental over time. ...

I thus think it proper, above all where history provides no clear answer, to look to other factors in considering whether a right is sufficiently "fundamental" to remove it from the political process in every State. I would include among those factors the nature of the right; any contemporary disagreement about whether the right is fundamental; the extent to which incorporation will further other, perhaps more basic, constitutional aims; and the extent to which incorporation will advance or hinder the Constitution's structural aims, including its division of powers among different governmental institutions (and the people as well). Is incorporation needed, for example, to further the Constitution's effort to ensure that the government treats each individual with equal respect? Will it help maintain the democratic form of government that the Constitution foresees? In a word, will incorporation prove consistent, or inconsistent, with the Constitution's efforts to create governmental institutions well suited to the carrying out of its constitutional promises?

25 | Other than history, what else should justices consider when interpreting the meaning of the Constitution?

26 | What rights should be considered to be "fundamental to the American scheme of justice"?

27 |

28 | How does incorporation of an amendment "remove it from the political process in every State"?

In your opinion, which of these questions is the most important for the Court to ask before incorporating an amendment?

[On judicial review and *Federalist* No. 78]

Note the connection here to required reading *Federalist* No. 78. From your reading of *Federalist* No. 78, which side of this case is better supported by Hamilton's view of the role of the judiciary?

29 Finally, I would take account of the Framers' basic reason for believing the Court ought to have the power of judicial review. Alexander Hamilton feared granting that power to Congress alone, for he feared that Congress, acting as judges, would not overturn as unconstitutional a popular statute that it had recently enacted, as legislators. The Federalist No. 78, p. 405 (G. Carey & J. McClellan eds. 2001) (A. Hamilton) ("This independence of the judges is equally requisite to guard the constitution and the rights of individuals from the effects of those ill humours, which" can, at times, lead to "serious oppressions of the minor part in the community"). Judges, he thought, may find it easier to resist popular pressure to suppress the basic rights of an unpopular minority.

[Incorporation and broader constitutional concerns]

This passage contrasts incorporation of the Second Amendment with other amendments incorporated previously.

Define *stare decisis*, and describe how the principle of *stare decisis* might be applied to this case.

30 Moreover, there is no reason here to believe that incorporation of the private self-defense right will further any other or broader constitutional objective. ... Unlike the First Amendment's rights of free speech, free press, assembly, and petition, the private self-defense right does not comprise a necessary part of the democratic process that the Constitution seeks to establish. ... Unlike the First Amendment's religious protections, the Fourth Amendment's protection against unreasonable searches and seizures, the Fifth and Sixth Amendments' insistence upon fair criminal procedure, and the Eighth Amendment's protection against cruel and unusual punishments, the private self-defense right does not significantly seek to protect individuals who might otherwise suffer unfair or inhumane treatment at the hands of a majority. Unlike the protections offered by many of these same Amendments, it does not involve matters as to which judges possess a comparative expertise, by virtue of their close familiarity with the justice system and its operation. And, unlike the Fifth Amendment's insistence on just compensation, it does not involve a matter where a majority might unfairly seize for itself property belonging to a minority.

31   Finally, incorporation of the right *will* work a significant disruption in the constitutional allocation of decisionmaking authority, thereby interfering with the Constitution's ability to further its objectives.

First, on any reasonable accounting, the incorporation of the right recognized in *Heller* would amount to a significant incursion on a traditional and important area of state concern, altering the constitutional relationship between the States and the Federal Government. Private gun regulation is the quintessential exercise of a State's "police power"—*i.e.*, the power to "protec[t] ... the lives, limbs, health, comfort, and quiet of all persons, and the protection of all property within the State," by enacting "all kinds of restraints and burdens" on both "persons and property."

32

Define reserved powers and describe how they are being invoked in this passage to make an argument about the balance of power under federalism.

[The problem with courts assessing gun regulation]

Second, determining the constitutionality of a particular state gun law requires finding answers to complex empirically based questions of a kind that legislatures are better able than courts to make.

33

Do you agree with the claim that creating gun regulations is the role of the legislature rather than the courts?

Government regulation of the right to bear arms normally embodies a judgment that the regulation will help save lives. The determination whether a gun regulation is constitutional would thus almost always require the weighing of the constitutional right to bear arms against the "primary concern of every government—a concern for the safety and indeed the lives of its citizens."

34

[Congress is better able to decide on gun regulation]

At the same time, there is no institutional need to send judges off on this "mission-almost-impossible." Legislators are able to "amass the stuff of actual experience and cull conclusions from it." ... They are far better suited than judges to uncover facts and to understand their relevance. And legislators, unlike Article III judges, can be held democratically responsible for their empirically based and value-laden conclusions. We have thus repeatedly affirmed our preference for "legislative not judicial solutions" to this kind of problem,..., just as we have repeatedly affirmed the Constitution's preference for democratic solutions legislated by those whom the people elect.

35

Do you agree that elected institutions such as Congress are preferable to tenured, appointed judges in determining what regulations are effective? Explain why or why not.

[Local control and federalism]

Third, the ability of States to reflect local preferences and conditions—both key virtues of federalism—here has particular importance. The incidence of gun ownership varies substantially

36

as between crowded cities and uncongested rural communities, as well as among the different geographic regions of the country.

37 The nature of gun violence also varies as between rural communities and cities. Urban centers face significantly greater levels of firearm crime and homicide, while rural communities have proportionately greater problems with nonhomicide gun deaths, such as suicides and accidents.

Summarize one argument for national control of the issue of gun regulation, and one argument for state/local control of the issue.

38 It is thus unsurprising that States and local communities have historically differed about the need for gun regulation as well as about its proper level. Nor is it surprising that "primarily, and historically," the law has treated the exercise of police powers, including gun control, as "matter[s] of local concern."

[Against incorporation]

39 In sum, the police power, the superiority of legislative decisionmaking, the need for local decisionmaking, the comparative desirability of democratic decisionmaking, the lack of a manageable judicial standard, and the life-threatening harm that may flow from striking down regulations all argue against incorporation. Where the incorporation of other rights has been at issue, *some* of these problems have arisen. But in this instance *all* these problems are present, *all* at the same time, and *all* are likely to be present in most, perhaps nearly all, of the cases in which the constitutionality of a gun regulation is at issue. At the same time, the important factors that favor incorporation in other instances—*e.g.*, the protection of broader constitutional objectives—are not present here. The upshot is that all factors militate against incorporation—with the possible exception of historical factors.

Is there anything in Justice Breyer's dissent that you believe a future Court may revisit and reevaluate? Describe what you think are the most important takeaways from this dissent.

[Summary of dissenting arguments]

40 In sum, the Framers did not write the Second Amendment in order to protect a private right of armed self-defense. There has been, and is, no consensus that the right is, or was, "fundamental." No broader constitutional interest or principle supports legal treatment of that right as fundamental. To the contrary, broader constitutional concerns of an institutional nature argue strongly against that treatment.

41 And, in the absence of any other support for its conclusion, ambiguous history cannot show that the Fourteenth Amendment incorporates a private right of self-defense against the States.

Impact of *McDonald v. Chicago* on gun ownership, interpretation of the Second Amendment, and federalism

McDonald v. Chicago reminds us of the active and ongoing work of constitutional interpretation. It is the latest in a line of cases, starting in the 1920s, that incorporated an amendment to the states, and in doing so, changed the balance of power between the state and federal governments.

A close 5-4 decision, the case is controversial. It reflects the partisan nature of the debate over gun control as well as how this issue demonstrates the natural policymaking tension between state and national governments in a federal system.

This case raises issues about the role of the courts in our political system and what Justices' role should be as appointed, tenured experts on the Constitution. What questions about and details of an issue such as gun rights are better left to elected institutions of government, and which should be decided by the Court? Consider how the power of judicial review changed the Court's role in the policymaking process. To what extent has Hamilton's vision of the role of the Court described in *Federalist* No. 78 been realized today?

Check for Understanding

1. Explain how this case affects the balance of policymaking power between the state and national governments.
2. Explain how this case, and the issue of gun control, illustrates both advantages and disadvantages of federalism.
3. Define selective incorporation, and describe at least two questions the Court may pose when deciding whether to incorporate part of the Bill of Rights.
4. Explain how this case illustrates tensions between the Court and elected institutions of government in deciding on issues like gun regulation.
5. Explain how the Court's role has been strengthened because of judicial review and modern interpretations of the Fourteenth Amendment.

SCOTUS Practice Question

In *District of Columbia v. Heller,* the respondent was a D.C. special policeman who had applied to register a handgun he wished to keep in the home but was denied under a D.C. law that forbade registration of handguns in most instances. Dick Heller brought suit against the city, claiming that the law, which also made it a crime to carry an unregistered weapon, and required residents to keep legal firearms unloaded at home, violated his constitutional rights.

In a 5-4 decision, the Supreme Court struck down the law as unconstitutional. Writing for the majority, Justice Scalia wrote: "The enshrinement of Constitutional rights necessarily takes some policy choices off the table. These include the absolute prohibition of handguns held and used for self-defense in the home."

A. Identify the constitutional clause that is common to both *District of Columbia v. Heller* and *McDonald v. Chicago*.

B. Based on the constitutional clause in part A, explain why the facts of *District of Columbia v. Heller* led to a similar ruling as the holding in *McDonald v. Chicago*.

C. Describe one way states may enact policies regulating gun ownership.

Brown v. Board of Education

▨ Focus on *Brown v. Board of Education* (1954)

Brown v. Board of Education of Topeka, 347 U.S. 483, is the unanimous Supreme Court ruling that overturned the "separate but equal" doctrine that had given legal cover to segregation policies for generations. This ruling applied only to legal segregation in public schools, but it helped to undermine Jim Crow policies that affected every part of life in the South. Many states were slow to comply with the ruling, and some did not integrate without federal enforcement. This decision is a victory for the African-American civil-rights movement, but its legacy is still up for debate today.

▨ Reader Alert!

This unanimous opinion is written in clear, straightforward prose. It is important to understand the significance of overturning such a longstanding precedent and also to gain a firm understanding of how the equal protection clause of the Fourteenth Amendment was interpreted and applied. This case is about constitutional interpretation as well as how to provide equal opportunity for students in school. Students may be asked in an FRQ to compare this case to a later case involving race, education, and the equal protection clause. Make sure you have a firm understanding of the meaning of the Fourteenth Amendment and the way that courts have interpreted it.

▨ Facts of the Case

The Court consolidated several different cases challenging legally segregated schools in Kansas, South Carolina, Virginia, and Delaware. In each case, African-American students had been denied entry to public school based on local segregation laws. The families affected were represented by the NAACP, a prominent civil-rights group that used litigation as one means of changing policy. Lower courts ruled with the varying school districts, finding that under the precedent set by *Plessy v. Ferguson* (1896), "separate but equal" educational facilities were constitutionally permissible.

▨ Issue

Does state-mandated racial segregation in public schools violate the equal protection clause of the Fourteenth Amendment?

■ Holding/Decision

"Separate but equal" educational facilities for racial minorities are *inherently* unequal, thereby violating the equal protection clause of the Fourteenth Amendment.

Excerpt from Majority Opinion

1   MR. CHIEF JUSTICE WARREN delivered the opinion of the Court.

[On the differences among the lower courts]

What factors should a court consider in determining whether or not schools are "equal"?

2   In each of the cases, minors of the Negro race, through their legal representatives, seek the aid of the courts in obtaining admission to the public schools of their community on a nonsegregated basis. In each instance, they had been denied admission to schools attended by white children under laws requiring or permitting segregation according to race. This segregation was alleged to deprive the plaintiffs of the equal protection of the laws under the Fourteenth Amendment. In each of the cases other than the Delaware case, a three-judge federal district court denied relief to the plaintiffs on the so-called separate but equal doctrine announced by this Court in *Plessy v. Ferguson,* 163 U.S. 537. Under that doctrine, equality of treatment is accorded when the races are provided substantially equal facilities, even though these facilities be separate. In the Delaware case, the Supreme Court of Delaware adhered to that doctrine, but ordered that the plaintiffs be admitted to the white schools because of their superiority to the Negro schools.

Explain why the Supreme Court ordered that African-American students be admitted to white schools in the Delaware case.

3   The plaintiffs contend that segregated public schools are not equal and cannot be made equal, and that hence they are deprived of the equal protection of the laws. Because of the obvious importance of the question presented, the Court took jurisdiction…

[History and purpose of the Fourteenth Amendment]

What factors, other than history, should the Supreme Court consider in determining the meaning of an amendment and how to apply it?

4   Reargument was largely devoted to the circumstances surrounding the adoption of the Fourteenth Amendment in 1868. It covered exhaustively consideration of the Amendment in Congress, ratification by the states, then-existing practices in racial

segregation, and the views of proponents and opponents of the Amendment. This discussion and our own investigation convince us that, although these sources cast some light, it is not enough to resolve the problem with which we are faced. At best, they are inconclusive. The most avid proponents of the post-War Amendments undoubtedly intended them to remove all legal distinctions among all persons born or naturalized in the United States. Their opponents, just as certainly, were antagonistic to both the letter and the spirit of the Amendments and wished them to have the most limited effect. What others in Congress and the state legislatures had in mind cannot be determined with any degree of certainty.

[Is separate always unequal?]

In the first cases in this Court construing the Fourteenth Amendment, decided shortly after its adoption, the Court interpreted it as proscribing all state-imposed discriminations against the Negro race. The doctrine of separate but equal did not make its appearance in this Court until 1896 in the case of *Plessy v. Ferguson,* supra, involving not education but transportation. American courts have since labored with the doctrine for over half a century. In this Court, there have been six cases involving the separate but equal doctrine in the field of public education. ... In more recent cases, all on the graduate school level, inequality was found in that specific benefits enjoyed by white students were denied to Negro students of the same educational qualifications. Missouri ex rel. Gaines v. Canada, 305 U.S. 337; Sipuel v. Oklahoma, 332 U.S. 631; Sweatt v. Painter, 339 U.S. 629; McLaurin v. Oklahoma State Regents, 339 U.S. 637. In none of these cases was it necessary to reexamine the doctrine to grant relief to the Negro plaintiff. And in *Sweatt v. Painter,* supra, the Court expressly reserved decision on the question whether *Plessy v. Ferguson* should be held inapplicable to public education.

In the *instant* cases, that question is directly presented. Here, unlike *Sweatt v. Painter,* there are findings below that the Negro and white schools involved have been equalized, or are being equalized, with respect to buildings, curricula, qualifications and salaries of teachers, and other tangible factors. Our decision, therefore, cannot turn on merely a comparison of these tangible factors in the Negro and white schools involved in each of the

5

Why didn't the Court have to reevaluate the "separate but equal" doctrine in cases involving graduate schools?

6

instant—brought at this moment

cases. We must look instead to the effect of segregation itself on public education.

7   In approaching this problem, we cannot turn the clock back to 1868, when the Amendment was adopted, or even to 1896, when *Plessy v. Ferguson* was written. We must consider public education in the light of its full development and its present place in American life throughout the Nation. Only in this way can it be determined if segregation in public schools deprives these plaintiffs of the equal protection of the laws.

[On the impact of segregation in a modern, democratic society]

8   Today, education is perhaps the most important function of state and local governments. Compulsory school attendance laws and the great expenditures for education both demonstrate our recognition of the importance of education to our democratic society. It is required in the performance of our most basic public responsibilities, even service in the armed forces. It is the very foundation of good citizenship. Today it is a principal instrument in awakening the child to cultural values, in preparing him for later professional training, and in helping him to adjust normally to his environment. In these days, it is doubtful that any child may reasonably be expected to succeed in life if he is denied the opportunity of an education. Such an opportunity, where the state has undertaken to provide it, is a right which must be made available to all on equal terms.

9   We come then to the question presented does segregation of children in public schools solely on the basis of race, even though the physical facilities and other tangible factors may be equal, deprive the children of the minority group of equal educational opportunities. We believe that it does.

10   In *Sweatt v. Painter,* supra, in finding that a segregated law school for Negroes could not provide them equal educational opportunities, this Court relied in large part on those qualities which are incapable of objective measurement but which make for greatness in a law school. In *McLaurin v. Oklahoma State Regents,* supra, the Court, in requiring that a Negro admitted to a white graduate school be treated like all other students, again resorted to *intangible* considerations ... his ability to study, to engage in discussions and exchange views with other students, and, in general, to learn his profession.

Explain how the Court determines the effects of segregation on students?

This passage emphasizes the fact that education has traditionally been a state and local issue. Under what circumstances should the Supreme Court become involved in state and local laws concerning education?

intangible—not a physical object, inherent qualities that cannot be touched or measured

How did legal segregation impact "intangible considerations" such as the ability to study or engage in conversations?

[On the effects of segregation on children]

Such considerations apply with added force to children in grade and high schools. To separate them from others of similar age and qualifications solely because of their race generates a feeling of inferiority as to their status in the community that may affect their hearts and minds in a way unlikely ever to be undone. The effect of this separation on their educational opportunities was well stated by a finding in the Kansas case by a court which nevertheless felt compelled to rule against the Negro plaintiffs. Segregation of white and colored children in public schools has a detrimental effect upon the colored children. The impact is greater when it has the sanction of the law, for the policy of separating the races is usually interpreted as denoting the inferiority of the negro group. A sense of inferiority affects the motivation of a child to learn. Segregation with the sanction of law, therefore, has a tendency to [retard] the educational and mental development of negro children and to deprive them of some of the benefits they would receive in a racial[ly] integrated school system.

11

Why is it crucial for the Court to consider the impact of segregation on younger students?

[Overturning the decision in *Plessy v. Ferguson*]

Whatever may have been the extent of psychological knowledge at the time of *Plessy v. Ferguson,* this finding is amply supported by modern authority. Any language in *Plessy v. Ferguson* contrary to this finding is rejected.

12

Courts are often reluctant to overturn precedent. Identify the legal principle that justices should adhere to precedent.

We conclude that, in the field of public education, the doctrine of separate but equal has no place. Separate educational facilities are inherently unequal. Therefore, we hold that the plaintiffs and others similarly situated for whom the actions have been brought are, by reason of the segregation complained of, deprived of the equal protection of the laws guaranteed by the Fourteenth Amendment. This disposition makes unnecessary any discussion whether such segregation also violates the Due Process Clause of the Fourteenth Amendment.

13

It is so ordered.

14

Impact of *Brown v. Board of Education* on education and on racial segregation

This case is regarded as a landmark ruling today, but it did not have an immediate impact in many segregated school districts. Many school districts did not in fact move "with all deliberate speed" to desegregate their facilities. (This famous phrase appeared in the Supreme Court's opinion in a second case named *Brown v. Board of Education of Topeka,* 349 U.S. 294 (1955, and sometimes called *Brown* II).) Most famously, it took the deployment of federal troops in 1958 by President Dwight Eisenhower to protect nine students who helped integrate Central High School in Little Rock, Arkansas. In other states, where less political pressure was applied by civil-rights groups, legal segregation did not end until well into the 1970s. *Brown v. Board of Education* was a test of whether state and local governments would comply with a controversial Supreme Court ruling and the willingness of the executive branch to help enforce it.

This case only applied to legal segregation in public schools, but it helped to bolster the civil-rights movement and undermine Jim Crow laws by removing the legal sanction of segregation. For this reason, Dr. Martin Luther King, Jr. referred to the case in "Letter from Birmingham Jail" (a required document) when he describes the goals and tactics of the movement.

Brown v. Board of Education of Topeka will be a major focus in Unit 3, especially Chapter 9, Civil Rights. In addition to its impact on the southern civil-rights movement, it also helped to frame later cases about race and schools. *Brown v. Board of Education* ended only *de jure* segregation (segregation by law). In later decades, the Court took up cases seeking to end *de facto* segregation (occurring because of neighborhood, history, and systemic housing discrimination) as well as cases about race-conscious college admissions policies, known as affirmative action programs. In an FRQ, you might be asked to compare one of these later cases with the ruling in *Brown v. Board of Education,* so you should have a solid understanding of the equal protection clause and how it has been interpreted differently over time.

Check for Understanding

1. Identify the constitutional clause at issue in this case, and explain why it was originally added to the Constitution. (See paragraph 4.)
2. Identify the case that served as precedent prior to *Brown v. Board of Education,* and describe the ruling made in this precedent. (Refer to paragraphs 2 and 5.)
3. Explain why the Court struck down the "separate but equal" doctrine.
4. Describe one way the *Brown* decision impacted the civil-rights movement.
5. Describe the long-term judicial impact of the *Brown* decision in cases concerning race and public schools.

▨ SCOTUS Practice Question

Allan Bakke, who was white, was twice denied admission to the University of California, Davis, Medical School. The school reserved sixteen spots in each class for members of underrepresented minority groups deemed qualified, as part of an affirmative action program to address historic discrimination in education and in the medical field. Bakke's college GPA and test scores exceeded those of every minority admitted under the program in the two years Bakke applied. Bakke challenged the decision, asserting that he was denied entry to the school solely on the basis of race.

The Court ordered the University of California to admit Bakke, ruling that an explicit racial quota system violates the Constitution. The ruling made clear, however, that public schools could still take race into account as one of many admissions factors, in order to further the goals of affirmative action.

A. Identify the constitutional clause that is common to both *Regents of the University of California v. Bakke* (1978) and *Brown v. Board of Education* (1954).

B. Based on the constitutional clause listed in part A, explain why the facts of *University of California v. Bakke* led to a different holding from the holding in *Brown v. Board of Education*.

C. Describe one way in which interest groups concerned with equity and access in education could further their policy goals.

Citizens United v. Federal Election Commission

Focus on *Citizens United v. Federal Election Commission* (2010)

Citizens United v. Federal Election Commission (558 U.S. 310) is generally considered a landmark case in the Supreme Court's interpretation of free speech as it relates to campaign finance. Critics believe that the ruling in *Citizens United v. Federal Election Commission* opened the door for unlimited election spending by corporations, allowing companies and businesses to unduly influence elections and promote candidates who will support their financial interests.

Reader Alert!

The opinions rendered in the 5-4 decision in *Citizens United v. Federal Election Commission* are lengthy and very detailed, comprising 183 pages, and often cite precedent from previous cases, such as *Austin v. Michigan Chamber of Commerce* (1990) and *McConnell v. Federal Election Commission* (2003). Five separate opinions were filed. The opinions include the majority opinion written by Justice Kennedy joined by Chief Justice Roberts and Justices Scalia, Alito, and Thomas. Chief Justice Roberts with Justice Alito wrote a concurring opinion. Justice Scalia was joined in part by Justices Alito and Thomas in an opinion criticizing Justice Stevens's dissent. Justice Stevens wrote the dissent, joined by Justices Ginsburg, Breyer, and Sotomayor. The holding in *Citizens United v. Federal Election Commission* was split along ideological lines within the Court, with conservative justices in the majority and liberal justices dissenting.

Facts of the Case

Billions of dollars are spent on congressional and presidential campaigns by candidates and outside groups. Congress, in an attempt to set limits on campaign fundraising and spending, passed the Federal Election Campaign Act (FECA) in 1971 and amended it under the Bipartisan Campaign Reform Act (BCRA), also known as the McCain-Feingold Act, in 2002.

The BCRA restricted corporations and labor unions from financing issue-based advertising on behalf of candidates and prohibited corporations and labor unions from funding "electioneering communications" from their general funds. Instead, they could

236

establish political action committees (PACs) made up of employees or members who could donate to the PAC, which could then donate directly to the candidates. Corporations and unions were prohibited from directly paying for advertisements supporting or opposing a candidate within 30 days of a primary and 60 days of a general election.

Citizens United, a conservative non-profit organization funded partially by corporate donations produced a highly critical documentary film entitled *Hillary: The Movie* in 2008, to persuade voters not to vote for Hillary Clinton in the Democratic presidential primaries. Citizens United wanted to distribute the film to cable company subscribers through video-on-demand services and wanted broadcast television stations to run advertisements for the movie within a 30-day period before the 2008 Democratic primary elections.

Distributing and advertising the film was a violation of Section 441b of BCRA because it was considered to be an "electioneering communication" aired within 30 days of a primary. Citizens United requested a preliminary hearing in district court for an injunction against the FEC to prevent the FEC from applying the act to *Hillary: The Movie*. Citizens United argued that the BCRA was an unconstitutional restriction on political speech by corporations and therefore violated the First Amendment's protections of free speech.

The district court denied the injunction based on precedent established in *Austin v. Michigan Chamber of Commerce* (1990) and *McConnell v. Federal Election Commission* (2003). Both of these cases upheld the authority of state and federal agencies to regulate campaign ads. Using special appellate procedures under BCRA, Citizens United appealed directly to the Supreme Court.

Issue

Do restrictions that prohibit corporate independent election expenditures (as applied to *Hillary: The Movie*) to advocate the election or defeat of a candidate violate the First Amendment's guarantee of free speech? Are the BCRA's disclaimer, disclosure, and reporting requirements constitutional?

Holding/Decision

In a 5-4 decision, the Supreme Court ruled that the BCRA ban on corporate and union spending for independent expenditures and electioneering communications was unconstitutional because it violates protections of free speech under the First Amendment. The majority argued that corporations and labor unions have free speech rights and their rights cannot be restricted any more than that of an individual.

In the majority opinion, Justice Kennedy wrote that political speech is "indispensable to a democracy, which is no less true because the speech comes from a corporation." The Court ruled that the prohibition on corporate spending for independent expenditures and electioneering communications was unconstitutional. The majority maintained that laws restricting political speech must be subject to strict scrutiny.

The Court ruled against the Federal Election Commission and reversed the ban on corporate spending. However, the ruling upheld the existing disclaimer and disclosure requirements. "The government may regulate corporate political speech through disclaimer and disclosure requirements, but it may not suppress that speech altogether."

Excerpt from Majority Opinion

1   Justice Kennedy delivered the opinion of the Court.

[Survey of the law and of previous rulings, *Austin* and *McConnell*]

2   Federal law prohibits corporations and unions from using their general treasury funds to make independent expenditures for speech defined as an "electioneering communication" or for speech expressly advocating the election or defeat of a candidate.... Limits on electioneering communications were upheld in *McConnell v. Federal Election Comm'n*, 540 U.S. 93, 203–209 (2003). The holding of *McConnell* rested to a large extent on an earlier case, *Austin v. Michigan Chamber of Commerce*, 494 U.S. 652 (1990). *Austin* had held that political speech may be banned based on the speaker's corporate identity.

Why were restrictions on independent expenditures upheld in previous decisions?

3   In this case we are asked to reconsider *Austin* and, in effect, *McConnell*. It has been noted that "*Austin* was a significant departure from ancient First Amendment principles," *Federal Election Comm'n v. Wisconsin Right to Life, Inc.*, ... We agree with that conclusion and hold that *stare decisis* does not compel the continued acceptance of *Austin*. The Government may regulate corporate political speech through disclaimer and disclosure requirements, but it may not suppress that speech altogether. We turn to the case now before us.

In *Austin*, the Court held that "political speech may be banned based on the speaker's corporate identity." See the next paragraph, in which the Court mentions an "antidistortion interest." This is the concern that large sums of money may easily distort the political process.

4   *Austin* "uph[eld] a direct restriction on the independent expenditure of funds for political speech for the first time in [this Court's] history." 494 U.S., at 695 (Kennedy, J., dissenting). There, the Michigan Chamber of Commerce sought to use general treasury funds to run a newspaper ad supporting a specific candidate. Michigan law, however, prohibited corporate independent expenditures that supported or opposed any candidate for state office. A violation of the law was punishable as a felony. The Court sustained the speech prohibition.

To bypass *Buckley* and *Bellotti*, the *Austin* Court identified a 5 new governmental interest in limiting political speech: an antidistortion interest. *Austin* found a compelling governmental interest in preventing "the corrosive and distorting effects of immense aggregations of wealth that are accumulated with the help of the corporate form and that have little or no correlation to the public's support for the corporation's political ideas."

The Court is thus confronted with conflicting lines of precedent: a pre-*Austin* line that forbids restrictions on political speech based on the speaker's corporate identity and a post-*Austin* line that permits them. No case before *Austin* had held that Congress could prohibit independent expenditures for political speech based on the speaker's corporate identity. Before *Austin* Congress had enacted legislation for this purpose, and the Government urged the same proposition before this Court.

In its defense of the corporate-speech restrictions in §441b, 7 the Government notes the antidistortion rationale on which *Austin* and its progeny rest in part, yet it all but abandons reliance upon it. It argues instead that two other compelling interests support *Austin*'s holding that corporate expenditure restrictions are constitutional: an anticorruption interest, see 494 U.S., at 678 (Stevens, J., concurring), and a shareholder-protection interest, see *id.*, at 674–675 (Brennan, J., concurring).

[Understanding the rules of the Bipartisan Campaign Reform Act]

Before the Bipartisan Campaign Reform Act of 2002 (BCRA), 8 federal law prohibited—and still does prohibit—corporations and unions from using general treasury funds to make direct contributions to candidates or independent expenditures that expressly advocate the election or defeat of a candidate, through any form of media, in connection with certain qualified federal elections. 2 U.S.C. §441b (2000 ed.); see *McConnell, supra,* at 204, and n. 87; *Federal Election Comm'n v. Massachusetts Citizens for Life, Inc.,* 479 U.S. 238, 249 (1986) *(MCFL)*. BCRA §203 amended §441b to prohibit any "electioneering communication" as well. 2 U.S.C. §441b(b)(2) (2006 ed.). An electioneering communication is defined as "any broadcast, cable, or satellite communication" that "refers to a clearly identified candidate for Federal office" and is made within 30 days of a primary or 60 days of a general

----

Justice Kennedy contends that *Austin* had gone too far in restricting corporations. Note also that Justice Kennedy is trying to resolve a conflict among the decisions.

Two other interests come into play: The anticorruption interest means not allowing organizations (or individuals) to give money in exchange for political favors. The shareholder-protection interest means preventing shareholders in a company from being forced to fund corporate speech that they may not agree with.

Note that previous legislation prohibited campaign donations from "general treasury funds"—the organization's regular budget.

Note the Court's definition of an "electioneering communication."

election. §434(f)(3)(A). The Federal Election Commission's (FEC) regulations further define an electioneering communication as a communication that is "publicly distributed." 11 CFR §100.29(a)(2) (2009). "In the case of a candidate for nomination for President ... *publicly distributed* means" that the communication "[c]an be received by 50,000 or more persons in a State where a primary election ... is being held within 30 days." §100.29(b)(3)(ii). Corporations and unions are barred from using their general treasury funds for express advocacy or electioneering communications. They may establish, however, a "separate segregated fund" (known as a political action committee, or PAC) for these purposes. 2 U.S.C. §441b(b)(2). The moneys received by the segregated fund are limited to donations from stockholders and employees of the corporation or, in the case of unions, members of the union. *Ibid.*

How may corporations fund electioneering communications? Note the use of the term *political action committee.*

[On the political action committee, Citizens United, and free speech]

9   Citizens United wanted to make *Hillary* available through video-on-demand within 30 days of the 2008 primary elections. It feared, however, that both the film and the ads would be covered by §441b's ban on corporate-funded independent expenditures, thus subjecting the corporation to civil and criminal penalties under §437g. In December 2007, Citizens United sought declaratory and injunctive relief against the FEC. It argued that (1) §441b is unconstitutional as applied to *Hillary;* and (2) BCRA's disclaimer and disclosure requirements, BCRA §§201 and 311, are unconstitutional as applied to *Hillary* and to the three ads for the movie.

10   Section 441b's prohibition on corporate independent expenditures is thus a ban on speech. As a "restriction on the amount of money a person or group can spend on political communication during a campaign," that statute "necessarily reduces the quantity of expression by restricting the number of issues discussed, the depth of their exploration, and the size of the audience reached." *Buckley v. Valeo*, 424 U.S. 1, 19 (1976) *(per curiam).* Were the Court to uphold these restrictions, the Government could repress speech by silencing certain voices at any of the various points in the speech process. ... If §441b applied to individuals, no one would believe that it is merely a time, place, or manner restriction

on speech. Its purpose and effect are to silence entities whose voices the Government deems to be suspect.

Speech is an essential mechanism of democracy, for it is the means to hold officials accountable to the people. See *Buckley*, *supra*, at 14–15 ("In a republic where the people are sovereign, the ability of the citizenry to make informed choices among candidates for office is essential"). The right of citizens to inquire, to hear, to speak, and to use information to reach consensus is a precondition to enlightened self-government and a necessary means to protect it. The First Amendment "'has its fullest and most urgent application' to speech uttered during a campaign for political office." *Eu* v. *San Francisco County Democratic Central Comm.*, 489 U.S. 214, 223 (1989) (quoting *Monitor Patriot Co. v. Roy*, 401 U.S. 265, 272 (1971)); see *Buckley*, *supra*, at 14 ("Discussion of public issues and debate on the qualifications of candidates are integral to the operation of the system of government established by our Constitution").

11 | Citing several cases Justice Kennedy confirms that the Court has recognized that political speech does not lose First Amendment protection "simply because its source is a corporation."

[Concerning First Amendment protections]

For these reasons, political speech must prevail against laws that would suppress it, whether by design or inadvertence. Laws that burden political speech are "subject to strict scrutiny," which requires the Government to prove that the restriction "furthers a compelling interest and is narrowly tailored to achieve that interest." *WRTL*, 551 U.S., at 464 (opinion of Roberts, C. J.). While it might be maintained that political speech simply cannot be banned or restricted as a categorical matter, see *Simon & Schuster*, 502 U.S., at 124 (Kennedy, J., concurring in judgment), the quoted language from *WRTL* provides a sufficient framework for protecting the relevant First Amendment interests in this case. We shall employ it here.

12 | Note the use of the term *strict scrutiny* and the definition that follows. Strict scrutiny is a difficult standard for the government to meet before it may restrict political speech.

Premised on mistrust of governmental power, the First Amendment stands against attempts to disfavor certain subjects or viewpoints. See, *e.g.*, *United States* v. *Playboy Entertainment Group, Inc.*, 529 U.S. 803, 813 (2000) (striking down content-based restriction). Prohibited, too, are restrictions distinguishing among different speakers, allowing speech by some but not others. See *First Nat. Bank of Boston* v. *Bellotti*, 435 U.S. 765, 784 (1978). As instruments to censor, these categories are interrelated: Speech

13

restrictions based on the identity of the speaker are all too often simply a means to control content.

14   Quite apart from the purpose or effect of regulating content, moreover, the Government may commit a constitutional wrong when by law it identifies certain preferred speakers. By taking the right to speak from some and giving it to others, the Government deprives the disadvantaged person or class of the right to use speech to strive to establish worth, standing, and respect for the speaker's voice. The Government may not by these means deprive the public of the right and privilege to determine for itself what speech and speakers are worthy of consideration. The First Amendment protects speech and speaker, and the ideas that flow from each.

15   We find no basis for the proposition that, in the context of political speech, the Government may impose restrictions on certain disfavored speakers. Both history and logic lead us to this conclusion.

16   The Court has thus rejected the argument that political speech of corporations or other associations should be treated differently under the First Amendment simply because such associations are not "natural persons." *Id.,* at 776; see *id.,* at 780, n. 16. Cf. *id.,* at 828 (Rehnquist, J., dissenting).

[Overruling *Austin* and *McConnell*]

17 The First Amendment does not permit Congress to make these categorical distinctions based on the corporate identity of the speaker and the content of the political speech.

18   Due consideration leads to this conclusion: *Austin,* 494 U.S. 652, should be and now is overruled. We return to the principle established in *Buckley* and *Bellotti* that the Government may not suppress political speech on the basis of the speaker's corporate identity. No sufficient governmental interest justifies limits on the political speech of nonprofit or for-profit corporations.

19   *Austin* is overruled, so it provides no basis for allowing the Government to limit corporate independent expenditures. As the Government appears to concede, overruling *Austin* "effectively invalidate[s] not only BCRA Section 203, but also 2 U.S.C. 441b's prohibition on the use of corporate treasury funds for express advocacy." Brief for Appellee 33, n. 12. Section 441b's restrictions on corporate independent expenditures are therefore invalid and cannot be applied to *Hillary*.

What does the First Amendment protect?

Given our conclusion we are further required to overrule the part of *McConnell* that upheld BCRA §203's extension of §441b's restrictions on corporate independent expenditures.

20 | Why does the Court overturn its recent decisions in *Austin* and *McConnell*?

Excerpt from Dissenting Opinion

Justice Stevens, with whom Justice Ginsburg, Justice Breyer, and Justice Sotomayor join, concurring in part and dissenting in part.

The real issue in this case concerns how, not if, the appellant may finance its electioneering. Citizens United is a wealthy non-profit corporation that runs a political action committee (PAC) with millions of dollars in assets. Under the Bipartisan Campaign Reform Act of 2002 (BCRA), it could have used those assets to televise and promote *Hillary: The Movie* wherever and whenever it wanted to. It also could have spent unrestricted sums to broadcast *Hillary* at any time other than the 30 days before the last primary election. Neither Citizens United's nor any other corporation's speech has been "banned," *ante*, at 1. All that the parties dispute is whether Citizens United had a right to use the funds in its general treasury to pay for broadcasts during the 30-day period. The notion that the First Amendment dictates an affirmative answer to that question is, in my judgment, profoundly misguided. Even more misguided is the notion that the Court must rewrite the law relating to campaign expenditures by *for-profit* corporations and unions to decide this case.

22

How could Citizens United have broadcast *Hillary: The Movie* without violating the law?

The basic premise underlying the Court's ruling is its iteration, and constant reiteration, of the proposition that the First Amendment bars regulatory distinctions based on a speaker's identity, including its "identity" as a corporation. While that glittering generality has rhetorical appeal, it is not a correct statement of the law. Nor does it tell us when a corporation may engage in electioneering that some of its shareholders oppose. It does not even resolve the specific question whether Citizens United may be required to finance some of its messages with the money in its PAC. The conceit that corporations must be treated identically to natural persons in the political sphere is not only inaccurate but also inadequate to justify the Court's disposition of this case.

23

The dissent makes a distinction between corporate and human speakers. Justice Stevens quotes Chief Justice John Marshall, "A corporation is an artificial being, invisible, intangible, and existing only in contemplation of law. Being a mere creature of law, it possesses only those properties which the charter of its creation confers upon it."

[Contrasting a corporation and a natural person]

24 In the context of election to public office, the distinction between corporate and human speakers is significant. Although they make enormous contributions to our society, corporations are not actually members of it. They cannot vote or run for office. Because they may be managed and controlled by nonresidents, their interests may conflict in fundamental respects with the interests of eligible voters. The financial resources, legal structure, and instrumental orientation of corporations raise legitimate concerns about their role in the electoral process. Our lawmakers have a compelling constitutional basis, if not also a democratic duty, to take measures designed to guard against the potentially deleterious effects of corporate spending in local and national races.

Justice Stevens contends that the Court deliberately disregards precedent and the principle of *stare decisis*. His general argument refers to the danger of weakening the voice of the individual against corporate political participation.

25   The Court's ruling threatens to undermine the integrity of elected institutions across the Nation. The path it has taken to reach its outcome will, I fear, do damage to this institution. Before turning to the question whether to overrule *Austin* and part of *McConnell*, it is important to explain why the Court should not be deciding that question.

[On the reasons for not overruling *Austin* and *McConnell*]

stare decisis—"to stand by things decided"; the legal principle of determining litigation according to precedent and not overturning settled doctrine. Note Justice Stevens's argument here and in the following paragraphs.

26 The final principle of judicial process that the majority violates is the most transparent: *stare decisis*. I am not an absolutist when it comes to *stare decisis*, in the campaign finance area or in any other. No one is. But if this principle is to do any meaningful work in supporting the rule of law, it must at least demand a significant justification, beyond the preferences of five Justices,

27   The Court's central argument for why *stare decisis* ought to be trumped is that it does not like *Austin*. The opinion "was not well reasoned," our colleagues assert, and it conflicts with First Amendment principles. *Ante*, at 47–48. This, of course, is the Court's merits argument, the many defects in which we will soon consider. I am perfectly willing to concede that if one of our precedents were dead wrong in its reasoning or irreconcilable with the rest of our doctrine, there would be a compelling basis for revisiting it. But neither is true of *Austin*, ...

28   Having explained why this is not an appropriate case in which to revisit *Austin* and *McConnell* and why these decisions

sit perfectly well with "First Amendment principles," *ante*, at 1, 48, I come at last to the interests that are at stake. The majority recognizes that *Austin* and *McConnell* may be defended on anti-corruption, antidistortion, and shareholder protection rationales. *Ante*, at 32–46. It badly errs both in explaining the nature of these rationales, which overlap and complement each other, and in applying them to the case at hand.

[Highlighting the anticorruption interest]

Undergirding the majority's approach to the merits is the claim that the only "sufficiently important governmental interest in preventing corruption or the appearance of corruption" is one that is "limited to quid pro quo corruption." *Ante*, at 43. This is the same "crabbed view of corruption" that was espoused by Justice Kennedy in *McConnell* and squarely rejected by the Court in that case. 540 U.S., at 152. While it is true that we have not always spoken about corruption in a clear or consistent voice, the approach taken by the majority cannot be right, in my judgment. It disregards our constitutional history and the fundamental demands of a democratic society.

29

On numerous occasions we have recognized Congress' legitimate interest in preventing the money that is spent on elections from exerting an "'undue influence on an officeholder's judgment'" and from creating "'the appearance of such influence,'" beyond the sphere of *quid pro quo* relationships. ... Corruption can take many forms. Bribery may be the paradigm case. But the difference between selling a vote and selling access is a matter of degree, not kind. And selling access is not qualitatively different from giving special preference to those who spent money on one's behalf. Corruption operates along a spectrum, and the majority's apparent belief that *quid pro quo* arrangements can be neatly demarcated from other improper influences does not accord with the theory or reality of politics. It certainly does not accord with the record Congress developed in passing BCRA, a record that stands as a remarkable testament to the energy and ingenuity with which corporations, unions, lobbyists, and politicians may go about scratching each other's backs—and which amply supported Congress' determination to target a limited set of especially destructive practices

30 How does Justice Stevens define corruption?

How does the dissent distinguish between corporations and people? What is the result of allowing corporations to run political ads until election day?

Consequently, when corporations grab up the prime broadcasting slots on the eve of an election, they can flood the market

31

with advocacy that bears "little or no correlation" to the ideas of natural persons or to any broader notion of the public good, 494 U.S., at 660. The opinions of real people may be marginalized. "The expenditure restrictions of [2 U.S.C.] §441b are thus meant to ensure that competition among actors in the political arena is truly competition among ideas." *MCFL*, 479 U.S., at 259.

[On the effects of too much money]

32   In addition to this immediate drowning out of noncorporate voices, there may be deleterious effects that follow soon thereafter. Corporate "domination" of electioneering, *Austin*, 494 U.S., at 659, can generate the impression that corporations dominate our democracy. When citizens turn on their televisions and radios before an election and hear only corporate electioneering, they may lose faith in their capacity, as citizens, to influence public policy. A Government captured by corporate interests, they may come to believe, will be neither responsive to their needs nor willing to give their views a fair hearing. The predictable result is cynicism and disenchantment: an increased perception that large spenders "'call the tune'" and a reduced "'willingness of voters to take part in democratic governance.'" *McConnell*, 540 U.S., at 144 (quoting *Shrink Missouri*, 528 U.S., at 390). To the extent that corporations are allowed to exert undue influence in electoral races, the speech of the eventual winners of those races may also be chilled. Politicians who fear that a certain corporation can make or break their reelection chances may be cowed into silence about that corporation. On a variety of levels, unregulated corporate electioneering might diminish the ability of citizens to "hold officials accountable to the people," *ante*, at 23, and disserve the goal of a public debate that is "uninhibited, robust, and wide-open," *New York Times Co. v. Sullivan*, 376 U.S. 254, 270 (1964). At the least, I stress again, a legislature is entitled to credit these concerns and to take tailored measures in response.

33   The majority's unwillingness to distinguish between corporations and humans similarly blinds it to the possibility that corporations' "war chests" and their special "advantages" in the legal realm, *Austin*, 494 U.S., at 659, may translate into special advantages in the market for legislation. When large numbers of citizens have a common stake in a measure that is under consideration, it may be very difficult for them to coordinate resources on behalf of their position. The corporate form, by contrast, "provides a

simple way to channel rents to only those who have paid their dues, as it were. If you do not own stock, you do not benefit from the larger dividends or appreciation in the stock price caused by the passage of private interest legislation." ... Corporations, that is, are uniquely equipped to seek laws that favor their owners, not simply because they have a lot of money but because of their legal and organizational structure. Remove all restrictions on their electioneering, and the door may be opened to a type of rent seeking that is "far more destructive" than what noncorporations are capable of. *Ibid.* It is for reasons such as these that our campaign finance jurisprudence has long appreciated that "the 'differing structures and purposes' of different entities 'may require different forms of regulation in order to protect the integrity of the electoral process.' "

In a democratic society, the longstanding consensus on the need to limit corporate campaign spending should outweigh the wooden application of judge-made rules. The majority's rejection of this principle "elevate[s] corporations to a level of deference which has not been seen at least since the days when substantive due process was regularly used to invalidate regulatory legislation thought to unfairly impinge upon established economic interests." *Bellotti*, 435 U.S., at 817, n. 13 (White, J., dissenting). At bottom, the Court's opinion is thus a rejection of the common sense of the American people, who have recognized a need to prevent corporations from undermining self-government since the founding, and who have fought against the distinctive corrupting potential of corporate electioneering since the days of Theodore Roosevelt. It is a strange time to repudiate that common sense. While American democracy is imperfect, few outside the majority of this Court would have thought its flaws included a dearth of corporate money in politics.

34 Why does the dissent believe that the majority decision endangers democratic values?

Impact of *Citizens United v. Federal Election Commission* on campaign financing

The AP® U.S. Government and Politics curriculum specifically requires you to understand the impact of federal policies on campaigning and how electoral rules continue to be contested by both sides of the political spectrum. This includes how campaign financing and spending affect the election process.

The decision in *Citizens United v. Federal Election Commission* generated controversy immediately. Proponents of a broad view of the First Amendment welcomed it as an unquestionable victory for freedom of speech, while critics saw it as an attempt to rewrite campaign finance law in a way that threatened free and fair elections.

In a related case, *SpeechNow.org v. Federal Election Commission* (2010), the U.S. Court of Appeals for the D.C. Circuit used the *Citizens United* case as precedent when it struck down limits on the contributions to groups that specifically supported political candidates. While contributions to PACs had previously been limited to $5,000 per person per year, spending became virtually unlimited, leading to the creation of super PACs. The result has been an outpouring of money into these super PACs and a dramatic rise in the cost of campaigning.

Check for Understanding

1. Describe the political activity Citizens United planned to engage in during the 2008 primary election.
2. Describe how the political activity Citizens United planned to engage in during the 2008 primary election was illegal under BCRA.
3. Describe how Citizens United could have avoided violating BCRA.
4. Explain why the Court ruled in favor of Citizens United.
5. Explain why *Citizens United v. Federal Election Commission* is considered a landmark decision.

SCOTUS Practice Question

The Michigan Campaign Finance Act prohibited corporations "from using treasury money for independent expenditures to support or oppose candidates in elections for state offices." The state had enacted the law because of "the unique legal and economic characteristics of corporations necessitate some regulation of their political expenditures to avoid corruption or the appearance of corruption." Although corporations were prohibited by state law from using their general funds to support the election or defeat of state-level candidates, corporations were allowed to set up independent funds designated exclusively for political purposes. The Michigan Chamber of Commerce wanted to use its general funds to publish a newspaper advertisement to support a candidate for the Michigan House of Representatives.

In *Austin v. Michigan Chamber of Commerce* (1990), the Court held by a vote of 6-3 that the prohibition, under the Michigan law, against corporations from making independent expenditures from their general funds did not violate the U.S. Constitution. The Court held that the Chamber of Commerce was similar to a business. Furthermore, the Court found that the Michigan Campaign Finance Act was narrowly constructed and implemented to achieve the important goal of maintaining "... a compelling state interest: preventing corruption or the appearance of corruption in the political arena by reducing the threat that huge corporate treasuries, which are amassed with the aid of favorable state laws and have little or no correlation to the public's support for the corporation's political ideas, will be used to influence unfairly election outcomes."

A. Identify the constitutional clause that is common to both *Austin v. Michigan Chamber of Commerce* (1990) and *Citizens United v. Federal Election Commission* (2010).

B. Based on the constitutional clause identified in part A, explain why the facts of *Citizens United v. Federal Election Commission* led to a different holding from the holding in *Austin v. Michigan Chamber of Commerce*.

C. Describe an action that Congress could take to limit the effects of *Citizens United v. Federal Election Commission*.

Baker v. Carr

Focus on *Baker v. Carr* (1962)

In the United States, each state is responsible for drawing their legislative district lines for both the state and federal legislatures. *Baker v. Carr,* 369 U.S. 186 (1962), is about whether federal courts could rule on the way states draw their state legislative district lines.

In the mid- to late twentieth century, populations began increasingly shifting from rural areas to cities. Many states did not redraw their state legislative district lines as populations shifted. The results were districts unequal in population size. Some voters filed lawsuits alleging inequity among districts with small and large populations, but the federal courts would not hear the cases because they viewed these as political questions (not suitable for judicial decision making). Cases questioning legislative apportionment were routinely dismissed.

Facts of the Case

In the Tennessee state legislature, each of the 95 counties elected one member of the state's general assembly, as determined by the 1900 census. The population distribution of the state changed substantially between 1901 and 1950. More people moved to Memphis, which is in Shelby County. Shelby County had one representative in the state legislature, and rural countries with smaller populations also had one representative, even though the population of Shelby County was substantially larger. The state constitution required revising the legislative districts every 10 years after the federal census, but the state lawmakers had not done so.

Charles Baker, a voter in Shelby County, believed that he and others in the district were being denied the Fourteenth Amendment guarantee of equal protection under the law because his vote in a district with a large population was "devalued" or diluted compared to the rural district with a smaller population.

The state of Tennessee argued that the courts could not provide a solution because this was a political question. The district court dismissed Baker's complaint on these grounds, and Baker appealed that decision to the Supreme Court.

Issue

Do federal courts have jurisdiction over cases of state legislative apportionment?

▓ Holding/Decision

The Supreme Court decided in favor of Baker holding that the federal courts have the authority to enforce the Fourteenth Amendment's equal protection of the law against state officials if the state legislative districts are disproportionately populated.

▓ Reader Alert!

The court did not decide whether Baker's vote was diluted, but it did decide that cases of legislative apportionment were justiciable (properly decided in court).

Excerpt from Majority Opinion

MR. JUSTICE BRENNAN delivered the opinion of the Court.   1

[Overview of the powers of the judiciary]

Article III, 2, of the Federal Constitution provides that   2

> "The judicial Power shall extend to all Cases, in Law and Equity,   3
> arising under this Constitution, the Laws of the United States, and
> Treaties made, or which shall be made, under their Authority. ..."

It is clear that the cause of action is one which "arises under"   4
the Federal Constitution. The complaint alleges that the 1901
statute effects an apportionment that deprives the appellants of
the equal protection of the laws in violation of the Fourteenth
Amendment. Dismissal of the complaint upon the ground of lack
of jurisdiction of the subject matter would, therefore, be justified
only if that claim were "so attenuated and unsubstantial as to be
absolutely devoid of merit,"... That the claim is unsubstantial
must be "very plain."... Since the District Court obviously and
correctly did not deem the asserted federal constitutional claim
unsubstantial and frivolous, it should not have dismissed the complaint for want of jurisdiction of the subject matter.

Why did the district court make a mistake in dismissing the case?

An unbroken line of our precedents sustains the federal   5
courts' jurisdiction of the subject matter of federal constitutional
claims of this nature. The first cases involved the redistricting of
States for the purpose of electing Representatives to the Federal
Congress.

[Who brought the suit, and can they bring such a suit?]

6   The complaint was filed by residents of Davidson, Hamilton, Knox, Montgomery, and Shelby Counties. Each is a person allegedly qualified to vote for members of the General Assembly representing his county. These appellants sued "on their own behalf and on behalf of all qualified voters of their respective counties, and further, on behalf of all voters of the State of Tennessee who are similarly situated. ..."

standing—legally, demonstrating a sufficient interest to bring or participate in a lawsuit

7   We hold that the appellants do have *standing* to maintain this suit. Our decisions plainly support this conclusion. Many of the cases have assumed, rather than articulated, the premise in deciding the merits of similar claims. And *Colegrove v. Green, supra,* squarely held that voters who allege facts showing disadvantage to themselves as individuals have standing to sue. A number of cases decided after *Colegrove* recognized the standing of the voters there involved to bring those actions.

capricious—unpredictable and unaccountable

8   These appellants seek relief in order to protect or vindicate an interest of their own, and of those similarly situated. Their constitutional claim is, in substance, that the 1901 statute constitutes arbitrary and *capricious* state action, offensive to the Fourteenth Amendment in its irrational disregard of the standard of apportionment prescribed by the State's Constitution or of any standard, effecting a gross disproportion of representation to voting population. The injury which appellants assert is that this classification disfavors the voters in the counties in which they reside, placing them in a position of constitutionally unjustifiable inequality *vis-à-vis* voters in irrationally favored counties. A citizen's right to a vote free of arbitrary impairment by state action has been judicially recognized as a right secured by the Constitution when such impairment resulted from dilution by a false tally, *cf. United States v. Classic,* 313 U.S. 299; or by a refusal to count votes from arbitrarily selected precincts, *cf. United States v. Mosley,* 238 U.S. 383, or by a stuffing of the ballot box, *cf. Ex parte Siebold,* 100 U.S. 371; *United States v. Saylor,* 322 U.S. 385.

vis-à-vis—with regard to, in comparison with

Why was Baker entitled to bring the case under the Fourteenth Amendment?

9   We conclude that the complaint's allegations of a denial of equal protection present a justiciable constitutional cause of action upon which appellants are entitled to a trial and a decision. The right asserted is within the reach of judicial protection under the Fourteenth Amendment.

The judgment of the District Court is reversed, and the cause 10
is remanded for further proceedings consistent with this opinion.

The holding of the Supreme Court did not require Shelby County's district to be redrawn. What happens after a case is remanded?

Excerpt from Dissenting Opinion

MR. JUSTICE FRANKFURTER, whom MR. JUSTICE HARLAN 11
joins, dissenting.

[On a differing view of the powers of the judiciary]

The Court today reverses a uniform course of decision established by 12
a dozen cases, including one by which the very claim now sustained
was unanimously rejected only five years ago. The impressive body
of rulings thus cast aside reflected the equally uniform course of our
political history regarding the relationship between population and
legislative representation—a wholly different matter from denial of
the franchise to individuals because of race, color, religion or sex.
Such a massive repudiation of the experience of our whole past in
asserting destructively novel judicial power demands a detailed analysis of the role of this Court in our constitutional scheme. Disregard
of inherent limits in the effective exercise of the Court's "judicial
Power" not only presages the futility of judicial intervention in the
essentially political conflict of forces by which the relation between
population and representation has time out of mind been, and now
is, determined. It may well impair the Court's position as the ultimate organ of "the supreme Law of the Land" in that vast range of
legal problems, often strongly entangled in popular feeling, on which
this Court must pronounce. The Court's authority—possessed of
neither the purse nor the sword—ultimately rests on sustained public confidence in its moral sanction. Such feeling must be nourished
by the Court's complete detachment, in fact and in appearance, from
political entanglements and by abstention from injecting itself into
the clash of political forces in political settlements.

[On intrusions by the judiciary into political matters]

Recent legislation, creating a district appropriately described as 13
"an atrocity of ingenuity," is not unique. Considering the gross

What is gerrymander-ing, and how does it create districts that are "an atrocity of ingenuity"?

inequality among legislative electoral units within almost every State, the Court naturally shrinks from asserting that, in districting, at least substantial equality is a constitutional requirement enforceable by courts. Room continues to be allowed for weighting. This, of course, implies that geography, economics, urban-rural conflict, and all the other non-legal factors which have throughout our history entered into political districting are to some extent not to be ruled out in the undefined vista now opened up by review in the federal courts of state reapportionments. To some extent—aye, there's the rub. In effect, today's decision empowers the courts of the country to devise what should constitute the proper composition of the legislatures of the fifty States. If state courts should for one reason or another find themselves unable to discharge this task, the duty of doing so is put on the federal courts or on this Court, if State views do not satisfy this Court's notion of what is proper districting.

14   We were soothingly told at the bar of this Court that we need not worry about the kind of remedy a court could effectively fashion once the abstract constitutional right to have courts pass on a statewide system of electoral districting is recognized as a matter of judicial rhetoric, because legislatures would heed the Court's admonition. This is not only a euphoric hope. It implies a sorry confession of judicial impotence in place of a frank acknowledgment that there is not under our Constitution a judicial remedy for every political mischief, for every undesirable exercise of legislative power. The Framers, carefully and with deliberate forethought, refused so to enthrone the judiciary. In this situation, as in others of like nature, appeal for relief does not belong here. Appeal must be to an informed, civically militant electorate. In a democratic society like ours, relief must come through an aroused popular conscience that sears the conscience of the people's representatives. In any event, there is nothing judicially more unseemly nor more self-defeating than for this Court to make *in terrorem* pronouncements, to indulge in merely empty rhetoric, sounding a word of promise to the ear sure to be disappointing to the hope.

[On restricting the powers of the states]

15 This is the latest in the series of cases in which the Equal Protection and Due Process Clauses of the Fourteenth Amendment have been invoked in federal courts as restrictions upon the power of

> Why are the dissenters wary of allowing federal courts to make decisions about legislative districts?

> *in terrorem*—filled with (empty) legal threats

the States to allocate electoral weight among the voting populations of their various geographical subdivisions.

A federal court enforcing the Federal Constitution is not, to be sure, bound by the remedial doctrines of the state courts. But it must consider as pertinent to the propriety or impropriety of exercising its jurisdiction those state law effects of its decree which it cannot itself control. A federal court cannot provide the authority requisite to make a legislature the proper governing body of the State of Tennessee. And it cannot be doubted that the striking down of the statute here challenged on equal protection grounds, no less than on grounds of failure to reapportion decennially, would deprive the State of all valid apportionment legislation and—under the ruling in *McCanless*—deprive the State of an effective law-based legislative branch.

16 | What problems in carrying out this decision do the dissenting justices anticipate? How do these problems relate to the principle of federalism?

Impact of *Baker v. Carr* on legislative apportionment

This decision was a dramatic break with former tradition of the Court not reviewing cases on legislative apportionment. This decision established a precedent that was followed by subsequent courts allowing residents to challenge their legislative districts, and today, challenges to legislative redistricting after the census are fairly common.

This case is important in the AP® U.S. Government and Politics course for several reasons. First, it supports the Essential Knowledge (EK) in the curriculum framework that "Gerrymandering, redistricting, and unequal representation of constituencies have been partially addressed by the Supreme Court decision in *Baker v. Carr*," which led to the "one person, one vote" doctrine in *Shaw v. Reno* (1993) (another required case in the AP® U.S. Government course). Second, this case reinforces the application of the Fourteenth Amendment's equal protection clause in the context of legislative districts.

Check for Understanding

1. Describe the facts of this case.
2. Identify the constitutional clause that is the basis for the Court's decision.
3. Describe the arguments made on behalf of the state of Tennessee.
4. Describe Baker's argument that the federal courts have the authority to review state legislative districts.
5. How will this ruling impact future redistricting cases?

▪ **SCOTUS Practice Question**

James Wesberry resided in a Georgia congressional district with a population two to three times greater than that of other congressional districts in the state. Wesberry argued that his vote was diluted as a result of the state's failure to reapportion the districts with equal population sizes. The constitutional question argued before the Supreme Court was whether or not Georgia's congressional districts violated the Fourteenth Amendment.

In a 6-3 decision in *Wesberry v. Sanders* (1964), the Court ruled for Wesberry and held that congressional districts must have roughly equal population sizes when this is feasible and that legislative apportionment was justiciable.

A. Identify the constitutional clause that is common to both *Wesberry v. Sanders* (1964) and *Baker v. Carr* (1962).

B. Based on the constitutional clause identified in part A, explain why the facts of *Baker v. Carr* led to a similar holding as the holding in *Wesberry v. Sanders*.

C. Describe one way in which states may draw legislative district boundaries to favor a particular group of voters.

Shaw v. Reno

Focus on *Shaw v. Reno* (1993)

Shaw v. Reno, 509 U.S. 630 (1993), deals with the issue of redistricting and racial gerrymandering. The district in question, North Carolina's Twelfth District, was drawn to create a minority-majority district with the intent that the district would elect a minority representative. This case required the application of a strict scrutiny standard to the use of race in drawing the boundaries of congressional districts. Laws subject to strict scrutiny require a government to prove that the measure or restriction furthers a compelling interest and is narrowly tailored to achieve that interest. This case limited the application of both Section 2 and Section 5 of the Voting Rights Act of 1965 (updated several times, most recently in 2006).

Reader Alert!

An idea that might be tricky in understanding *Shaw v. Reno* (1993) is that the Supreme Court did not rule on the constitutionality of the congressional district in question. (This is similar to the ruling by the majority in *Baker v. Carr*.) The Court remanded the case back to the district court with instructions to apply a strict scrutiny standard. When using this standard, the policy must serve a "compelling government interest," be "narrowly tailored" to achieve that interest and must use the least restrictive means necessary. While the district court upheld the congressional district in question, the district was again challenged in *Shaw v. Hunt* (1996) and, in another 5-4 decision, was found a second time to violate the Fourteenth Amendment's equal protection clause. These decisions have been used to limit the use of race in drawing congressional districts.

Facts of the Case

North Carolina gained a twelfth congressional district as a result of the 1990 census. As a result, the North Carolina General Assembly engaged in the process of redistricting, in which the state redraws congressional district boundaries to reflect internal changes in population and, in this case, the addition of another congressional district. The North Carolina General Assembly created one minority-majority district in the redistricting plan. North Carolina had to submit the redistricting plan to the federal government for approval as a result of the Voting Rights Act. Section 5 of the Voting Rights Act required certain jurisdictions with a history of discrimination against African American voters to submit changes in voting processes, such as redistricting, for approval to ensure that the changes did not disadvantage minority voters. The U.S. attorney general at the time, Janet Reno, sent the plan back the General Assembly with the requirement that the assembly create another minority-majority district. The General Assembly did so. The resulting district, the Twelfth Congressional District stretched, "approximately 160 miles along Interstate 85 and, for much of its length, is no wider than the I-85 corridor." This oddly shaped district led five North Carolina residents to sue. They argued the district was drawn in an unconstitutional manner. The district court dismissed the case, and the residents appealed to the Supreme Court.

Issue

Does the Twelfth Congressional District of North Carolina, which was drawn as a minority-majority district, violate the equal protection clause of the Fourteenth Amendment?

Holding/Decision

In a 5-4 decision, the Court sent the case back to the district court with the instruction to use a strict scrutiny standard. Using this standard, the district court ruled the Twelfth Congressional District of North Carolina fulfilled a compelling governmental interest in complying with the Voting Rights Act and was, therefore, permissible. The district was challenged again in *Shaw v. Hunt* (1996) and the Supreme Court found it unconstitutional a second time.

Excerpt from Majority Opinion

[On gerrymandering and strangely shaped districts]

1   JUSTICE O'CONNOR delivered the opinion of the Court.

2   The first of the two majority-black districts contained in the revised plan, District 1, is somewhat hook shaped. Centered in the northeast portion of the State, it moves southward until it tapers to a narrow band; then, with finger-like extensions, it reaches far into the southernmost part of the State near the South Carolina border. District 1 has been compared to a *"Rorschach ink-blot test," Shaw v. Barr, 808* F. Supp. 461, 476 (EDNC 1992) (Voorhees, C. J., concurring in part and dissenting in part), and a "bug splattered on a windshield," Wall Street Journal, Feb. 4, 1992, p. A14.

Rorschach ink-blot test—a psychological test involving complicated shapes

[On the shape of the Twelfth District]

The second majority-black district, District 12, is even more unusually shaped. It is approximately 160 miles long and, for much of its length, no wider than the 1-85 corridor. It winds in snakelike fashion through tobacco country, financial centers, and manufacturing areas "until it gobbles in enough enclaves of black neighborhoods." 808 F. Supp., at 476-477 (Voorhees, C. J., concurring in part and dissenting in part). Northbound and southbound drivers on 1-85 sometimes find themselves in separate districts in one county, only to "trade" districts when they enter the next county. Of the 10 counties through which District 12 passes, 5 are cut into 3 different districts; even towns are divided. At one point the district remains *contiguous* only because it intersects at a single point with two other districts before crossing over them.

3 Why does the majority opinion describe the peculiar shape of the Twelfth District?

contiguous— adjacent, sharing a border

[Considering the historical background of voter suppression]

"The right to vote freely for the candidate of one's choice is of the essence of a democratic society. ..." *Reynolds v. Sims,* 377 U.S., at 555. For much of our Nation's history, that right sadly has been denied to many because of race. The Fifteenth Amendment, ratified in 1870 after a bloody Civil War, promised unequivocally that "[t]he right of citizens of the United States to vote" no longer would be "denied or abridged... by any State on account of race, color, or previous condition of servitude." U.S. Const., Amdt. 15, § 1.

4

But "[a] number of states... refused to take no for an answer and continued to circumvent the fifteenth amendment's prohibition through the use of both subtle and blunt instruments, perpetuating ugly patterns of pervasive racial discrimination."

5 How did the Voting Rights Act protect African Americans in exercising the right to vote guaranteed by the Fifteenth Amendment?

[On the content of the appellants' claim]

Our focus is on appellants' claim that the State engaged in unconstitutional racial gerrymandering. That argument strikes a powerful historical chord: It is unsettling how closely the North Carolina plan resembles the most egregious racial gerrymanders of the past.

6

An understanding of the nature of appellants' claim is critical to our resolution of the case. In their complaint, appellants did not claim that the General Assembly's reapportionment plan

7

unconstitutionally "diluted" white voting strength. They did not even claim to be white. Rather, appellants' complaint alleged that the deliberate segregation of voters into separate districts on the basis of race violated their constitutional right to participate in a "color-blind" electoral process.

Is a color-blind constitution an achievable goal? Should it be?

8   Despite their invocation of the ideal of a "color-blind" Constitution, see *Plessy v. Ferguson,* 163 U.S. 537, 559 (1896) (Harlan, J., dissenting), appellants appear to concede that race-conscious redistricting is not always unconstitutional. ... That concession is wise: This Court never has held that race-conscious state decisionmaking is impermissible in *all* circumstances. What appellants object to is redistricting legislation that is so extremely irregular on its face that it rationally can be viewed only as an effort to segregate the races for purposes of voting, without regard for traditional districting principles and without sufficiently compelling justification. For the reasons that follow, we conclude that appellants have stated a claim upon which relief can be granted under the Equal Protection Clause.

What might constitute a "sufficiently compelling justification" for a race-conscious policy?

[On the negative impacts of racial gerrymandering]

9   Classifications of citizens solely on the basis of race "are by their very nature odious to a free people whose institutions are founded upon the doctrine of equality." *Hirabayashi v. United States,* 320 U.S. 81, 100 (1943). Accord, *Loving v. Virginia,* 388 U.S. 1, 11 (1967). They threaten to stigmatize individuals by reason of their membership in a racial group and to incite racial hostility. *Croson, supra,* at 493 (plurality opinion); *UJO, supra,* at 173 (Brennan, J., concurring in part) ("[E]ven in the pursuit of remedial objectives, an explicit policy of assignment by race may serve to stimulate our society's latent race consciousness, suggesting the utility and propriety of basing decisions on a factor that ideally bears no relationship to an individual's worth or needs").

What are the negative impacts of race-based policies, especially racial gerrymandering?

10   A reapportionment plan that includes in one district individuals who belong to the same race, but who are otherwise widely separated by geographical and political boundaries, and who may have little in common with one another but the color of their skin, bears an uncomfortable resemblance to political apartheid. It reinforces the perception that members of the same racial group-regardless of their age, education, economic status, or the

community in which they live-think alike, share the same political interests, and will prefer the same candidates at the polls. We have rejected such perceptions elsewhere as impermissible racial stereotypes. See, *e. g., Holland v. Illinois,* 493 U.S. 474, 484, n. 2 (1990) ("[A] prosecutor's assumption that a black juror may be presumed to be partial simply because he is black... violates the Equal Protection Clause" (internal quotation marks omitted)); see also *Edmonson v. Leesville Concrete Co.,* 500 U.S. 614, 630-631 (1991) ("If our society is to continue to progress as a multiracial democracy, it must recognize that the automatic invocation of race stereotypes retards that progress and causes continued hurt and injury"). By perpetuating such notions, a racial gerrymander may exacerbate the very patterns of racial bloc voting that majority-minority districting is sometimes said to counteract.

The message that such districting sends to elected represen- 11 tatives is equally pernicious. When a district obviously is created solely to effectuate the perceived common interests of one racial group, elected officials are more likely to believe that their primary obligation is to represent only the members of that group, rather than their constituency as a whole. This is altogether antithetical to our system of representative democracy.

Excerpt from Dissenting Opinion

JUSTICE WHITE, with whom JUSTICE BLACKMUN and 12 JUSTICE STEVENS join, dissenting.

[Distinguishing two types of voting cases]

The grounds for my disagreement with the majority are simply 13 stated: Appellants have not presented a *cognizable* claim, because they have not alleged a cognizable injury. To date, we have held that only two types of state voting practices could give rise to a constitutional claim. The first involves direct and outright deprivation of the right to vote, for example by means of a poll tax or literacy test. See, *e. g., Guinn v. United States,* 238 U.S. 347 (1915). Plainly, this variety is not implicated by appellants' allegations and need not detain us further. The second type of unconstitutional practice is that which "affects the political strength of various groups," *Mobile v. Bolden,* 446 U.S. 55, 83 (1980)

cognizable—within the jurisdiction of the court

What are the two types of voting practices that give rise to constitutional claims?

What forms of political participation can groups engage in other than voting?

(STEVENS, J., concurring in judgment), in violation of the Equal Protection Clause. As for this latter category, we have insisted that members of the political or racial group demonstrate that the challenged action have the intent and effect of unduly diminishing their influence on the political process. Although this severe burden has limited the number of successful suits, it was adopted for sound reasons.

14   ...a number of North Carolina's political subdivisions have interfered with black citizens' meaningful exercise of the franchise and are therefore subject to §§4 and 5 of the Voting Rights Act. Cf. *UJO, supra,* at 148. In other words, North Carolina was found by Congress to have "'resorted to the extraordinary stratagem of contriving new rules of various kinds for the sole purpose of perpetuating voting discrimination in the face of adverse federal court decrees'" and therefore "would be likely to engage in 'similar maneuvers in the future in order to evade the remedies for voting discrimination contained in the Act itself.'" *McCain v. Lybrand,* 465 U.S. 236, 245 (1984) (quoting *South Carolina v. Katzenbach,* 383 U.S. 301, 334, 335 (1966)).

credulity— believability

15   In light of this background, it strains *credulity* to suggest that North Carolina's purpose in creating a second majority-minority district was to discriminate against members of the majority group by "impair[ing] or burden[ing their] opportunity... to participate in the political process." *Id.,* at 179 (Stewart, J., concurring in judgment)... The State has made no mystery of its intent, which was to respond to the Attorney General's objections, see Brief for State Appellees 13-14, by improving the minority group's prospects of electing a candidate of its choice. I doubt that this constitutes a discriminatory purpose as defined in the Court's equal protection cases—*i. e.,* an intent to aggravate "the unequal distribution of electoral power." *Post,* at 678 (STEVENS, J., dissenting). But even assuming that it does, there is no question that appellants have not alleged the requisite discriminatory effects. Whites constitute roughly 76% of the total population and 79% of the voting age population in North Carolina. Yet, under the State's plan, they still constitute a voting majority in 10 (or 83%) of the 12 congressional districts. Though they might be dissatisfied at the prospect of casting a vote for a losing candidate—a lot shared by many, including a disproportionate number of minority voters—surely they cannot complain of discriminatory treatment.

How does Justice White use statistics to contrast voting rights of whites with those of African Americans under the redistricting plan?

Wright is relevant only to the extent that it illustrates a proposition with which I have no problem: that a complaint stating that a plan has carved out districts on the basis of race *can*, under certain circumstances, state a claim under the Fourteenth Amendment. To that end, however, there must be an allegation of discriminatory purpose and effect, for the constitutionality of a race-conscious redistricting plan depends on these twin elements. In *Wright*, for example, the facts might have supported the contention that the districts were intended to, and did in fact, shield the 17th District from any minority influence and "pack" black and Puerto Rican voters in the 18th, thereby invidiously minimizing their voting strength. In other words, the purposeful creation of a majority-minority district could have discriminatory effect if it is achieved by means of "packing"—*i. e.*, overconcentration of minority voters. In the present case, the facts could sustain no such allegation.

16 | How did the facts in the *Shaw* case differ from those of the *Wright* decision? According to the dissent, why is it important to consider the intent of the legislature in creating minority-majority districts?

Impact of *Shaw v. Reno* on redistricting and on the makeup of districts

The AP® U.S. Government and Politics curriculum requires you to know about redistricting and gerrymandering and its impact on congressional policymaking. The *Shaw* decision had a significant impact on the redistricting process. As a result of the *Shaw* decision, race cannot be used as the main factor in drawing congressional districts. This decision has resulted in fewer congressional districts in which a majority of the voters are minorities, which by extension has most likely led to fewer minority members of Congress.

Check for Understanding

1. Identify the constitutional clause that was the basis for the Court's decision in the *Shaw* case.
2. Explain why race-based policies, such as racial gerrymandering, are subjected to a strict scrutiny standard.
3. Explain why Justice O'Connor argues that assuming that racial groups vote alike is dangerous and simplistic.
4. Describe the arguments made by the dissent in favor of upholding the minority-majority district.
5. Describe the impact of the decision in *Shaw v. Reno* on membership and party control in the House of Representatives.

■ SCOTUS Practice Question

In the 1980s, Georgia had ten congressional districts, only one of which was majority African-American. In the 1990 census, Georgia was awarded an eleventh congressional district, and the U.S. Justice Department held that Georgia was required to add additional minority-majority districts to comply with the Voting Rights Act of 1965. After several attempts, Georgia created a map with three minority-majority districts, one of which was the Eleventh Congressional District, which stretched from Atlanta to Savannah on the coast. White voters in this new district sued the state of Georgia, arguing that the district was unconstitutional. The voters won their case in district court, and the state appealed the decision to the U.S. Supreme Court.

In 1995, in *Miller v. Johnson* (1995), the Supreme Court, in a 5-4 decision, ruled that the Eleventh Congressional District was unconstitutional. Justice Kennedy wrote "The court found it was 'exceedingly obvious' from the shape of the Eleventh District, together with the relevant racial demographics, that the drawing of narrow land bridges to incorporate within the district outlying appendages containing nearly 80% of the district's total black population was a deliberate attempt to bring black populations into the district..."

Based on the information above, respond to the following questions.

A. Identify the constitutional provision that is common to both *Shaw v. Reno* (1993) and *Miller v. Johnson* (1995).

B. Based on the constitutional clause identified in part A, explain how the facts of *Shaw v. Reno* (1993) led to a similar holding in *Miller v. Johnson* (1995).

C. Describe an action that interest groups and social movements could take to increase minority representation despite the decisions in *Shaw v. Reno* (1993) and *Miller v. Johnson* (1995).